'Three weeks after the take-over seventy Army officers and more than 2000 men had died. Within three months 10,000 civilians had been slaughtered. Crocodiles basked beneath the Karume Falls Bridge, the Bridge of Blood, spanning the River Nile. They grew both fat and lazy. Idi Amin Dada cancelled elections and filled his prisons. Bataringaya was to die. Benedicto Kiwanuka, appointed chief justice, was to be dragged from his chambers at Kampala's Law courts and savagely murdered.

The honeymoon was over. Uganda turned to the horror of Amin's

LUST TO KILL.'

The authors and publishers gratefully acknowledge the kind co-operation and assistance of CAMERAPIX, NAIROBI, KENYA for all the photographs contained in this book.

LUST TO KILL

The Rise and Fall
of
Idi Amin

Joseph Kamau and Andrew Cameron

LUST TO KILL: The Rise and Fall of Idi Amin
A CORGI BOOK 0 552 11058 2

First Publication in Great Britain

PRINTING HISTORY

Corgi edition published 1979

Corgi Books are published by
Transworld Publishers Ltd.,
Century House, 61–63 Uxbridge Road,
Ealing, London W5 5SA
Typesetting by Westchester Book Composition
Printed by Offset Paperback Mfrs. Inc., Dallas, Pa.,
U.S.A.

TO THOSE
WHO HAVE
DIED

CHAPTER I

'The time is now ripe for us very seriously to consider how best we can ensure that there is a permanent return to a sense of unity, freedom and liberty in Uganda.'

Major General Idi Amin Dada

Daybreak came abruptly—and with it, gunfire. Battle prepared troops lay in position around Parliament building. Swiftly, soldiers threw up road blocks on the approaches, shooting out the tyres of cars parked in nearby streets. Overshadowing the crack of sporadic gunfire and the clatter of soldiers boots as they dispersed to key positions was the rumble of tanks, on the move before 3:00 a.m., churning up the city's thin tarmacadam.

The day: January 25, 1971. The place: Kampala, capital of Uganda. It was a moment in which yet again the history of Africa was changing—being written in violence and blood.

Down the road from Parliament, which was due to resume soon after President Milton Obote returned from the Commonwealth Prime Ministers' Conference in Singapore, a crack Uganda squad, the Mbuya Hill Battalion, stormed the Voice of Uganda radio station.

An early morning announcer, sub-machine pistol pressing into his ribs, fumbled to put on martial music. Jeeps squealed to a halt at the main post office complex. Telephone and telex lines were disconnected.

Twenty two miles to the south, a military convoy rumbled towards Entebbe Airport. A mile or two ahead of it, a saloon car was carrying four Catholic priests. One of them, Father Gerard Guerts, of the Canadian Order of the White Fathers of Africa, was saying his farewells to his three brothers-in-Christ.

They were early. The Sabena flight which would carry Father Guerts to Europe en route to Canada had not yet arrived.

The friends relaxed in the airport lounge, talking over small, intimate matters.

Volleys of machine gun fire broke the calm, followed by the thump of artillery. A shell burst through the airport's main entrance killing two of the priests instantly.

Outside, soldiers quickly laid barbed wire across the runway, encircled the airport buildings and kicked their way into the control tower.

Today Father Guerts would not be going back home to Canada.

An NCO ordered three of his men to drag the shrapnel-torn bodies of the two white priests down to the banks of Lake Victoria. Crocodiles would soon find floating corpses.

Foreign tourists bound for Murchson Falls stood against a wall with their hands up.

'Go back to your hotels. Do not move until you are told.'

Overhead the sun was nearing its zenith. Along the road not far from Entebbe Airport, crowds of flies had begun to swarm. The doors of the Hippo Bar remained shuttered. The flies had found more corpses to feast upon.

Mortar fire punctuated the rattle of automatic weapons in Kampala. A Land Rover carried seven bodies away from Parliament precincts. The door of the

President's office inside had been broken down. After bursts of shooting an armoured car positioned itself in the compound at the residence of French Ambassador Albert Thabault. City residents who had set out for work were told by soldiers to go home.

British High Commissioner Richard Slater warned his nationals not to venture out.

Fifty miles to the east fighting flared between soldiers of the Uganda Army 3rd battalion at Jinja. The victors moved on to seize the Owen Falls Hydro-Electric dam and, that secure, began marching towards Kampala. The 2nd battalion headed for the city too—from its Mbarara base 150 miles to the south-west.

Soldiers surrounded the ruins of Mengo Hill palace where Acholi and Langi troops loyal to President Milton Obote were camped. Other detachments cordoned off Nsamba police barracks and the police training college a mile from the centre of Kampala. In a radio studio at the Voice of Uganda, Warrant Officer Class 2 Sam Aswa ran his eyes down a roughly prepared announcement. Aswa's voice faltered.

'The Uganda Armed Forces have this day decided to take over power from Obote and hand it to our fellow soldier Major General Idi Amin Dada . . . and we hereby entrust him to lead this our beloved country of Uganda to peace and goodwill among all.'

The transmission faded momentarily. 'We call upon everybody. . . . to continue with their work in the normal way. We warn all foreign governments not to interfere in Uganda's internal affairs. Any such interference,' Aswa stammered, '. . . . will be crushed with great force . . . because . . . we are ready.' The Warrant Officer read a list of 18 grievances within the Army. 'Power is now handed over to Major General Idi Amin and you must await his statement which will come in due course. We have done this for God and our country.'

Aswa pushed his cap to the back of his head.

Idi Amin Dada had listened to the announcement with inordinate satisfaction. A Sherman tank stood in the driveway of his luxury mansion built on the crown of one of Kampala's seven imposing hills. Amin placed machinegunners on the roof of the building and paratroopers indoors. He renamed his home in Prince Charles Drive The Command Post. Amin walked out onto the sun terrace overlooking the city. Bodyguards shuffled behind him, keeping their distance. This was his moment. He was on top, looking down—at last. He eased his 6 ft. 3 in. 230 lbs. frame into an armchair pulled onto the terrace. The afternoon was dry and crisp. He loosened his belt and leaned forward to ease the pistol that had squeezed into his hip. Sweat stains mottled his olive-green fatigues. A young officer reported that Amin's instructions that a curfew would be imposed from 7:00 p.m. to 6:30 a.m. had been carried out.

But the curfew was not observed. Towards dusk crowds flooded into the Kampala streets. Baganda cheer-leaders whipped up choruses of anti-Obote slogans. Patrolling Army jeeps crawled through the throng. Soldiers smiled, people shook their hands, kissed them, hugged them.

'Oyiieeh! Thanks to God. Hail our saviour, Idi Amin. We are behind Major General Amin.'

'Obote Afude!' (Obote is dead!)

Motorcades of private cars appeared: the cars were crammed, decorated with banana leaves and coloured paper, and towing tin cans. Passengers shouted happily. Small children tagged along, waving banana leaves. The soldiers at roadblocks were apologetic. Occasionally they loosed off shots into the air. An Army jeep drove through the campus at Makerere University, its crew firing rifle shots into the air too.

Rural people arriving in Kampala swelled the carnival—they came in busloads, car-loads, on bicycles and on foot. In the countryside around the city, they said, the homes of Obote supporters had been burned, their cattle had been taken.

Buildings burned in Kampala too. Acrid smoke hung over the city; the fires glowing in the evening twilight. The crowds tore down portraits of Obote, smashed them, jumped on them. They brought out crumpled pictures of the Kabaka of Buganda to tack up instead.

In a toilet in the recently built 12-storey Apollo Hotel named after Milton Obote, a medium built man in neat lounge suit was cowering. Basil Bataringaya, Obote's Minister for Internal Affairs, had cause to be frightened. He hoped he would not be found. It was a forlorn wish. He was known to too many who had reason to hate him.

He did not have long to wait. A whisper here, a message there and soon a small group of soldiers was breaking down the door to drag him out and beat him until he was unconscious.

Nearby in the lounge Obote's wife Mira sipped tea, watched over by eager-eyed soldiers, as she scribbled messages to family and friends saying she and the children—6-year-old Akeno, 4-year-old Atoke and three-year-old Engena—were unharmed. As she wrote on hotel stationery, she tried to shut out the mounting noise from the street outside—the screams of abuse about the man she loved.

She had married Milton Obote as a young aspirant politician in Uganda's colonial days. She had been by his side as he had steered Uganda first to Independence and then himself to the Presidency.

Today he was five thousand miles away in Singapore. Briefly the news had reached Obote. As his wife was under guard in the Apollo, he was swiftly packing, leaving his suite in the Singapore Hilton to board East African Airways flight EC 733 for Entebbe via Bombay.

Soon after the Super VC 10, one of three which were the flag carriers of East African unity, took off he reclined his seat in the first class cabin and closed his eyes.

His 27 colleagues—aides, ministers and secretaries—watched him closely. Two hours later he went to the aircraft toilet, washed and returned to his seat to sleep once more. Few around him were able to relax. Nobody spoke. As passengers in the economy section behind ordered lunch and drinks, the sad, sombre Uganda party refused food—and nobody ordered drinks.

There was nothing to celebrate.

At Bombay, Indian soldiers surrounded the aircraft. Indian officials handed Obote a Press Trust of India report. Information was still sketchy. Another ninety minutes passed before Obote joined Captain David Powell in the cockpit to hear up-to-the-minute radio messages. He emerged with tears in his eyes.

'It is a great shame,' said an air hostess. 'I cannot help but pity the situation.'

Foreign Minister Sam Odoka walked down the aisle. 'I don't really know what to say. We don't know much. We hope whatever happened prosperity and stability will continue. That is what we have all worked for. That is the President's wish. It is a private hell for all of us not knowing what is happening.'

The aircraft touched down at Kenya's Embakasi airport at Nairobi at exactly 7:10 East African time. A tight police cordon—supervised personally by Kenya Police Commissioner Bernard Hinga—surrounded the jet-liner and within minutes Milton Obote was being driven at speed towards Nairobi's Panafric Hotel. Installed overnight in top-floor rooms Obote received news that he and his principal aides would face execution by the Uganda Army should they return home. Kenya vice president Daniel arap Moi visited the top-floor.

Downstairs police and security men refused to allow newsmen to enter the hotel, remained tight lipped when questioned. Later, after midnight, Obote's delegation left their rooms and came downstairs to be driven by the same escort back to the airport.

Moi went too. He had strict instructions for the flight crew of the EAA Comet jet. Pilot Colin Skillett was ordered to take the Uganda party to Dar es Salaam.

But, asked Skillett, what if Tanzania refuses landing permission? 'I don't care,' said Moi. 'Take him anywhere—but do not bring him back to Kenya.'

With President Julius Nyerere visiting India on his way back from the Singapore Commonwealth summit meeting Obote's East African Airways comet was met by Tanzania's second vice president Rashid Kawawa. Kawawa embraced a stooping, strained and gaunt Obote. The Ugandan wore a black suit and a blue shirt without a tie. The Ugandan flag fluttered from a masthead at Dar es Salaam airport and the Ugandan presidential standard flapped on the wing of the black Rolls Royce which took Obote to Nyerere's state house. The contrast to Embakasi was pointed.

CHAPTER II

'Uganda is a fairy tale. You climb up a railway instead of a beanstalk and at the top there is a wonderful new world. The scenery is different, the climate is different and most of all, the people are different from anything elsewhere to be seen in the whole range of Africa.'
                                   Winston Churchill.

Uganda, the cradle of the River Nile, sits high in the heartland of Africa. The Ruwenzori Mountains—the Mountains of the Moon—rise 17,000 feet to their equatorial snowfields. The foothills, pitted with volcanic craters and salty lakes, flatten down to the Maramagambo forests and wide, rolling plains. Ishaha lion stretch out on tree boughs, vividly plumed birds call out, gorillas command their domain, Virunga peaks.

Eastwards, a pattern of rivers carves through the lush plains of the Pleistocene plateau—joining the myriad of lakes to the greatest of them all, Lake Victoria. Fish eagles circle above the shores, Bantu canoe-men flee a squall which dies as suddenly as it is born.

Lake water pours north, descending in a series of tumbling cascades, cataracts and lagoons until it plunges through a narrow ravine at Murchison Falls and fans into marsh. Hippopotamus barge each other in muddy still-pools. The crocodiles creep to their lair.

Dashes of tropical flowers, woven by bees and butterflies, embroider the gentle hills beyond.

In arid, scrubby Karamoja flash floods turn sand-rivers into torrents. Mount Elgon nudges up at the other, warmly-vegetated corner of the high plateau.

The first explorer's caravan had reached a part of this land to find an ancient kingdom—a kingdom whose fortune, by legend, followed victory in fearsome wars with the neighbour kings of Bunyoro, Toro, Ankole and Kigezi. Journeying inland from the exotic, spice-scented Indian Ocean harbour of Zanzibar John Hannon Speke marvelled at the erect, proud Baganda.

'I cut a poor figure in comparison. They wore neat bark cloth cloaks resembling the best yellow corduroy cloth, crimp and well set, as if stiffened with starch, and over that as upper cloaks, a patchwork of small antelope skins, which I observed were sewn together as well as any English glovers could have pierced them; whilst their head-dresses generally were abrus turbans, set off with highly polished boar tusks, stick charms, seeds, beads or shells.'

Permanent highways led between the wood and grass houses of the Baganda, between the reed stockades. And the monarch, Kabaka Mutesa I, ruled with a cruel hand.

Arab slavers and ivory traders—at the head of them, Snay Bin Amir—had already come to Mutesa's court. The Kabaka read and wrote Arabic and could muster 150,000 warriors for slave-gathering forays.

Mutesa excelled his father Suna as despot and butcher. On his accession to the royal palace at Mengo, he commanded the death of his brothers by burning at the stake and the ceremonial mutilation of scores of slaves. The dynastic king decreed vicious death for those defying royal rules: to be cut up and scorched over slow fires; royal knifemen seared away the cheeks, the lips, the eyelids and the ears of court defaulters; other victims were simply buried alive in sacrifice.

Speke handed the king a carbine as a gift. Mutesa

15

knew firearms . . . the Zanzibari slavers traded muskets for men. Testing his gift he loaded the rifle, passed it to a young boy and demanded the shooting of the first person he saw outside the palace gatehouse.

Missionaries set out for Mutesa's capital, Rubaga. They were to challenge the Lubare paganism of the Baganda and the seeds of Islam and homosexuality planted in it by Arabs from both the eastern seaboard and the northern territories, Sudan on to Egypt. Robert Pickering Ashe brought the first bicycle and dared Baganda to race him: zealous Alexander Mackay presented Mutesa with a less lethal gift—a music box playing Haydn's Creation.

The Kingdom took quickly to Christianity, even if understanding of its doctrines was slow. The Church Missionary Society vanguard was joined by priests of the White Fathers order directed by an ardent French cardinal. Hence begun Catholic-Protestant rivalry, with Islam a sharp and ever present thorn to both.

All along Mutesa himself stood intrigued but aloof from the new creed. Once, suffering then from advanced syphilis, Mutesa proclaimed he would only grant the missionaries absolute freedom to teach in return for a daughter of English royalty.

Acting under a special charter from Lord Salisbury's government, and assigned the task of drawing the kingdom of Mutesa's successor, Mwanga, into the nascent British sphere of influence in East Africa, the Imperial British East Africa Company despatched Captain Frederick Lugard to Buganda. Mutesa's death had plunged the region into civil religious wars. Observed Lugard of the Baganda: 'They are a people of great courage and amazing loyalty who would face death by mutilation or burning rather than forsake the religion they had adopted and who would not be disloyal to their Kabak no matter how despicable he might be.'

He added later: 'Their intelligence stands proven by the standard of political organisation evolved without foreign aid.'

16

Lugard established his first camp not far from Mengo on a rise to be known as Kampala Hill. A treaty with Mwanga—albeit a shaky one—signed and sealed, Lugard led Buganda armies against Bunyoro, Toro and Ankole. But uprisings against its outposts and continued religious strife soon drained both the Company's resolve and its finances.

Of the IBEAC's withdrawal the British Foreign Office lamented in a cabinet memorandum: 'When we gave a charter ... the aim had been to take Uganda, and so prevent the Germans from linking up their West Coast sphere across the Upper Nile to their East African possessions.'

An imperial commissioner was appointed and Buganda declared a Protectorate. British authority rapidly spread to absorb the Nilotic and Hamitic tribes of the Nile, Madi, Acholi, Lango, Teso and Karamoja regions to the north and east. In the main Baganda chiefs administered the territory under British overseers. Their assistance to quell troublesome Bunyoro reaped further reward when, at the turn of the century, a formal agreement with the British endorsed Buganda ownership over chunks of its neighbours' land.

And the railway—the Iron Snake—was pushing up from the coast.

Britain ruled the Protectorate with uncharacteristic detachment at first. Having put down rebellions by Mwanga and Bunyoro king Kabarega concern was more with 'fostering the growth of native products including cereals and fruits suited to the climate' and with the introduction of coinage 'to obviate the tedious and laborious method of payment by trade goods' than enticing white settlers to its fertile farmlands already under a traditional system of fixed cultivation and land ownership.

Most attractive of all was the strategic value of the Protectorate in Britain's imperial designs. The French, the Belgians and the Germans were near, while control of the Nile headwaters offered Britain security for Egypt and the new route through Suez to India. The railway gave scope to move troops and supplies to the Protectorate as and when the need arose.

Buganda prospered.

Mwanga's son, Daudi Chwa, learned from Church tutors and grew up in a neat English-style house decorated inside with prints and portraits of Queen Victoria and King Edward.

Revenue from cash crops—tea, coffee and cotton—paid off administration costs, and then colonial military expenditure. Slaving was over, giant elephant tusks were no longer exchanged for a handful of beads and in the kingdoms education had emphasis. The ferocious, spearweilding Karamajong were forced to sell their cattle to government agents. Soldiers of Tae colonial Army's Kings African Rifles went to Karamoja to try and stop cattle raiding between villages.

To royal drums and to fanfares, Edward William Frederick David Walugembe Luwangula Mutesa II became the 35th Kabaka of Buganda, Professor of Almighty Power and Knowledge, Lord of the Clans and the Land, The Father of All Twins, The Blacksmith's Hammer, The Cook With All The Firewood, The Smelter of Iron, The Power of the Sun, First Officer of the Order of the Shield and Spears. . . .

Choirs, clergy and bishops headed the colourful procession to Thanksgiving at Namirembe Cathedral. The band of the Kings African Rifles struck up Handel's Largo. The 18-year-old Kabaka wore his flowing white Kanzu robe. The year . . . 1942.

Kabaka Mutesa II was not able to stave off political change in Uganda for long. A breathing space at the end of World War Two gave rise to the emergence of coherent, modern political groupings.

The Church had been recognised as a political force nearly half a century before. Many posts of power had gone to the Protestants. The late 1940s now saw the beginning of the end of Uganda's traditional power structure.

The initial change was rooted in legislation promul-gated by the British and sanctioned by the Buganda parliament, the Great Lukiiko, which—through zone laws and the Produce Marketing Ordinance—restricted the activities of small African farmers. Producers of cotton and coffee, they encouraged cash crops, had no control over the processing and distribution of their harvests. Instead, Government representatives dealing through middlemen—many were Asians who had worked on the railway—had the monopoly. They transported the coffee and ran the cotton ginneries.

Anger built up until it could be held back no more. Rioting spread throughout Buganda. The main targets: Indian ginnery owners and Colonial government officials.

Crowds mobbed anyone suspected of being a dupe of the government or the favoured few. Joe Kiwanuka, editor of the White-owned vernacular newspaper, *The Uganda Post*, was beaten by crowds and left for dead. Kiwanuka recovered to receive a certificate of loyalty from the Colonial government and a handsome sum in compensation. The money enabled him to buy his own printing press and launch a newspaper which was to become the administration's most vociferous opponent.

Out of the riots was born the powerful Farmers' Union. Labour unions sprang up too.

Regions other than Kingdoms still retained only secondary importance for educational, social and economic organisation. Both inside and outside the Kingdoms nationalists marshalled themselves. Milton Obote formed the Uganda People's Congress and Benedicto Kiwanuka the predominantly Catholic Democratic Party, both as a butt to the Buganda party, Kabaka Yekka.

The test of national unity came in 1953 in the form of suggestions by the Colonial Office for a Federation of East Africa incorporating Uganda, Kenya and Tanzania which, Buganda feared, would inevitably come under the domination of Kenya's white minority. Mutesa and the Great Lukiiko immediately demanded the transfer of Buganda from the Colonial Office to the Foreign

19

Office and a timetable for the separate independence of Buganda.

Even after the proposed East African federation was abandoned Britain's newly-appointed Uganda governor, Sir Andrew Cohen, was unable to allay the Kabaka's fears that measures to draw Uganda's region into a united whole were in fact a clever prelude to federation after all. Mutesa's dealings with Sir Andrew were, at best, difficult. Mutesa refused to cooperate with the governor, who eventually chose to withdraw Britain's recognition of the Kingdom's authority. With Baganda support for their Kabaka unswerving the protectorate government then felt it safer to deport Mutesa to England.

Mutesa left Mengo under escort on November 30. That day Kampala came to a standstill. Baganda gathered in groups on the streets in silence. Women wept. More important, the Kabaka's detractors were angered. The Uganda National Congress, ever eager to denounce the British Government, sent representatives to Britain to press for Mutesa's release.

The Kabaka's triumphant return to Buganda two years afterwards concluded in an agreement which gave the Kingdom a large measure of internal self-government. By signing the agreement Mutesa allowed Buganda to be represented on the Legislative Council of Uganda, the symbolic national embryo he had steadfastly shunned.

In the next seven years up to independence three constitutional commissions and two conferences were held. Britain granted Uganda internal self government and elections boycotted by Buganda swept Democratic Party leader Ben Kiwanuka to office as first prime minister.

Full independence was declared 17 months later.

But Britain had left the new Uganda a complex constitutional legacy. It gave the kingdoms semi-autonomous status, with their own parliamentary machinery, under a Federal parliament. The kingdoms maintained many of their own services, the treasury and police: their parliaments appointed members for the Federal body.

Independent Uganda set off on an unsure footing. In fresh elections Milton Obote's UPC had ousted Kiwanuka's Democratic Party—but only by a slim margin of seats. It was left to Obote to strike an alliance with Buganda's Kabaka Yekka to give him the majority strength he needed in the national parliament. Kabaka Yekka had been allocated 21 seats in the 82-seat house.

Obote paid dearly for the alliance. He agreed to Mutesa's wish that Buganda should have its own High Court with equal jurisdiction to that of national court as well as other economic and political privileges. Baganda believed the Kabaka kept the supremacy of kingship intact. At the same time the marriage of convenience earned Obote resentment outside the kingdoms. From the outset King Freddie of Buganda and Milton Obote were on a collison course.

The Democratic Party had been beaten down. In opposition it charged that in economic development Buganda had received unfair advantage at the expense of other regions. After all, Buganda centered on the country's economic and social and cultural hub. Baganda were the largest single ethnic group— accounting for roughly one sixth of the total population. More than other groups they had risen to key civil posts and were generally better off in educational opportunities. Baganda comprised the largest number of undergraduates at Kampala's Makerere University, East Africa's premier seat of learning.

Festering resentment erupted periodically. Obote appointed five Kabak Yekka members to his cabinet, giving two of them the critical portfolios of Finance and Economic Affairs. Photographs were published soon after the appointments showing the ministers—one a European businessman—lying flat in obeisance before the Kabaka.

Constitutional amendments in 1963 made King Freddie president of Uganda, replacing Queen Elizabeth of England as titular head, and Sir William

21

Nadiope, the king, or Kyabazinga, of Bunyoro vice president, with Obote still prime minister. Uganda remained in the Commonwealth.

The amendments reaffirmed the Kabaka's supremacy in the eyes of the Baganda. But the presidential stamp did not stave off King Freddie's downfall. If anything, it hastened it.

Inherent in the Federal parliamentary system was the belief by the kingdoms they were safeguarded. Fragile as the UPC—KY alliance was it received a number of jarring jolts. Principal among them was KY executive chairman Michael Kintu's policy to nominate only conservatives and ultra-loyalists to the national assembly. This alienated progressive KY politicians who had begun to align themselves with Obote's more radical line. Concurrent with inducements from Obote—reputed to include senior posts in parastatal companies—nine KY MPs crossed the floor of the Assembly to join UPC.

Defections from the Democratic Party were to follow—the most notable being that of opposition leader in the house, Basil Bataringaya.

The issue of the "Lost Counties", however, led the Kabaka and Obote into direct confrontation. Bunyoro had never forgiven Buganda for seizing its land during Captain Lugard's invasion three quarters of a century before. The problem had simmered as long—and had to be settled once and for all. It could no longer be brushed aside.

Obote decided on a referendum giving the counties the chance to decide whether to go back to Bunyoro. King Freddie immediately made it clear he would have none of it. Baganda feeling: The counties had been acquired through bloodshed and could only be taken away through bloodshed. The British conceded the Lost Counties dispute as having just the ingredients that could spark civil war in Uganda.

Leading up to the referendum Mutesa II gave land to some 4,500 Baganda World War II veterans eager to fight and stay in the "Lost Counties". Bunyoro armed its ex-servicemen. Predictably Mutesa refused to sign the referendum bill. Obote sacked two Kabaka Yekka cabinet ministers and KY MPs walked out of parliament in protest at a motion setting the date of the referendum.

At last, the KY-UPC alliance was formally dissolved. The referendum went ahead as scheduled. Two counties voted to return to the jurisdiction of Bunyoro. A month after the poll seven Bunyoro officials were shot dead by Buganda veterans settled by the Kabaka near Ndaiga. Bunyoro responded by attempting to seize Baganda property in the disputed area and at the same time the Baganda would not give up: Baganda chiefs arrested Bunyoro who resisted their administration.

The political crisis deepened when Kabaka Yekka secretary general Daudi Ocheng moved a parliamentary motion calling for an immediate inquiry into charges of illicit gold, ivory and coffee dealing with rebels of the Soumaliot uprising in the Congo. The charges accused Obote, minister of planning Odoko Neykon (Obote's cousin) and minister of defence Felix Onama of profiting from the trade of arms to the rebels in return for gold and ivory seized from fallen Congolese towns.

Also named by Ocheng Deputy Army Chief of Staff Colonel Idi Amin.

In the National Assembly the motion was greeted with uncertainty and confusion. Prime Minister Obote was not present to hear it. But was on a 'meet the people' tour of Northern Uganda. The motion, which also demanded Colonel Amin's suspension until after the inquiry, was passed unanimously.

Obote continued with his tour of West Nile and Acholi. Two weeks passed before the Kabaka Yekka, using the corruption charges in the hope of bringing down Obote, tabled another motion calling for the resignation of the named officials because nothing had yet been done to start the inquiry.

Events quickened.

Army commander Brigadier Shaban Opolot, an

Iteso married to a Muganda who appeared to entertain profound Buganda sympathies, was sent north to 'persuade' Obote to return to the capital. This created suspicion among Obote's closest supporters and Colonel Pierino Okoya, Obote's friend and fellow Acholi, rallied loyal troops in Kampala.

Obote, vehement in his denial of complicity in the gold and ivory affair, challenged cabinet ministers who supported Ocheng's resolution to resign. The challenge met with no response. On February 22, 1966, a police detachment streamed into a cabinet meeting and arrested Grace Ibingira, minister of state and secretary general in Obote's party, together with four other ministers. The prime minister further declared that King Freddie had sinisterly approached foreign diplomats for military supplies and assistance.

The crisis had precipitated. Prime Minister Obote suspended both the 1962 independence constitution and Parliament and announced that he was taking over full control. He invited judges and lawyers from Kenya and Tanzania to conduct an independent inquiry into the gold and ivory charges. The jurists found insufficient substance in them but left considerable doubt hanging over one name.

That name: Colonel Idi Amin, newly-promoted Army Chief of Staff.

Obote, sympathetic to the Congolese rebels, had authorised Amin to deal directly with them. Amin's promotion was a logical result of Obote's suspicions about Opolot—although it seemed incongruous in the light of Ocheng's revelations. Rivalry verging on mutual fear existed between Opolot and Amin but in Amin Obote thought he had a more loyal officer at a time when he knew elements in the military would have welcomed and aided his ousting.

What the corruption inquiry did not clear up included large payments into Amin's personal bank account. Copies of Amin's bank statements showing deposits and withdrawals apparently on behalf of the

Congolese rebels had been released by Ocheng. Without any real cohesion within his party Obote now found himself relying on the military as a power base.

And Amin received the benefit of the doubt.

Meanwhile the Baganda, who were comparatively poorly represented in the Army, had become desperately agitated by Obote's latest manipulations. Buganda attempted to secede. The Lukiiko ordered the Central Government out of the kingdom. On paper the Lukiiko decision meant the government would have to close its offices in its own capital, Kampala and that Buganda was, in effect, an independent state.

Buganda was in revolt. Rioting flared up in Kampala amid rumours that Buganda loyalists were being issued with arms at the Kabaka's Mengo Hill palace.

Obote's hand had been forced.

He summoned Amin to his Lodge and ordered him to beseige the Kabaka's palace at Mengo Hill. Early the following morning Amin's troops launched their attack. Baganda veterans put up stiff resistance for several hours, keeping the soldiers pinned down with small arms fire. It was not until mid-afternoon that an eager Amin sought permission from Obote to shell the palace.

The shells smashed through the stockades. Explosions ripped through the Kabaka's residence, the Great House, and smoke poured from the other buildings.

A first wave of troops began an assault. Amin was angered by the stubborness of the Baganda and saw no cause for restraint...

The heavy skies could no longer hold their weight. Sheets of rain drove down. In the confusion of the storm, the gunfire, the explosions Mutesa—dressed as a commoner—slipped from the palace. With two armed bodyguards he sheltered in a nearby house until dark.

Soldiers were looting the palace. Wounded Baganda lay where they fell. Many had been crushed by fallen stonework, many had been buried in the rubble. Soldiers were searching for Mutesa.

They saved the Kabaka's presidential flag and found

the ceremonial headress signifying the president as nominal commander in chief of the Uganda armed forces.

After nightfall Mutesa escaped to the swamps. He stayed in hiding there for nearly a month. Loyalists brought their king food, blankets and news.

Looting at Mengo Hill had lasted several days. The palaces at Bamunanika and Masaka had also been burned and looted.

The Kabaka fled to Burundi. Thence to Britain.

The number of dead after Amin's Mengo attack was officially put at forty seven. But Baganda said at least 1,500 died in Amin's relentless onslaught.

Colonel Idi Amin later boasted that Kampala streets had been "full of bodies" on that May day in 1966.

Milton Obote had been in a corner. Amin gave him elbow room. A state of emergency was declared in Buganda which subsequently was to be extended over the entire country.

Mengo Hill confirmed Obote as the enemy of the Baganda and strengthened his reliance on the Army in general and, for the time being, Amin. The seige had finally lost him any prospect of Baganda support. He knew Baganda accounted for about one quarter of the country's electorate. Given his unconstitutional dissolution of parliament he needed Amin's muscle to help steer his future course. He declared Uganda a republic with himself as executive president, saying Mutesa had been planning a coup d'etat and the action was necessary for national unity.

Ugandans were sceptical. Virtually overnight the country had become a near-military dictatorship. The Army put on continual shows of strength in potential trouble spots—ostensibly taking the form of route marches and map reading exercises. With Amin's encouragement Army commander Opolot was arrested and detained: Amin moved into his office. Twenty two people—mostly Baganda—were arrested and charged with planning a coup against Obote.

Thus began systematic arrests of political undesirables.

CHAPTER III

*'He was just the type that the British liked, the
type of African that they used to refer to as
from the "warrior tribes": black, big, uncouth,
uneducated and willing to obey orders.'*
Dr Atieno Odhiambo

January 1, 1928.

IT WAS The twilight hour, the brief span between
the end of another African day and an African night.
Inside, the hut was already dark, fetid with the smell of a
woman's labour. She lay on the wicker bed moaning and
sweating. The village midwife grunted as she wiped the
woman's brow. It was going to be a difficult birth. The
baby was bigger than normal. Aiyee, moaned the
woman as another pain convulsed her.

The little village not far from Koboko, a few beehived
huts of mud and wattle and earthen floors, a few sparse
vegetable plots, was far off the beaten track, one of a
hundred such hamlets the visitor stumbled on along the
winding dirt road that disappears across the border into
the scrub and swamp wastes of south Sudan.

A great agony racked her body. The midwife
struggled, stumbling in the dark as night came down
swiftly.

The labour continued far into the night while the midwife cursed and comforted, and the father snored away his fatigue in another hut. In the morning the long hours of pain were ended. The new baby was at least 12 pounds in weight, if not more, and the women who crowded into the hut were overcome with awe.

Outside the men of the village laid down their tools and dressed only in genital cloths, tall of carriage, proud and erect, settled down to celebrate the birth. Elation followed swiftly as they drank the water of yakan, a raw native liquor for elders only, mixed with a drug extracted from a local plant. Soon elation became frenzy. Inside the mother nursed her son and dozed, exhausted. She was sick of the pain and the struggle for existence. The soil around Koboko in Northern Uganda is either swampy or rocky, hard to break, slow to yield, malnourished for centuries, laid waste by the endless hunger of the goat. Maize, millet, ground nuts and sweet potatoes grew in protest. The meals were plain, eaten only once a day, lacking in protein, strong in calories. Soon, thought the woman, clutching her infant son, soon we will leave.

Later she packed her scanty belongings and hoisting the boy on her back in a sling began the long walk to the main dirt road to wait for the occasional bus. Days later the strange woman and her son arrived in Lugazi. Others of her tribe were living in the town on the main Kampala-Jinja road.

There would be business, she was sure, for her ripe, overflowing body and for the ancient alchemies she had learnt from her mother's lips even when she was at the breast. Soon the customers were eagerly seeking her out for love charms and potions, for malignant curses on an hated enemy and some for more physical comforts. The boy could walk now and was filling out.

When his mother was busy he would play outside. School was not for him or his agemates. They wrestled in fun and played ancient games, but sometimes the witch's boy could be rough. If any displeased him he would resort to painful methods of showing his anger. It was an indolent childhood, an education of gossip and tribal legends and of superstition and fear. He learnt many dark arts from his mother and in play he had discovered the secret of power. At 12, he was well established as the leader of the village children—a domineering, resourceful, brute-strong youth with a pronounced streak of sadism. In the sundown hours of play he would overcome any opposition by simply grasping his opponent's genitals and crushing them in his great bear paw of hand. Not far away, across the bush, as the sun slipped quickly below the horizon, elephants on the banks of the majestic Nile guarded their young as they played gentle games with each other, teasing, impish, but in the wisdom of their primeval ancestry, never brutal.

Kampala had grown in the 30 years since Winston Churchill had visited it. Roads had been laid from Entebbe, on the shores of Lake Victoria, ribbons of metal through white clad fields of cotton and tall avenues of proud blue eucalyptus and jacaranda trees. Houses climbed up and down the hills of Kampala, shaded everywhere by abundant trees. The streets, laid out with neat precision, pronounced the gusto of empirical commerce. Hawkers crowded every corner selling their wares—fruit and vegetables from the fertile lands of Uganda's lake basins, colourful cloth for headgear and dresses. All was bustle and progress.

Jinja was a colonial town, on the banks of the Ripon Falls, the source of the Nile, and an army town. From his earliest days, when soldiers came to visit his mother, Amin was impressed by the smart uniforms of the King's African Rifles. The barracks nearby drew him like a magnet. Unwittingly, it was the KAR that was to act as the catalyst for Amin's primitive lust for power learned in the tussles with his friends. It was to provide him the opportunity to indulge it.

In the young Idi Amin the British officers of the 4th Battalion, Kings African Rifles, found all the qualities for which they were looking. Intelligence was not one.

The main criteria used for the selection of African troops were height, physique and the ability to shut one eye—the prerequisite of being able to shoot a rifle.

Enlisted as a private in 1946 it took Idi Amin seven years of dogged soldiering to make lance-corporal. His boots were always immaculately polished, their toecaps shining like mirrors. His starched khaki uniform crackled, its creases were like razors. Amin showed respect and admiration for his superiors, he became assiduously loyal and pro-British and developed a fierce regimental pride. He was a boon on the sportsfield, but above all he obeyed commands unquestioningly.

To the British officers Amin was ideal KAR material. "Not much grey matter," as one of the officers put it, "But a splendid chap to have about."

Major Iain Grahame, then a young subaltern seconded to the KAR, met Lance Corporal Amin in 1953. 'It was clear even in 1953 that Idi was an outstanding leader. He was brave, showed initiative, was tremendously loyal and a great athlete. He couldn't speak any English, except to say "Good Morning, Sir," but it was obvious he would get promoted fairly rapidly, despite the fact that he was terribly handicapped by his obvious lack of education.'

Recalled a British sergeant major in the KAR. 'He was rather quiet, not the rowdy type at all and the only thing that perhaps distinguished him from the other Askari was his zest for military knowledge. Everyone really liked him, especially the Europeans—they thought the world of him.

'I remember one incident very well, which I think shows what kind of soldier he was. Out on a company exercise one day we organised a race between the platoons to carry a crate of beer from point A to point B. The winners were to be allowed to drink the beer.

'Idi detailed two of his soldiers to carry it first, but they weren't doing too well, so he got two NCOs to take over. Still they didn't go fast enough, so he grabbed the crate from them, lifted it onto his shoulders and doubled for about three miles with the platoon running behind him. They won.

'While he was very good to his men, he was also a very strict disciplinarian. If a soldier got out of line it was standard practice among the Africans to give him a switching—two NCOs would hold the offender while a third beat him with a thick length of rope. I never actually saw Idi do that but I am sure he would have done it at some time or other.'

THE TRUCK rumbled through Eastern Kenya. Corporal Amin sat with his feet over the tailboard, eyes scanning the horizon. Adventure followed adventure. He thought back to the year just finished where he had been on duty in his home territory in northern Uganda.

The scrub kept up the same monotonous panorama. Blue mountains loomed far away, shimmering, vanishing. Occasionally he talked to his troops in Swahili, lapsing into silence, remembering the night three months before when he and his small squad had stumbled on a group of cattle rustlers at their lunchtime camp Amin had indulged himself, bringing roars of laughter from his men, as he twisted the scrotums of his captives before bayoneting them and leaving them to bleed to death.

The uniform of the KAR was a protective shield which gave him strength. He could hear again the screams of the victims as he prolonged the pleasure of his torture. Too bad, he regretted, that one of the privates had reported his behaviour to the RSM. Amin had marked the man for vengeance, after his facile explanation and respectful manner had cleared him with the officers who had questioned him. White men responded to respect. It did not do to let them see your thoughts. He twisted around to gaze ahead, towards Somalia.

Army life, the incessant discipline, the barrack-room cameraderie, for the illiterate and the uneducated, soon becomes a form of expression. The drill takes on the mystique of communication. The platoon takes on the distinction of group identity. Amin relished the army as

32

it relished his uncluttered but simple intelligence. He was quick to respond to the discipline. The 5:45 a.m. reveille, the early breakfast, the morning parade, were part of his environment. Sun up and sun down are the natural parameters in Africa between work and sleep or relaxation. His behaviour at Langata soon marked him as a natural soldier—a mute, unquestioning obedience, a reflex arm of the law, of government, of colonial domination. Amin was dependable. He spent his training weekends on short passes, travelling to the Nairobi areas of Kibera, Eastleigh, Eastlands, where his own tribesmen gathered, drinking the clear alcohol called changa, known as kill-me-quick, sleeping with the ten-a-penny whores who crowded the stone-built, cockroach-infested buildings. He took little notice of politics, the rising crescendo of the cries for Uhuru, the irrepressible yearning for freedom. He was secure. His pay, though little, was regular. His food, though plain, was plentiful and often. He took an interest in the sports of the army, displaying great strength if little finesse at physical training, enjoying the inherent brutality of the boxing ring, the close bodily contact in the rough and tumble of the Rugby field. Sometimes in the scrum he would resort to his old boyhood trick of squeezing one of the opponent's genitals. He never resented, or showed resentment, if the opponents replied in kind. Sheer strength, an unquestionable charisma, made certain Amin had been marked for other things by his superiors.

MOGADISHU was hot and primitive, a small outpost of Italian and British colonialism, in the middle of a land of nomads—tall handsome, fine-boned people, grandly aloof, volatile, quick to anger; elegant women, slender, feline in long flowing robes. The cries of the morning prayer call from the minarets woke Amin who after the fashion of his faith, though his head was pounding with the alcohol he had consumed the night before, rose and knelt before the window of the squalid shanty bordello and bowed his head in prayer to the East. The full-breasted woman in the bed snored

33

heavily. Amin's piety was outraged. She was a Muslim, too, though not of the orthodox faith. He rose and walked across to the bed and grabbed her long, fine black hair and pulled her from the bed. She woke as her body thumped on the floor. Half pulled, half rising she got to her feet, bleary eyed: 'Pray you Moslem bitch,' Amin ordered in Swahili. His hand slapped across her face, leaving an ugly weal. Obediently, unresistingly, the woman knelt to answer the discipline of the Prophet. Amin peered in the cracked mirror and was satisfied. The indulgence of last night did not show. A sybaritic smile creased his lips and without a backward glance he left the room. He was back in the camp before 6:15 and ignored the inquisitive looks of his men as he paraded them fifteen minutes later.

They were pulling out that day, moving across arid stunted semi-desert land, west towards the border with the Kenya colony where bands of lawless shifta were raiding the bomas of the other tribes and rustling livestock, sheep, goats, cattle and camels. Amin kept his eyes alert, frowning against the glare of the sun, as the trucks carrying him and his fellow Kakwa trundled along the rough, sandy trail. He was considering the intricacies of his scheme to unseat Private Samuel Adaka whose reports to his English Officers, which Amin regarded simply as an attempt to curry favour, had given Amin those uncomfortable moments of inquiry about his tactics. Amin had decided to bide his time. In the manner of the African peasant, he had let Adaka see his displeasure but until he formulated a plan of revenge he was content simply to make his life uncomfortable, harassing him during kit inspection, on parade and bluntly rebuffing him during off-duty hours. It was a source of amusement to the rest of the platoon. Amin was a convivial NCO, given to moments of immense mirth which they all shared. Adaka had been the butt of some very crude jokes. Now he plotted Adaka's demise. Although he could not yet think of a scheme that was infallible, Amin with his crude logic was sure that he would see the moment when it arose and also that he would respond.

The soldiers camp was situated round a waterhole some 50 miles from the border. Not far away a herd of camels were tethered around the makeshift camp of a band of nomadic tribesmen. It was to be three days later, during a night patrol, that Amin was given the opportunity he had been seeking. With nine soldiers, he had trekked through the bush, starting in the late afternoon, searching for a gang of shifta which the nomads had reported were in the area. Adaka was one of the men. Sundown found them six or seven miles from the camp. Amin sought the cover of a bunch of doum palms, stunted and fading, on the bank of a dry donga. The perennial drought was at its height. Later, after cooking a meal on a camp fire, as they relaxed drowsily on their sleeping bags, talking idly in low voices and smoking cigarettes, they heard the slow, stealthy shuffle of feet some distance away. Amin, whose reflexes were superb, quickly threw sand on the fire and raised his finger for quiet. Grabbing his rifle he bent low and beckoned his men to follow him in a night lit by the glow of a full moon. Two hundred yards away Amin nearly fell on the gang as he crept through the thorn bush and found them walking across his trail. There were fifteen or so, with knives and old Lee Enfield first world war rifles. Amin let them pass, called up his troops and gave them quickly whispered instructions. His plan was crude and simple. They would follow the shifta and when they paused Amin would give the signal to fire. While they followed they must keep all together.

It was after 10 and the men crept along, boots slung around their necks, barefoot, avoiding the dry twigs underfoot, keeping low to avoid even a shadowy silhouette against the star-peckled horizon. The Shifta were heading back towards the army camp and that of the nomads. Later, much later it seemed to the tense soldiers, the gang paused, possibly to elaborate their plan of surprise. Amin listened, then beckoned his men forward by touch signalling them to maintain complete silence. In the glimmering dark, the shifta emerged whispering shadows, about twenty feet away. Amin, flat on the ground raised his rifle, waited until the others were in position and then opened fire. Flashes of light from the powder lit the bush. The shifta took off. Amin ordered Adaka and the others to follow and seeking Adaka in the dark, found him and fell behind him. Adaka may have thought the tall fellow Kakwa whose bobbing head he was following at a jog trot was Amin, but whatever his thoughts, they were brief. Running behind him, Amin placed his rifle against his back and fired. Adaka fell dead. Amin almost tripping over the body and calling Halt at the same time, ordering his men back. In the melee, confused by the sudden shot after the silence of the chase, they whispered to each other in their tribal tongue as Amin ordered them to see who had fallen. The others soon realised it was Adaka who was the victim.

None knew what had happened but in the frenetic excitement of the moment, nobody thought to question Amin's bland explanation that Adaka must have been the victim of return fire from the fleeing shifta. Amin ordered them to return to the ambuscade where they found five corpses and two badly injured shifta. The squad made camp for the night, after clumsily dressing the wounds of the two survivors and, with two on guard each four hours, they settled down to wait for sun-up when they would bury the dead shifta and carry the other two back to base for interrogation. Adaka's body was covered with a blanket.

If the young British lieutenant in charge of the patrol thought there was something odd about the hole in Adaka's back when he examined the victim next morning he soon forgot it in the process of questioning the shifta prisoners through an interpreter and in organising a hasty funeral for the late private with full military honours. In his report later, he was to commend the initiative and courageous devotion to duty of Corporal Amin. For Amin, the experience was salutary.

He had learnt that he could kill and that, with guile, he could do so with impunity.

Chege Kariuki was one of more than a million Kikuyu who had taken the Mau Mau oath by the end of 1953. He lived on his family's shamba near Fort Hall in Kenya's well-watered Central Province.

Under their self-styled General Kago Mau Mau fighters struck out from the southern Aberdares—from the Kinangop across the mountains to Fort Hall Reserve. Armed with Pangas, simis, home-made rifles of piping and captured .303s and sten guns they attacked police and loyalist guard posts.

Kariuki had turned 19. A jagged sheet of paper nailed to a tree carried the scrawled warning: 'We are called Mau Mau. Our oath, with the symbols of cats, dogs and chickens, is valid for seven years. People who take the Government oath must die. Anyone who does not take the Mau Mau oath must die. Anyone reporting a person to the government must die. Anyone reporting or removing this poster must die. Anyone who can read this poster and does not pass on this message must die.'

African soldiers found the poster and tore it down. Again they came to the shamba. Again they gathered the people in, clubbing them with rifle butts. They dragged Kariuki's sister away.

The sergeant grunted commands in Swahili. Kariuki's father, frail with age, broke from the group, fell, scrambled weakly towards the girl's screams until he was beaten prostrate.

This time the village escaped lightly.

Kariuki joined Kago. He was not to set eyes on the hulking sergeant for more than a year—a year of stalking through the bush with the guerrilla's animal stealth, a year in which the colonial troops dealt rough and arbitrary justice to real or imagined Mau Mau sympathisers.

Searching for suspects the soldiers razed the homes of Kikuyu villagers—by fire or with explosives. Methods of interrogation were basic, but effective—beatings, panga slashings, castration, burnings with red hot embers. From the garrison at Kandara the sergeant led his men to nearby villages to steal livestock and food, and for women.

Kariuki was captured in a sweep operation and taken to the barbed wire compound at Fort Hall. The sergeant's detail was guarding the compound. Young Kariuki had been made a Mau Mau major by Kago.

'Major, huh!' Sergeant Idi Amin said disdainfully, smashing his giant elbow into Kariuki's face.

In 1959 Amin was promoted to 'Effendi,' a warrant officer rank created in anticipation of the forthcoming independence of the East African territories. A special training course for the new Effendi was held in Kenya and Amin was awarded the Sword of Honour. Two years later a small group of warrant officers were commissioned.

'We looked along the ranks of our soldiers and thought: "Who the hell are going to be the officers?"' said Major Grahame. 'On recruiting safaris we always went for the chaps who were tough and strong and ran quicker than anyone else. It was a terrible mistake. Faced with the prospect of finding African officers we had a choice between the loyal, long service chaps who were absolutely reliable but incredibly limited by their lack of intelligence—Idi was a typical example—or newly recruited chaps with slightly more intelligence but absolutely no experience.'

Two Ugandans, between whom bitter personal and tribal enmity existed, were chosen for promotion to lieutenant in the 4th Battalion, Idi Amin and Shaban Opolot. Amin was posted to Major Grahame's company at Jinja. One day Grahame suggested the newly commissioned lieutenant should open a bank account.

Amin found the purpose of having a bank account extremely difficult to understand. The Jinja bank manager did his best to explain the principles involved and watched as Amin ineptly practised his signature.

Lieutenant Amin deposited his first week's pay, just over £10.

'I think he must have called in at every shop of his way back to the barracks,' said Grahame. 'He ordered a car here, a sewing machine there, a new suit, crates of drink and Lord knows what else. By the time he got back he had run up an overdraft of about £2,000. From then on no cheque of his was valid unless I countersigned it.'

As Uganda's independence approached the ruin of Amin's military career seemed imminent. British authorities in Kenya had pieced together evidence of a number of murders in north west Kenya by KAR troops under Amin during operations against Turkana cattle rustlers. One small village had been completely wiped out, and bodies discovered in shallow graves showed some of the tribesmen had been hideously tortured.

But a political expedient saved Amin's career. It was decided not to instigate criminal proceedings against one of only two Ugandan army officers on the eve of the country's independence. Ironically it was a decision with which Milton Obote, prime minister at the time, concurred.

At independence Amin assumed command of one of the new Uganda Army's two battalions. Opolot commanded the other. Amin, now a captain, was sent to Britain to undergo a commanding officer's course at the School of Infantry in Wiltshire.

Amin returned to Uganda without completing the course after the army mutiny quelled by British troops from Kenya in 1964.

Amin was sent to Israel for a parachute course. He did not complete that either. He refused to make even one jump. But the Israelis gave him his wings anyway.

CHAPTER IV

*'My first twinge of foreboding came as I
watched Milton Obote raise the flag of
independence. My anxiety had no precise form
or cause. It was more the sensing of an
unfamiliar shift of emphasis, a gap between
what was fitting and what was not.'*

Sir Edward Mutesa,
the Kabaka of Buganda (King Freddie)

December 19, 1969.

The conference ended mid-evening. At Obote's
instigation the ruling Uganda People's Congress agreed
to a resolution that Uganda should become a one party
state.

A month before King Freddie had died in poverty in
London. An inquest concluded his death had been
caused by alcoholic poisoning. At home, however,
Baganda believed the Kabaka's wine had been poisoned.

Knots of people gathered outside the Kampala
meeting hall some cheered and clapped as Obote came
down the steps.

A single pistol shot rang out. The bullet smashed
through Obote's jaw, passing out through his cheek. A
grenade hurled at the President's entourage failed to go
off.

Even as Obote was being driven to Mulago Hospital troops threw up roadblocks throughout Kampala. Cars were held up for hours; lucky drivers were simply manhandled. Others were forced to lie in the ditch, to be clubbed with rifle butts.

A British family heading for a diplomatic reception at the High Commission turned for home. Soldiers at one roadblock fired volleys into the air. A car was burning. Three corpses lay on the verge.

Shooting continued throughout the night. The death toll rose. Seven bodies were officially taken to the city mortuary. Many more were hastily buried in the moist soil of Kampala's outskirts.

Just at the moment the assassin levelled his pistol at Obote, Idi Amin was resting, shoes off and tunic open, in the living room of his home not 500 yards from the conference hall.

He heard the shot, the commotion. . . . and the voices of soldiers approaching. Amin dashed through the back door and scaled a barbed wire fence lining the ill-kept garden. The barbs tore into his legs and hands as he clambered up . . .

He reappeared the next day and said he had feared it was an assassination attempt against *him*.

Amin's extraordinary flight was to have critical repercussions.

It snapped his already strained relationship with deputy army commander, Brigadier Okoya who bitterly criticised Amin, accusing him of behaviour tantamount to desertion. He also quarreled with Amin over his handling of investigations into the attempt on Obote's life.

For Okoya the row was to prove fatal. Five weeks after the shooting incident Okoya visited his home near Gulu air base north of the capital. The Brigadier slumped dead from a pistol shot fired at close range as he stood on the porch of the house after dark. The assailants burst into the house and gunned down Okoya's wife, Anna.

Police launched an inquiry into the murder. Initial

investigations implicated Amin. But statements by a group of soldiers to that effect were withdrawn—on the grounds they had been made under duress.

Army commander Amin did his utmost to thwart the police investigations. He barred police access to Army personnel for questioning and was able to divert the investigations.

In the meantime six Baganda were sentenced to life imprisonment for plotting the assassination of Obote.

Obote out of hospital and back at work, was to escape a second assassination attempt. The attackers, armed with a machine gun, fired at the wrong car—that of vice president John Babiiha. He was unharmed.

The time of Obote's estrangement from Amin was drawing closer. The two men had not so much been friends as collaborators. To the President's annoyance Amin had taken it upon himself to give material support to Anyanya guerrillas fighting a long rebellion in Southern Sudan.

He had broadened his own power within the army by stepping up the recruitment of Nubian and Sudanese from his West Nile region.

Obote censured Amin for going behind his back and secretly sent men of the paramilitary General Service Unit to police the border with Sudan'...at the prompting of his cousin, Akena Adoko.

When Amin thought of Adoko he was angry. Adoko, an avowed communist, masterminded the formation of the president's 'private armies', the GSU and Special Force. Adoko headed the secret police and had created a petticoat brigade of Mata Haris spying in almost every office, bar and corner cafe.

Furthermore, Adoko wanted to boost the strength of Acholi and Lango in the Army with preferential promotions for them.

Politically, Obote pressed ahead with his 'Move to the Left' programme of socialist change. His 'Common Man's charter' envisaged an end to capitalism, foreign economic control and labour inequalities. In its place: a new order based on collectives and state control of industry and trade.

Since independence, medical services had tripled in Uganda. Primary and secondary education reached out over most of the country and Makerere University offered twice as many places. The gross national product was increasing by more than ten per cent annually, compared with less than four per cent in 1962.

The transition Obote envisaged would inevitably be traumatic. The first 85 companies were nationalised on May 1. One immediate effect was the withdrawal of some foreign capital.

Other problems broke the surface in town and country alike. Kondoism, or violent robbery, had reached an unprecedented pitch. Law-abiding Ugandans, who formed 'stomping gangs' of vigilantes against the Kondos, thought Adoko's police network was too pre-occupied with political intrigue to enforce the law.

To instil grass-roots socialism in the populace as a whole, Obote announced the introduction of compulsory national service and the formation of youth cadres. In the eyes of many, Obote's motives were suspect. With Kondoism increasing total national service ignored social factors which would have arisen as a result. With its male members away from home for long periods the security of families was in jeopardy.

Unemployment was also increasing; earnings falling. The common man felt the prick of higher taxes. The civil service was top-heavy: Acholi and Langi were getting lucrative sinecures and Government officials did not give up their Mercedes Benz limousines. Corruption in high places seemed to go unchecked.

Amin and Obote drifted further apart...two main issues in dispute between them: the growing powers of Adoko's paramilitary forces and Obote's determination to force Langi and Acholi promotions in the Army.

Amin concluded he was being squeezed out. His successors—perhaps Langi officers like Lieutenant Colonel Oyite Ojok—were being groomed. Adoko's informants in the services were trying to discredit Amin.

Amin's 'promotion' to Army Commander did little to alter his conclusions. In effect, he lost operational control of his troops. He was also particularly angered by the promotion of a northerner, favoured by Obote, to the post of Army Chief of staff.

Finally a major reorganisation of Uganda's armed forces was scheduled to take place when Amin was away representing the Government at Nasser's funeral in Cairo.

While Amin made a pilgrimage to Mecca after the funeral, Kampala buzzed with rumours that he would face arrest on his return. To meet this possibility units of troops loyal to him mounted guard at Entebbe airport for Amin's return and escorted him to Kampala in a heavily armed convoy.

Obote prepared to leave for Singapore. As he did so, he left an ultimatum for Amin and Defence Minister Onama. The auditor general's report had shown 40 million shillings was missing from defence funds.

Obote wanted an explanation. And he wanted the Okoya murder cleared up.

The stage was set.

Amin was in the corner. He began preparations.

Obote ordered Amin's arrest.

Amin moved first.

January 25—a year to day after Okoya died—Amin's loyal Malire Mechanised Battalion moved on the armouries.

In Uganda and elsewhere the events of Monday, January 25 sank in overnight.

During the night forces loyal to Obote fled into the bush around Kampala, pursued by Amin's men. The city awoke early. Obote's chauffeur was found and hacked to death. Government officials were rounded up: some were stripped of their trousers, knocked to the ground and beaten with sticks. Taxis towing empty buckets joined the street processions. Obote once publicly pledged he would live to carry the King of

Buganda's head in a bucket. Now the Buganda brought out traditional drums which had been silent since the Kabaka's death in exile. More green foliage, an ancient sign of rejoicing, bedecked cars, trucks and the handlebars of bicycles followed. Even pedestrians hung twigs and leaves around their necks.

Entebbe parish priest Joseph Keyeyune had a more sombre task. He was making arrangements for the burial at Kusubu White Fathers Cemetary of Father Jean Paul Demers and Father Gerard Perreault, whose bodies had been retrieved from Lake Victoria.

At the traditional burial grounds of the Buganda kings crowds burned effigies of Obote: they crushed melons crudely painted to signify his head. And they chanted 'Kabak Yekka'... King only.... the name of the defunct Buganda kingdom party.

Soldiers searched the houses of Obote men. In the garden of a villa used by the presidential guard they found an armoury well-stocked with Russian arms and ammunition, including .82mm mortars, which had been shipped to Uganda through Dar es Salaam in crates marked: A Gift from the Red Cross of the Soviet Union. Told of the discovery, Amin declared: 'It proves Obote is a communist. That is why he has gone to Tanzania.' In turn, Obote responded that Amin had personally ransacked his Kampala residence. 'He blew down the door and then went in and took everything—including my underpants and my books—some 7,000 volumes. I don't know whether he is going to read them.'

Amin summoned chiefs of staff and civil servants to the Command Post. The atmosphere became tense. Wilson Oryema—Inspector General of Police under Obote and, like Obote, from the Acholi region—looked at his fingernails. Amin sat on the corner of his chair pointing his finger accusingly at the men assembled on the sun terrace. He had been on a hunting trip in northern Uganda, he said. He returned to Kampala on Sunday evening to find an Army half-track vehicle parked at the gate of his home. In it waited a bleeding soldier who reported tribal fighting had broken out within the Army. Acholi and Langi troops, they had told him, were marching on Kampala.

'I saw this was serious and immediately directed there would be no troop movement without permission,' Amid said. 'A mechanical battalion arrived in Kampala in a confused state. Other soldiers who had been misled by their officers surrendered. Others have fled with their arms into hiding ... They should come out. They will not be disciplined. All they did was to obey orders. Their officers will be courtmartialled."

Before Amin convened the meeting he had issued an order to his tank troops. Shortly before Oryema arrived at Amin's Command Post, a tank had pulled up in front of Oryema's house—and fired a single shell into it.

Now, in the meeting, Amin swung in the swivel chair to face the police chief who was sitting on his left.

Would Oryema support him? Already, Oryema had heard the news. He nodded. His 6,000 man force would back Amin.

Amin swung back to tell the rest of the meeting:

'I had this man brought to me. I could have had him killed. But I didn't. I gave him coffee.'

Amin swivelled again and opened out his arms. 'You see,' he said, 'I am not ambitious. Nor am I a tribalist. I have three wives—all from different tribes—living with me here in this house.' He stopped speaking, his eyes darting to the faces around him.

'I have ordered the soldiers to help the people. If all people die who is left to rebuild Uganda?' A burst of gunfire sounded outside. 'That is my men firing into the air,' Amin added quickly. 'They are very joyful.'

Soon Idi Amin Dada held another briefing at the Command Post. 'The instantaneous public jubilation that everywhere greeted the take-over has left everybody in no doubt whatsoever that the take-over is a very popular move indeed. What is the cause of all this public joy and excitement? The public reacted this way because they felt a great relief at the overthrow of an oppressive

46

and unpopular regime. A great heavy weight has been lifted off the shoulders of the general public so they went almost wild with joy.'

From Dar es Salaam Obote countered: Oryema's pledge to Amin had been influenced by the murder of his father by Amin thugs.

Buganda demanded the removal of Obote's portrait from Independence arch at the entrance to Kampala's parliament . . . and a new name for the Appollo Hotel.

'I am not a man who wants to remove the portrait of one man and replace it with mine,' Amin said. 'If we start doing things that way we cannot write the history of Uganda.'

Already, the burly ex-British army private had begun to make momentous sayings which he himself in the years to come would contradict alone by his actions.

There were some things, however, even he could not erase by words. He did it by murder and terror.

Augustine Kamwa, Kampala branch chairman in Obote's Uganda People's Congress party, fled a mob which attacked his house. The mob ransacked each room before setting the building alight. Shops and properties belonging to UPC members were broken into and gutted. Rioters burst into the Florida Night Club— owned by an Obote sympathiser—smashing all the glass doors and windows and breaking up the furniture. Stores near Kampala's main bus station were looted.

In the days which followed the coup Amin began to enjoy the eminence which an unsuspecting world— unaware of his terrorism and cold blooded murder— attached to his words. At various meetings on different occasions he was to say:

'Obote's regime was one of great hypocrites,' Amin said. 'Obote was anything but a socialist. Obote had two palaces in Entebbe, three in Kampala, one in Jinja, one in Tororo and one in Mbale. All these places had to be furnished and maintained at great public expense, and yet all but one remained idle and unused almost all the time. It is no wonder that the people of Jinja in their

47

great joy attacked and damaged the so-called President's palace at Jinja, total destruction of the palace only being prevented by the Army...

'Obote's mode of living was also anything but socialist. He heavily indulged in drink, smoking and women and carried a big retinue wherever he went. This idle living was also indulged in by his chief of Intelligence Napthali Akena Adoko.'

Amin came to their "crimes". Corruption, he said, was so widespread it was taken for granted. Ministers and public servants owned fleets of cars, buses, scores of houses for tenting, bars, petrol stations, taxi businesses, butcheries, aeroplanes...

Amin puffed out his chest and cheeks. 'Obote's Move to the Left, the Common Man's Charter is a lot of hot air. What is most instructive is that he never dared bring out what was perhaps the most urgently needed proposal—relating to a code of conduct for his ministers. That was a subject he never dared tackle...'

Amin basked in their adulation. 'I have received hundreds of messages congratulating the Armed Forces. These messages continue to pour in and for us who are now responsible for the good and proper running of Uganda affairs this is a source of great encouragement...'

Amin made his vows. 'The masses who are rejoicing at the overthrow are remembering Obote's misdeeds, also his inaction, his ineptitude and political impotence at times of great need,' Amin said slowly. 'Time will without doubt reveal more of his weaknesses galore. For my part, I can only wish great luck and good sailing to the Uganda Second Republic. My Government will at the right time make arrangements for honest, fair and completely free general elections... I shall then go back to the barracks and take orders from whoever is elected president. My Government firmly believes in peace and the international brotherhood of man... I will maintain good relations with all countries of the world... I don't believe in a one party system. The president cannot be a proper leader if no-one is opposing him . . .'

Between the speeches, perhaps made with the world outside in mind, Amin was most conscious of one thing. He needed to maintain his image in Uganda.

In the days immediately after the coup, he often left the Command Post in one open jeep. He wore dark glasses. It was time to be seen by the people—and the soldiers—in the streets. He saw an Army captain breaking down the door of a general store. Amin stopped his jeep and lumbered over to the captain. He tore off the captain's epaulettes, buttons and insignia of rank and ordered him back to barracks as a private.

With all the show his displays easily won Amin had an over-riding fear. His old adversary was still alive.

Tanzania could attempt to reinstate Obote. Nyerere's commanders would as a matter of course mobilise units along the two countries' 100 mile common border. Amin put the Uganda Air Force on standby. He made a radio broadcast. 'Our Air Force is good, our Army is mechanised. We are preparing a warm reception for invaders. We are waiting for them. These are not rumours—but the Ugandan people should not be afraid. We will be able to repel any attempt to interfere with the internal affairs of our country. We will fight them and we will fight them effectively. We will meet them on the ground.'

Amin's soldiers dug slit trenches at Entebbe. Others in the capital distributed copies of a circular letter purporting to have been found at the villages of Banda and Ntinda. Addressed to President Nyerere, State House and Cabinet secretariat, P.O. Box 9102, Dar es Salaam, the letter began: 'There is no doubt we the common men are behind General Idi Amin. When you authorise, which we hope you will not do, your army to attack Uganda you would be declaring war on the common men. You will not be fighting the Uganda Army alone but the whole people of Uganda, young and old, men and women. We shall all fight behind General Amin. We are ready to die rather than be ruled again by dictators. The coup is no longer an Army coup but the people's coup. The common man is ready to fight and defend his fatherland.' A note on the top of the letter stated: If you agree with this please sign it, get as many friends to sign it, put it in an envelope and post it.

Near Gulu air base north of Kampala, where more than 100 Soviet military advisors and technicians were stationed for training Ugandans on a newly-delivered MIG fighter squadron, troops spread out into the bush to attack units of Obote's General Service Unit and the paramilitary Special Force. The hard corps put up resistance outside Kampala and to the West.

The soldiers guarding Parliament withdrew. They were replaced by six Securicor askaris with shotguns. The Sherman tank drove away from Amin's Command Post.

'I need hardly add' Amin told a gathering of diplomats, 'that the military government is now firmly in control of the whole country. Some confused men fight for a lost cause. Why continue useless opposition causing bloodshed?'

Fifty thousand people streamed out to Kololo airstrip. Two armoured cars made a way through the crowd for Amin's jeep. Cheers welled up.

'Dada, Dada, You have saved us. Long Live Dada.'

Women waved banana leaves: one broke through, hurled herself at Amin and kissed him. Sixty released political detainees were swept in on the swell. Held shoulder high Benedicto Kiwanuka, once prime minister and leader of the opposition Democratic Party, waved, just keeping his balance. Princess Nalinya Ndagire, the Kabaka's sister, wept and stopped in prolonged embraces. Grace Ibingira, jailed secretary general of Obote's UPC, called out: 'I am more convinced now that dictatorship cannot survive in Uganda. Wounds Obote gave Uganda have been healed by the courage and wisdom of General Amin. I pray that dictatorship may never come back to Uganda again.' Five years previously Ibingira and four other ministers,

Mathias Ngobi, Balak Kirya, George Magezi and Dr Emanuel Lumu, had been arrested during a cabinet meeting.

Amin stepped onto a makeshift rostrum. 'The government will not tolerate any form of lawlessness. I have decided that all forms of political activity such as public discussions, meeting and rallies will not at the moment be permitted. They are therefore suspended with immediate effect. As soon as the security situation warrants the resumption of these political activities they will be immediately allowed.'

Amin looked at Joseph Kiwanuka, a sitting MP detained after an attempt on Obote's life two years before, and Shaban Opolot, a former Brigadier and commander of the Uganda Army whom Obote believed sympathised with Buganda royalists in 1966.

What Amin was to say and what his actions were to signify were different.

In Nakasero Road, a quiet residential street, 100 soldiers opened fire with rifles and machine guns at the house of Obote's brother-in-law, Dr Abeni. In the Newfield Nursery school next door 80 terrified children and white-haired Scottish schoolmaam Jennie Smith pressed themselves to the floor of the tin-roofed schoolhouse. The walls of Abeni's house disintegrated under the barrage of gunfire, the windows hung from shattered frames, the building caught fire. Two bodies were brought out of the house and a third man, cowering in a corner, gave himself up. A platoon commander said a single shot had been fired at the soldiers from the house.

Meanwhile, the affairs of state had to continue.

Amin summoned civil servants and Cabinet ministers to the Command Post. He stripped 18 Obote ministers of their responsibilities and ordered government business to be handled by Permanent Secretaries in each ministry. The ministers would no longer be allowed bodyguards and would return all Government property, including their cars. 'Now you had better be good boys,'

51

Amin wagged his finger at them. A soldier jostled in Basil Bataringaya, his face bruised and unshaven. He sat two chairs away from Amin.

'You were one of those fellows who started all this trouble,' Amin said. 'You know that on the 11th of January a secret meeting was held at the home of Maitum Engena at which a decision was taken to murder me and a lot of other people....This was confirmed in a telephone conversation between you and the president in Singapore on Saturday. Arrangements were complete for the murder of me and others...' Amin paused, nodding at his aide de campe, Captain Valerie Ochima. Ochima motioned armed guards to escort Bataringaya out.

The session ended.

Bataringaya was to live in suspense some time yet.

'The general had been magnanimous,' Finance Minister Lawrence Sattala remarked outside. 'I thought we would all be arrested.'

A dozen members of Uganda's Singapore delegation returned to Kampala. President Julius Nyerere returned to Tanzania from India. Welcoming demonstrators carried banners: Amin Go To Hell. Obote had committed Uganda to follow a socialist and truly independent path. Once again an African Army had resorted to the bullet to oust the leader of a nation and his Government. A successful coup d'etat in Uganda would be a bitter blow to African unity and the struggle to liberate Southern Africa—an act of treason.

Milton Obote had been one of the formost champions of unity and opponents of colonialism and racism. 'Let it be known that for us the African revolution is all we exist for. That revolution has no frontiers. That revolution tolerates no traitors....The cruel and ruthless hand of imperialism has been responsible for this criminal coup....'

Sir Wilberforce Nadiope and Benedicto Kiwanuka led a procession from Kampala's High Court to Nakivubo Stadium.

The released detainees presented a gift to Lieutenant Colonel Obitre Gama for Amin—a bible and a koran.

'General Amin has delivered this country from tyranny, oppression and political enslavement just as Moses delivered the Jews from Pharoah's bondage.' In 70 years of colonial rule British authorities detained 35 Ugandans. In nine years Obote detained 4,000. 'Such was the man who posed as a democrat, a socialist and the champion of the common man.'

Attorney General Nkambo Mugerwa urged: 'Obote supporters should join hands to build a new Uganda based on democratic ideals in which tribalism and religious intolerance will have no part.'

Amin prepared to bring back the body of Sir Edward Mutesa II, the Kabaka of Buganda, for a state funeral. 'Sir Edward was the first president of Uganda and an honorary colonel in the Grenadier Guards. He should be given a decent burial with full military honours.' he said.

The body of the Kabaka, known as King Freddie to the powerful Buganda, lay in state at Namirembe Cathedral. Home from his private school in Britain for the funeral the Kabaka's son, Prince Ronnie Mutebi, was overwhelmed by Buganda. Travelling into the capital his Mercedes was lifted off the ground by the milling crowd. Again, Amin received wild applause.

Eighty Langi teenagers caught crossing the border into Tanzania admitted they were going to join pro-Obote forces there. 'No harm will befall you,' Amin told them. 'You were misguided but caught before you could betray your country.'

Amin toured country districts. In a Langi village he met the father of G.S.U. Chief Akena Adoko. The old man complained that soldiers smashed his furniture and stole his wireless. Amin wrote out a personal cheque to cover the losses. Commented a veteran British observer: 'I have never encountered a more benevolent and apparently genuinely popular leader as General Amin.'

Three weeks after the take-over seventy Army officers and more than 2,000 men had died. Within three

53

months 10,000 civilians had been slaughtered. Crocodiles basked beneath the Karume Falls Bridge, the Bridge of Blood, spanning the River Nile. They grew both fat and lazy. Idi Amin Dada cancelled elections and filled his prisons. Bataringaya was to die. Benedicto Kiwanuka, appointed chief justice, was to be dragged from his chambers at Kampala's Law courts and savagely murdered.

The honeymoon was over. Uganda turned to the horror of Amin's Lust to Kill.

CHAPTER V

*'I am not a politician but a professional soldier.
Ours is not a political government. It is a
government of action.'*
                    Major General Idi Amin Dada.

Just as soon as Amin had grabbed power the tyranny
began.

Amin issued a directive. It gave all members of the
General Service Unit—as well as 'all persons who have
been on the payroll or who have in any way received
payment from the General Service Unit'—twenty four
hours to turn themselves in and surrender arms.

On the face of it, the directive looked like a brief
amnesty. It wasn't. Those who took it as such—mainly
civil servants engaged in paperwork for Adoko's special
forces—were beaten, jailed and ultimately killed.

Amin issued a decree. It empowered his troops to
arrest anyone on suspicion of any crime. It gave soldiers
carte blanche for unprecedented sprees of looting and
killing which, together with continuing clashes between
Kabaka loyalists and Obote sympathisers settling old
scores, annointed Amin's Uganda with blood.

Any hint of opposition to Amin, even simple
reservations about a military take-over, were crushed

with ferocious brutality by extermination squads drawn from the Nilotic and Sudanic units Amin had so painstakingly nurtured within the Army.

The killer squads swept through the Army camps dragging out suspected Obote men. Acholi and Langi soldiers and civilians were the first victims. The civilians were taken from their offices and homes.

In the beginning the killers had no regard for secrecy or subtlety. They came in the day-time. They asked for lists of office staff. They chose names starting with "O". That was a common characteristic of Acholi and Langi family names.

Then they came at night ... rapping on the doors, not waiting for the doors to be opened, smashing them down. They took their victims to Kampala's Makindye prison, headquarters of the Military Police.

Or to Naguru, three miles from the city centre, which was to become headquarters for Amin's terror police ironically named the Public Safety Unit.

Or to Nakasero in Kampala, the barracks of the secret police, shortly afterwards known as the State Research Bureau, one of Amin's principal torture and slaughter groups.

Or they were taken to Army barracks scattered throughout the country.

Troops loyal to Obote held out at Moroto barracks. After several weeks they were overpowered and liquidated—to a man. In Kampala, army chief of staff Brigadier Hussein Suleiman—the northerner whose promotion Amin had bitterly opposed three months before—was captured as he tried to escape. Taken to Luzira maximum security prison the Brigadier died slowly, beaten with rifle butts and slashed with pangas and steel wrenching tools.

Hundreds of prominent Ugandas were 'disappearing.' Amin's prisons were full. Prisoners were 'removed' to make way for more in the already overcrowded cells.

Not since the Nazis had used terror to overcome democracy had there been such stark brutality. If it was to be years before the world was to know the extent of Amin's mass murder machine, the innocent unsuspecting Acholi and Langi soldiers who had applauded his seizure of power were to know now.

Lined up in Makindye, their limbs and skulls were smashed with sledgehammers and car axles. Those who took hours to die were shot. Prisoners from neighbouring cells loaded the bodies into light trucks and washed the concrete floor, collecting up teeth, bone, brain tissue and eyeballs in water pails.

When the trucks returned they too were cleaned of the thick, coagulating blood ...

Corpses were driven to Mabira forest, east of Kampala on the road to Jinja. Trucks, buses and jeeps also took corpses to nearby Lugazi sugar plantation and the Namanve cedar plantation and to Nandere forest, near Murchison Bay prison, the Sebize River and Paradise Island.

The next destinations of the convoys of death: Karume Falls—Bridge of Blood—and Nakasolo, near Gulu.

The names of the dead were perhaps known only to their families or friends. But as the massacres continued Amin was appointing his first cabinet—many of whom would join the list of dead and vanished which was to signify his years of rule.

Idi Amin Dada nominated himself as Head of State, Minister of Defence and commander in chief of the armed forces. Charles Oboth Ofumbi, formerly secretary for Defence, joined the council of ministers as minister of state for Defence. Lieutenant Colonel Obitre Gama, officer commanding the Paratroopers school, became minister of Internal Affairs. A young lawyer, Wanume Kibedi, became Foreign Affairs Minister.

The list contained 18 names. Inspector General of Police Wilson Oryema accepted the portfolio of Mineral and Water Resources. Swearing in, by Chief Justice Sir Dermot Sheridan, was to take place on February 5. The Mechanised Reconnaissance Regiment would mount a guard of honour.

Amin sent emissaries to seek international recognition for his government. All he had so far were messages from inside Uganda. These were in plenty, if they were cautions and obsequious some of them:

'We respectfully assure your Excellency of our loyalty and full co-operation. We shall continue our efforts with renewed vigour in helping to achieve Uganda's goal of economic independence under Your Excellency's wise and courageous leadership.'

'We congratulate Your Excellency, the Military Head of State, on the assumption of your new onerous duties and the wise choice of Cabinet ministers and wish to assure Your Excellency and the new government of the Board's unswerving loyalty and devoted service to the new Government and all the people of Uganda.'

On swearing-in day Britain recognised Amin's government, a lead soon to be followed—oblivious of Amin's bloodletting. News of it seemed not to have spread: Ugandans themselves who knew seemed not to want to believe it.

Idi Amin arrived at Kololo airstrip for the swearing-in to the sound of a 21-gun salute, traditional drums and horns and booming applause. Amin stood in an open car without the usual escort of motor-cycle and police cars. Holding the bible in his right hand Amin swore he would 'truly exercise all functions of the Head of Government and do right to all manner of people without fear, favour or ill-will.'

Fourteen cabinet ministers—three were still out of the country canvassing for diplomatic recognition—took the oath of allegiance that they would 'to the best of my judgement give counsel and advice to the military Head of State for the good management of public affairs' and vowed they would not directly or indirectly reveal any state secrets which would. come to their knowledge in the course of their duties.

Amin briefly addressed the crowds. Tanzania was preparing military action against Uganda, he said, and

Sudanese Air Force planes had bombed Ugandan villages along the northern border.

'Tanzania and the Sudan are meddling in the internal affairs of Uganda. We have no intention of sending troops to fight them,' Amin said. 'We shall keep our tempers cool and strive to deal with those countries as members of the Organisation of African Unity.'

The bombings, Amin claimed, followed a visit by Dr Obote to Khartoum, where he met Sudanese leaders and visited the Sudanese leaders and visited the Sudanese Air Force operational centre.

'We do not yet know how many homes have been destroyed and how many people have died,' he said. 'Obote is not acting as a true son of Uganda.'

Amin shook hands with diplomats—all but the Chinese chief of mission attended the ceremony—and sped off to host a reception at State House, Entebbe, Milton Obote's former residence.

His triumph, it seemed, was complete.

To Ugandan commentators Amin had pledged to restore liberty and democratic institutions for the country's ten million people. He had given a chance for a country where once people seemed intent on pulling each other apart to pull together ... a chance to restore genuine democratic institutions instead of paper socialism ... a chance to nourish liberty and freedom in place of despotism and fear ... a chance to build an economy tailored to Uganda's needs and not to those of doctrinaire inspiration ...

'Can a big, bluff extrovert General succeed where a shrewd, introvert and sinuous politician failed in uniting a country divided by tribalist and royalist loyalties, a people whose confidence in themselves and trust in their brothers has been badly shaken by the police state techniques of the Obote regime ...?'

'Uganda, after the coup, immediately became a less furtive place where every word need no longer be guarded or one's colleague suspect ...'

'General Amin's removal of this oppressive and

59

stultifying mantle of fear and suspicion is his first decisive action on achieving power. It demonstrates a high degree of confidence in himself and his fellow countrymen...'

'The disbandment of the GSU and the abolition of government by keyhole must be widely acclaimed..."

Released from detention by Amin the former secretary general of Obote's UPC party Grace Ibingira addressed an open letter to Tanzania's President Nyerere:

'It is because of the persistent rumours intended to mislead you and all Tanzanians about the nature of Mr Obote's overthrow that I address myself to you as one of the persons who has for long admired your illustrious leadership and vision for a harmonious unified East Africa. If I talk to you justifying the coup in Uganda it is not because General Amin got me out of prison, although I am most grateful for it. It is because our brother Obote for a long time and presumably unknown to you set out systematically to corrupt and destroy most things you or any honest East African would feel most unwilling to lose.

'As you know I was a very close colleague and friend of Obote from the time we formed the UPC till the time he arrested me without charge together with four other ministers. So I talk to you of matters within my personal knowledge.

'It is to your credit that not only have you rejected "political courts under a tree" but people you have charged with grave crimes of treason have been tried by impartial judges in open court. In contrast Obote had locked up half his original cabinet by the time he was overthrown. In my almost five years of detention I have seen hundreds of innocent villagers hurled into jail. You may not know it but it is true that Obote, tragically, is a man driven to all his excesses by a deep sense of inferiority... Under the cover of unifying Uganda he introduced the deepest and most grievous rifts among Uganda people...

'Obote set out to practice nepotism of the worst kind. Uganda, which had been a free society, was riddled with gestapo spies in such fantastic numbers that it cost millions of shillings yearly to maintain this network . . .

'From 1963, I can tell you, he confided in me he would never relinquish power by constitutional means. . . . It is most painful that General Amin's revolution should be distorted as being foreign (western) engineered. It is my belief that in fact the Army delayed far too long.

'I can tell you that some of the most trusted Langi prison warders who were looking after us in jail could confide in us the fact that Obote had forfeited the respect and confidence of the whole country.

'There is a lot more I could say about why Obote had to fall but decency forbids me to state them in an open letter. I appeal to you not to support a fallen, disgraced dictator . . . General Amin has given liberty to the masses in the most convincing style. The fall of Obote is as much a fact as your being President Julius Nyerere of Tanzania. I refuse to believe that you could possibly be under pressure of external force to cling on to Obote. With respect, you are too sensible a leader to be misled.'

Ibingira, later to flee Uganda, signed off: 'I am, Sir, yours respectfully, and a companion in the struggle for African emancipation from both black and white oppression.'

Other letters had been written to Ugandan leaders in the past which, in many ways, were to become prophetic.

'In the end I shall return to the land of my fathers and my people,' wrote the Kabaka of Buganda Mutesa II in exile after Amin's soldiers attacked Mengo Hill in 1966.

King Freddie came home to a hero's welcome. He was dressed in the uniform of a major general and accompanied by a guard of honour from his old regiment, the Grenadier Guards. His aircraft, a chartered Boeing 707, was escorted by four Uganda Air Force jet fighters.

Idi Amin met him at Entebbe. The Kabaka got a 73-gun salute . . . 21 for a former president, 42 for a former king and 10 more, perhaps, because he was dead.

In Namirembe Anglican Cathedral Amin stood beside King Freddie for 30 minutes. King Freddie, almost perfectly preserved, lay in a transparent coffin. For four days thousands of Buganda—in queues three miles long—filed past their king.

The Kabaka's favorite son and chosen heir Prince Ronnie Mutebi came home, too, from his British private school, Bradfield—where the Uganda government paid a quarter of the annual £700 fees and 'The Friends of Freddie' (formed mostly of Grenadier Guards after the British Government refused a pension to the fallen king they'd knighted and made a Commander of the British Empire) paid the difference.

Ronnie received a hero's welcome too . . .

On the way from Entebbe to Kampala for his father's state funeral the Mercedes limousine carrying 16-year-old Ronnie was lifted off the ground several times by jubilant Buganda.

It was a very different scene to the cold, foggy London night 17 months before when the young black prince moved slowly through the gloom and shadows wavering in candlelight at the West London undertakers. He shook hands with a small group of mourners, moved over towards the rough wooden coffin and then stepped ahead of the rest.

A black-frocked lay preacher murmured a prayer. Ronnie drew a brown bark cloth over the coffin of his father.

He thought, then, of what might have been if Uganda had not been caught up in the wake of freedom from colonialism.

The great fire, the Eykoto, should have been lit to mark the death of a king. The 500 royal drums of Buganda should have sounded. Now there was only the grey dreariness and squalor of London.

The undertaker's men cleared out the simple personal belongings from King Freddie's cramped flat in

London's dockland. Ronnie stood by as the Kabaka's solicitor Martin Flegg read a short statement: 'Following the late Kabaka's wishes Prince Ronald Mutebi has now assumed the office of Kabaka subject to other formalities being completed.'

Flegg's words prompted a sincere but embarrassed cheer from the small, loyal audience. A serving of tea in the lawyer's office concluded Ronnie's 'coronation.'

A modest funeral service was held for Freddie at the Guards chapel, in Kensal Green.

What future for Ronnie in Amin's Uganda? His father's state funeral and interrment in the Muzibu-azaala Mpanga, the historic grass hut in Kampala where Mutesa I, Mwanga and Daudi Chwa were laid to rest, was a shrewd and immensely popular move by Amin. Despite indications by Amin that the kingdoms would not be restored to their traditional authority . . . that the Kingdoms had died with the unfortunate King Freddie . . . Uganda's Bantu hoped some vestige of the ancient lore would remain.

Ronnie himself was uncertain. At Bradfield College the prince was a model schoolboy—'intelligent and good at games.' He had been taken in by the upper-class British family of Captain Ronald Owen, his guardian and former aide de camp to the Kabaka.

Prince Ronnie could stay at home in Uganda—as could other Buganda royalists, Amin declared.

'It's marvellous news,' said Captain Owen. 'But at present the Prince has no intention of doing anything but staying in Britain to finish his O levels.'

Added Fred Mpanga, the former Buganda attorney general who followed the Kabaka into exile: 'That the boy will complete his studies in Britain does not rule out a visit to Uganda during the school holidays. It should be remembered that when the Kabaka was studying in Britain he frequently returned for a visit, and a regent was appointed in his absence.'

Ronnie's friends were being cautious and circumspect. They had noticed Amin's regime called itself the military government of the Second Republic: Uganda

63

would keep its republican constitution. They recalled that the Army which had toppled Milton Obote was the same that had shelled the Kabaka's palace, beginning his exile.

Then in command, as now: Idi Amin

Buganda gave King Freddie an emotional farewell. Buganda chiefs who attended a thanksgiving service after Amin's coup, still held themselves superior to other tribes and clung to their power. Freddie's funeral had been a risk. It could have heated up Buganda sentiments to boiling point again. But Amin was confident.

He made it known that discussions were being conducted with Flegg on the administration of King Freddie's estate and properties sequestered by the Obote Government. In a public ceremony Amin gave Prince Ronnie his father's old motor cruiser which had been renovated.

At a meeting of 1000 Buganda elders a petition was drawn up urging the military government to restore the kabakaship. Amin promised to set up a committee to examine the question, and left it at that.

It was not until the October Independence Day anniversary celebrations that Amin finally laid the restoration issue to rest. Addressing a mass rally at Kololo airstrip he pronounced:

'I want to take this opportunity to state clearly and categorically that the kingdoms will not be reintroduced and Uganda will not go back to the 1962 constitutional set-up.

'It is my wish and, after all, the wish of the vast majority of Ugandans that Uganda should remain a strong and united country.

'We are inaugurating a year which will be characterised by the promotion of human understanding. This demands, among other things, that every Ugandan must free himself from the clutches of factionalism and tribalism. Uganda must remain a strong, viable and united republic.'

THE soldiers knew they were going to die. They were herded together at gunpoint and jostled aboard the trucks.

Near Karuma Falls they were bayonetted and shot and their bodies were thrown into the Falls.

Their only crime: they belonged to the Acholi and Langi tribes.

Amin's trooper scoured Acholi and Langi districts for soldiers who had ignored orders to return to their barracks. The troops looted stores and homes.

Two Americans, Nicholas Stroh, a correspondent of the *Evening Bulletin,* Philadelphia, and a sociology lecturer at Makerere University, Robert Seidle, drove to Mbarara in the south west to investigate the reported deaths of hundreds of Acholi and Langi soldiers at the barracks there. It was the last journey the two men were ever to make. An affidavit by an officer stationed at Mbarara, Lt. Silver Tibihika later described the following events.

'The journalist came again to the barracks, I think at about 9.00 o'clock in the morning. I saw him drive in and stop at the Quarter Guard. I was at the Quartermasters' building nearby. About 15 minutes later I saw the car still there but did not see the journalist. About lunchtime I saw him with his clothes covered in mud being forced by two military policemen to run with his hands above his head towards the orderly room.

'I never saw him again but later heard officers in the mess say that the European was "kalasi", which is a term used by Nubians to indicate that a person is dead.'

That afternoon another Army officer drove Stroh's car away from the barracks.

'About four days later I was instructed to go with Intelligence officer Lt Taban to burn the car,' Lt Tibihika said under oath. 'We went to Rugaga military training area about 50 miles away and there we burned the journalists car using eight gallons of oil and 20 gallons of petrol. Lt Col Alli had told us to soak the upholstery with oil and then pour the petrol, so it would be more destructive.

'Lt Col Alli told us about two days later, after he had been to Kampala, that the matter of two missing Americans had become serious. He told Lt Taban and myself to collect the remains of the two Americans and burn them to ashes.

'We collected the remains in two sacks and drove to the barracks. It was about ten at night and no one was in the mess. We burned the remains behind the mess using oil and petrol. The remains were almost entirely reduced to ashes except that the next morning I saw a piece of arm bone and other small pieces of bone when we again put the ashes into sacks. We put the sacks into a room in the mess. That night Lt Taban and myself took the sacks to the river.'

The affidavit was submitted to an official inquiry, convened under Uganda High Court judge David Jeffreys Jones, after US government pressure.

Although the Uganda government eventually admitted responsibility for the killings every attempt was made by the government to frustrate the work of the inquiry. Judge Jones resigned from the High Court and secretly fled Uganda.

AMIN left Uganda for Israel and Britain, stopping over in Addis Ababa and Paris. From his earliest Army days Amin admired British style. He had reason to woo the Israelis: they had taught him to be a paratrooper, they were training Ugandans in civil and military spheres and, the story had it, may have been whispering in his ear all along. In Uganda Israel had access to the Sudan and the soft underbelly of the Arab world.

A 72-man guard of honour greeted Amin at Lod airport. He stepped out along the red carpet to meet foreign minister Abba Eban and defence minister Moshe Dayan. Accompanied by his own foreign minister Wanume Kibedi, Amin sped away for talks with Israeli prime minister Golda Meir. Amin wanted Israel to expand its military training programme in Uganda and sell him 'selective arms.'

The hour-long meeting was cordial. Amin expansively thanked Israel for her help. The Israelis appreciated that at least one black African country was openly on their side.

At dinner, at Dayan's Zahala home, Amin got down to the nuts and bolts of Uganda's requirements. The following day Amin was ushered into meetings with Dr Ya'acov Hertzog, director general in the prime minister's office, Simcha Dinitz, Mrs Meir's political advisor, Brigadier Israel Lior, the prime minister's military secretary, Ya'acov Shimon of the Foreign Ministry and Brigadier Yitzhak Bar-On, from Israel's defence ministry.

Israel was taking Amin very seriously indeed.

For his send-off at the end of the visit there was a full ministerial line-up and the guard of honour with regimental colours flying. Amin boarded his Israeli-built white Commodore executive jet. At the controls was an Israeli pilot, Colonel Shapiro.

The honeymoon, however, was only a prelude to disaster and estrangement.

In Britain Amin was accorded an equally warm and businesslike welcome. The Ugandan party drove quickly from Gatwick airport to a London hotel where he changed before attending a dinner at Prime Minister Edward Heath's official residence, No 10 Downing Street. Amin shed out of his uniform, squeezing himself into a dinner jacket and starched white shirt complete with bow tie.

The dinner party might have been awkward for the brutish Amin. But Heath was not going to make it difficult for him. His last African dinner guest, Zambia's President Kenneth Kaunda, had stormed from the table after Heath's ill-chosen remark that Zambia depended on South Africa. Now Heath could only warm to the man who deposed one of his bitter detractors at the Singapore Commonwealth summit.

With vitriol Milton Obote had attacked the British government's proposals to sell arms to South Africa and had threatened to pull Uganda out of the Commonwealth over the matter. Indeed, it had been the arms sales issue that made it imperative for Obote to travel to Singapore to add his voice to black Africa's clamour against Heath's intent...

Amin did not take brandy after dinner. Sir Alec Douglas Home and Réginald Maudling were there to make polite conversation. The Ugandans said goodnight to their hosts shortly after 11 o'clock.

The next day Amin saw Defence Minister Lord Carrington. They talked of Harrier jets and Saracen armoured cars. To aid Minister John Wood, Amin suggested Britain 'prolong' loan agreements to Uganda affecting some £30 million in debt repayments.

Britain showed willing by announcing an additional £10 million aid programme for Uganda.

Amin threw a party at the plush Hyde Park Hotel which Prime Minister Heath attended. He spoke to Uganda students in the conference hall at London's Uganda house:

Uganda, he said, could not afford to go through with the nationalisation programme begun by Obote. If lawlessness was to be overcome priority had to be given to security...

Amin lunched with Queen Elizabeth and Prince Philip at Buckingham Palace. He visited the Royal Military Academy, Sandhurst, and then boarded an aircraft of the Queen's Flight bound for Edinburgh—where he was to be guest of the G.O.C. in Scotland Sir Henry Leask. He was taken to Holyrood, the historic castle of the Kings of Scotland and the Ugandan flag flew over Edinburg Castle when Amin took the salute at a memorial service for Scots who died in the two world wars.

He wanted to swim in the sea—but, in the spring chill, settled for a shopping spree along Princess Street with his wife Malyami and son Moses.

Two-year-old Moses appeared later in a kilt at a Beating of Retreat by the King's Own Scottish Borderers at the British Army's Scottish headquarters.

AT MAKINDYE the man watched through a crack in the cell door. The guards were jeering and laughing in the corridor. One of them wore a black cloak which trailed behind him on the stone floor. When he had been brought in the man had seen the distinctive Sudanese tribal scars on the faces of the guards.

They had pushed him into a cell already crammed with another 30 men. He had become accustomed to the smell of their urine now. The bucket in the centre of the dark cell was futile. Some of the men's clothing was in tatters, their skin showing the welts of the whips. A young boy had been groaning all night long: his leg was broken, one of his elbows crushed. He crawled through the slime and pressed his face at the bottom of the door to draw in air.

Others slumped on the floor inertly—exhausted, staring blankly, shocked, hypnotized by fear.

The guards jeered more loudly at the four naked men standing along the wall outside. The man could hear the double-lashes of the hippo tail whips and see the men cowering on their hands and knees. The whips peeled open their skin. A second guard, crouching low, beat at their genitals with an iron rod.

They hauled the men up: half-leaning, half-falling, half-standing at the wall. The man saw the glint of a knife.

At last, the cloaked guard plunged the knife into the belly of each man. After the last had fallen, he licked the blade.

IN BRITAIN and Israel Idi Amin made out that his country was facing external threats—from Tanzania in the south and Sudan in the north. He accused Tanzania's Nyerere and Sudanese leader general Gaafer Nimeiri (himself brought to power in a military coup) of drawing together a seven-nation 'war council' to return Milton Obote to power.

Amin cried 'wolf'. He had claimed that guerrillas from the Sudan had fought battles with Uganda troops which left 600 dead. Missionaries and aid personnel, however, reported, no military activity on the border. It was also clear that Soviet-manned Uganda Air Force MIG Squadrons had not taken off from their Gulu base during the time Sudanese bombing raids were said to have taken place in northern Uganda.

Amin maintained the Russian pilots refused to give chase.

IF THERE was going to be a casualty of Amin's elusive wars it looked as if it would be the East African Community, an economic common market linking Tanzania, Uganda and Kenya.

Tanzania had already pulled out the plugs of its telegraph grid to Uganda and stopped direct air flights between the two countries. Kenya, in the meantime, took no drastic action: 'wait and see' was their policy.

With the Community in danger of collapse, Amin's takeover also began to gnaw at the consciences of African heads of state further afield.

Obote-hired Yugoslav contractors were building Kampala's Organisation of African Unity conference centre. The £6 million complex was to have been a showpiece—a symbol of African solidarity.

Amin ordered the work to go on. Within six months the conference hall for 2000 delegates, small halls, catering, interpreting and broadcasting facilities and a 140 room luxury hotel with separate VIP residences, was complete.

Only OAU delegates were missing.

Zambia, Tanzania, Somalia and Guinea would not recognise Amin as a 'club' member. It was determined diplomacy by Nigeria's General Gowon, ironically toppled from power attending the summit in 1975 when Kampala finally got its OAU delegates, which averted an irrevocable split in the Organisation over recognition of Amin.

THE MAN'S turn came as he knew it would. First, they pulled him from the cell and beat him with clubs...to the wheel torture.

His head was forced into the centre of the metal wheel rim of a truck. A boot on his neck, guards holding his legs.

They whipped his back. They struck the rim of the

wheel with iron bars until the man collapsed from the pain in his ears and brain.

Laying the foundation stone of the Aru Falls Hotel in East Acholi Amin said the ceremony was a step forward for Uganda's economic development. Regional development had been neglected in the past and his military government would ensure balanced development throughout the country.

The General moved on to the north west to open the hilltop Kitgum Hotel. 'I am determined to develop the hotel industry as soon as possible to meet the needs of tourist and others coming to Uganda,' he proclaimed.

But before the end of the first year of Amin's rule, Uganda's tourist industry had been all but stifled. In the four years up to the coup d'etat the number of visitors increased to 80,000 a year—and the Uganda Tourist Development Corporation had projected the country could play host to as many as a quarter of a million tourists by 1976.

Amin was later to ban tourism under the pretext that he was reorganising the industry. When the two year ban was lifted tourists returned not in their thousands, but in tenacious handfuls, only to find facilities more run down than reorganised. The trickle of visitors then dried up almost completely.

Not only did tourism suffer in Amin's first months of rule. The farming economy, accounting for some 90 per cent of exports—mainly in Arabica and Robusta varieties of coffee, cotton and tea—began feeling the effects of a new blight . . . Amin's dictatorship.

Despite his promises, Amin had indefinitely cancelled elections and a return to civilian rule. He continued with the sabre-rattling of which he was to become a master, stressing threats to Uganda's territorial integrity from its neighbours: Sudan to the north and Tanzania to the south. He seized upon a lesson from history: threats from without forged national unity and covered up internal shortcomings.

And they obscured the killings.

'I would be happy to meet President Nimeiri of Sudan for discussions that might lead to a complete normalisation of relations between Uganda and Sudan," Amin pronounced to the Sudanese Charge d'Affaires in Kampala, Mr Birido.

Amin had summoned the Sudanese representative to thank the Khartoum government for its belated recognition of his regime and the welcome given to Ambassador Weni, head of Uganda's diplomatic mission to Khartoum, when he presented his credentials to Nimeiri. Amin told Birido of his intention to make the mission a top-grade one as soon as necessary finances were available. In addition, a commercial attache would be despatched to the southern Sudanese centre, Juba.

Amin, however, was not one to let an opportunity slip away. Relations between the two countries had been strained—and, he reminded the diplomat pointedly, the common border remained closed to normal traffic. For his part, Amin said, he would not allow Uganda soil to be used by any subversive elements in their design against the recognised, legitimate government of Sudan. By the same token, he did not expect Sudan to harbour his opponents. If Sudan was not yet ready to take up his offer to send a high-level delegation to Kampala to discuss mutual differences—in particular, the border issue which had been unresolved since 1969—he could at least lay on an aircraft to fly Birido and embassy officials to the border.

'We will give you a car to travel to places where the plane cannot land,' Amin offered.

Next, Amin flew to Kisangani in north eastern Zaire to meet President Mobutu Sese Seko. It was the first meeting of the two Generals since Amin seized power. The meeting was good humoured and cordial. Amin told the leader of his vast eastern neighbour state he had opened Uganda's border with Tanzania the month before only on the advice of Mobutu himself, Kenya's President Jomo Kenyatta and Emperor Haile Selassie of Ethiopia—but Uganda was still being attacked by guerrillas operating from Tanzanian territory.

Visiting Kabamba Military Training area to watch a military exercise Amin thanked Israel for providing military assistance to the Uganda Army. To the sound of booming artillery he congratulated the Ugandan commander of the artillery course for his 'effort and zeal'. Uganda soldiers had achieved high standards in various specialised units—and only four Israeli instructors remained in Uganda. Amin told his soldiers to work hard and not to lapse into complacency. 'The war is not over. Therefore you should always be prepared, day and night.'

Hosting a luncheon at the Command Post, supposedly for soldiers wounded during the Army take-over, General Amin kept to the same tack. Guerrillas bent on ousting the Army would be met by 'Ugandan countermeasures'. The Armed Forces were prepared for any eventuality and opponents should give up any idea of challenging him. Curiously invited to lunch was the Papal Pro-nuncio Archbishop Luigi Bellotti.

On Christmas Eve Amin drove to Kasubi tombs, burial place of the Kabakas. A festive crowd ran to greet him. Amin shook hands and slapped backs, until he was hoisted shoulder high. Impressed by what he took to be spontaneous appreciation Amin ordered a group of soldiers from the Mechanised Battalion to distribute 1000 shillings among Buganda tending the tombs. A further gift to them was to be a bull.

Uganda radio broadcast that the General had received a flood of Christmas messages from his 'personal friends'. Names in this bland category were Edward Heath, President Kenyatta, President Kamuzu Banda of Malawi and Gambian Prime Minister Sir Dauda Jawara. The radio appealed to Ugandans to celebrate Christmas 'in peace'.

Just after Christmas the Chinese Charge D'affaires in Kampala, Mou Ping, received a formal invitation asking Chairman Mao Tse Tung to attend celebrations a month afterwards marking the first anniversary of the Uganda coup. Amin hoped Chairman Mao would find it convenient to come 'to the heart of Africa during our

73

auspicious occasion.'

A few days later Amin strolled along one of the capital's main thoroughfares, Kampala Road, with a group of ministers and government officials. Business in central Kampala came to a standstill as the filling streets resounded with shouts of 'Dada Yekka'. The President had wanted to inspect the city's preparations for the anniversary.

If foreign governments chose to disbelieve the first inklings of Amin's excesses the man in the street was apparently still largely unaware of them.

Amin, after 12 months of bellicose rule, was still the hero of the hour.

CHAPTER VI

*'I have repeatedly emphasised there is no room
in Uganda for hatred and enmity. I have stated
I will not victimise or favour anybody. Our aim
must be unity and love.'*

Idi Amin Dada

February 1972

Former Criminal Investigation Department chief
Mohamed Hassan had been moved from Luzira to
Mutukula prison, near Uganda's south-western border
with Tanzania. Hassan was severely weakened by
dysentery—a condition worsened by a three day period
without food.

'Don't worry about your food,' the soldier said.
'Tomorrow you will have a good diet.'

The following day the stumbling police detective was
led into the sun-baked prison courtyard and summarily
executed in a burst of rifle fire. And of another 510
Acholi and Langi army personnel taken to Mutukula,
only 102 remained alive. The dead had suffered the same
fate as Hassan—but en masse, starting with officers.

A group of at least 42 officers had been locked in an
outlying prison building stacked with explosives. A
series of simple charges were simultaneously detonated

both inside and outside the building. The officers had been forced, after beatings, to endorse statements confessing treason.

Acholi and Langi servicemen numbered roughly 5,000 at the time of Amin's take-over. In a year an estimated 4,000 of them had been killed as well as an unknown number of General Service Unit men, which Internal Affairs Minister Charles Oboth Ofumbi, during Amin's absence in West Germany, described Obote's GSU as 'a giant organisation of terror and suppression serving power hungry and selfish despots.'

Such killings did not go unnoticed—by the potential victims; rather than die unprotesting they plotted to escape.

A soldier collecting the urine pail from a Mutukula cell scoffed at the inmates: 'You have urinated for the last time.'

But as soon as he had left, the prisoners turned back to their furious work on the stone wall. Using broken blades from table knives, metal handles of mugs, they finally broke through.

Machine gun fire cut into the waves of escapees charging for freedom. Mortars opened fire on the prison, followed by artillery from emplacements beyond the perimeter. Still, 19 out of 100-or-so prisoners in the breakout reached Tanzania. They were treated at Bukoba hospital for serious wounds.

FAR AWAY in Kampala, leaders of Uganda's Asian community felt their own forebodings. Some 12,000 Asians applying for Uganda citizenship had their applications suddenly and inexplicably cancelled. The military authorities were known to be mulling over new naturalisation conditions believed aimed at the 50,000 strong Asian community, a large proportion of which held dual British-Uganda nationality.

A census of Asians resulted in the issue of a special identity pass, known as the Green Pass, without which all movment by Asians was forbidden. Amin convened a special conference of Asian leaders and harangued them

76

about business malpractices.

The Asians lived with their uncertainty for another six months. Then, Amin—true to his idiosyncratic manner of Government—called together troops at Tororo barracks in Eastern Uganda and announced he had been instructed by God to throw out the entire Asian population. The divine guidance had come to him in a dream.

Hours later Uganda television cameras swept over proceedings at Kampala's OAU conference centre. Representatives of Ugandan Cooperative Societies had gathered for International Cooperative Day. Amin's bulky figure filled the screen: the microphones amplified placatory remarks directed at the delegates.

'Asians came to Uganda to build the railway. The railway is finished. They must leave now.'

Amin gave them 90 days to pack up and go. Asians were incredulous. It could not have been a serious announcement. Such mass expulsion was not possible. Surely, it was a joke.

Not to Idi Amin. Uganda radio and television began an intense hate campaign. News broadcasts were framed by a new signature tune and song. The words of the song went: 'Farewell Asians, farewell Asians, you have milked the economy for too long.' The broadcasts themselves contained a string of decrees, which were wavering and contradictory. Asians holding British, Indian, Pakistani and Bangladesh passports would be forced out. But Uganda citizen Asians would not be affected.

The community breathed a measured sigh of relief.

Another broadcast said all non-citizen Asians—including those holding Kenya and Tanzania passports—must go. Another said professional Asians were exempt. Yet another broadcast then screamed: There will be no exemptions.

Citizen Asians were still safe. Or were they? The previous year's survey had recorded some 20,000 Uganda citizens within the Asian community. But such was the hostility of the campaign against Asians as a

77

whole that few citizens trusted either their future or Amin.

The Asians were told to report to the Immigration Department and produce documentary evidence confirming their citizenship—and thus their clearance to stay. It was a pretext.

Thousands of Uganda passports held by Asians were pronounced illegal. Rights to citizenship were withdrawn on the flimsiest excuse or invalidated by hastily enacted conditions of residence, family relationship and birth.

Amin was clearly going for the clean sweep. In the end, only about 6000 Asians were deemed bona fide citizens. But even for them, their troubles were not over. Amin's officials did not let up in their programme of Asian-baiting and harassment. Some whose citizenship could not be blocked by trumped-up technicalities became officially stateless when their papers were torn up by vindictive officials. Nor was their confidence helped by the fact that Amin—seemingly for publicity reasons—rescinded an order that all Asians, regardless of their citizenship, would be expelled. That, in essence, had been his intention all along.

The whimsical General dubbed his expulsion measures Uganda's 'Economic War'. Asians were wealthy, Asians had exploited the economy, Asians discriminated against Africans, Asians did not mix with Africans. The Asians were a British responsibility...

At Independence in Uganda probably as much as 80 per cent of the country's small businesses were owned and run by Asians. Indeed, the entrenched position of Asian traders, artisans and clerks had been the cause of resentment by aspirant Africans not only in Uganda—but in independent Tanzania and Kenya, too. For centuries Asians had settled along the East African coast, rarely venturing inland until the Europeans opened up the interior. For their part, the British found indigenous Africans either unwilling or unable to make up the construction gangs necessary to build the Kenya-Uganda railway, starting in 1895. The first batch of 350 Indian coolies were hired on contract with an understanding that after the work was finished they would be free to return to India or settle in East Africa.

The Asians that stayed in East Africa—about 10,000 of them by 1910—were quick to learn, adaptable and enterprising. They found biggest scope in the small retail and trading businesses. The British settlers and Colonial officials were careful to exclude Asians from any but the lowest positions in their ruling hierarchy—but encouraged them in small trading. Moreover, the settlers saw the Asians willing to operate on a profit margin which would have been considered derisory by a European.

Poor Africans with little or no economic influence inevitably developed a hatred of the prosperous traders. As the countries of East Africa attained their independence Asians were faced with the choice of taking up the citizenship of the independent territories or retaining British nationality. As it turned out, neither option was particularly advantageous.

Living in their insular religious and ethnic communities the Asians, it was true, had stood aloof from the Africans. In 1968 Kenya introduced a work permit system to eliminate non-Kenyans from sectors of the economy it was felt should be controlled by Africans. Asians retaining their British nationality believed Britain would take them unreservedly and felt betrayed when the British Government introduced immigration restriction under which 3,500 'vouchers' were issued annually allowing British Asians to enter the United Kingdom.

If anything, the Kenya precedent impressed upon Uganda Asians that they too would be an unwanted people. They also saw that, in Kenya, Asians who chose African citizenship—including the wealthy Ismaili community, following the advice of their spiritual leader, the Aga Khan—were taunted as 'paper citizens' not commited as Black Africans to national development and interested, instead, only in their own prosperity.

AS THE three-month deadline for their departure ticked closer the Uganda Asians were the butt of torrents of abuse from Amin. Their crime was economic sabotage—although little direct evidence of tax evasion, corruption or illegal dealings was ever produced. Certainly, there was no conclusive proof that business malpractices were any more common among Asians than other communities.

Uganda, however, was tottering towards economic crisis causes in part by the often-ineptly handled nationalisation policies of Milton Obote, the transition under Amin's military rule, increased spending on military hardware since the take-over, in addition to the inexpert control of economic affairs by Amin himself and soldiers elevated to important positions for bolstering his power.

Emanuel Wakhweya, a highly experienced economist and fiscal administrator, later to quit as Amin's Finance Minister, complaining that all his advice and planning had been 'scornfully rejected', was regarded as one man who could have saved the economy despite ruinous defence spending and the disruption of agriculture and industry under Amin.

The Asians provided Amin with a scapegoat.

Foreign exchange reserves had fallen and public spending dropped. The annual Army budget soared from US $20 million under Obote to nearly $100 million . . . mainly to please the soldiers by whose grace, of course, Amin was ruling Uganda.

Far from being a cure for Uganda's economic ills, the immediate effect of the expulsions was the closing down of many thriving businesses—with a consequent jump in urban unemployment. Amin's idea was that the Asians' businesses should immediately be transferred to black Ugandans.

Kampala Road, winding 2½ miles through the city centre, lost its bustle. The bars and barbers' shops and the stores and haberdasheries once stocked with rich-smelling spices and bolts of brightly-printed cloth had been shuttered up. It was clear to no-one just how the Asian property would be shared out . . .

Small African-owned shops remaining open did

roaring trade until their goods ran out. Pressed for replacements African shopkeepers began pushing up their prices, sometimes doubling them—a practice earning the shopkeepers the derisory accusation of being 'black Patels', a reference to a common Asian family name.

Street-hawkers haggled over their wares—cheap clothing, pots and pans and other small items—until they too could not replace supplies. Once they had been told to go, Asian wholesalers had not bothered to re-order goods and had cancelled outstanding orders on their books.

Schools staffed by Asian teachers were closing. In total, some 700 Asian teachers were to leave Uganda. Asian children were to vacate about 15,000 school places.

Asian residential areas—frequently nicknamed 'Bombay' by the Africans—emptied. Garages ran short of spare parts and servicing was more difficult to get. The mechanics, like electricians, plumbers, tailors, foremen, accountants, engineers, photographers, hair-dressers, pharmacists and doctors, were departing. African doctors in both private practice and hospitals worked feverishly to fill the gap.

Asian staff at Makerere University resigned from their posts. A newly-formed State Trading Corporation battled to reorganise Uganda's import trade, while the Uganda Development Corporation, already riddled with bureaucracy and inefficiency, took over abandoned enterprises—including a rayon textile mill, engineering firms, a soap works, a biscuit factory and a hotel.

Asians running sugar estates—sugar being one of the country's important secondary cash crops started in the first quarter of the century by the Mehta—were among those expelled. Other agricultural processing and essential consumer industries had also been reliant on Asian staff for the maintenance of machinery.

Britain had flown a special team to its Kampala High Commission to set about issuing entry certificates to all

81

Uganda Asians with British passports. Daily queues formed outside the office—one for people whose applications to go to Britain had been approved, the other for those whose Ugandan citizenship had been invalidated.

Passing Ugandans made their satisfaction obvious. 'The British brought Asians here to exploit us,' they called. 'Asians keep us in economic slavery.'

A common assumption at the time—which could not be disproved in the same way Amin could not prove it—was that well-to-do Asians foreseeing trouble ahead safely salted away private fortunes out of the country. Ever eager to play on his countrymen's prejudice against Asians Amin perpetuated the hatred with more claims of their treachery.

Account books, he said, had been kept in Hindi and Gujerati languages to deliberately hide irregularities from Government scrutineers. At one rally supposedly celebrating 'victory' in the economic war Amin bellowed above the noise of the drums and the dancing: 'If even I associated with Asians I would be rejected in a minute.'

As Britain prepared to receive the bulk of the misplaced Asians, smaller groups were scattered world-wide.

For instance, Canada and India agreed to take 6,000 each; the United States 1,000.

And the United Nations said it would look after Asians with nowhere to go after the expiry of Amin's deadline. (Within 24 hours of the deadline the UN organised 12 special flights to ferry 2,000 people to hastily-established transit camps in Europe.)

The exodus graphically showed up the nature of Amin's dictatorship. In an early declaration the regime promised 'foreign nationals' leaving Uganda they would be allowed to take personal belongings and 'a reasonable amount of cash'. There would be no confiscation of property: it would be sold and credited to the owners, whose bank accounts would remain intact. There would be no 'physical maltreatment' of affected persons, nor would those who inadvertently remain after the deadline suffer consequences. But they should renew their efforts to leave. This last pledge blatantly contradicted a remark by Amin himself that defaulters would be subject to severe and appropriate measures.

Predictably, the pledges were worthless. Some owners were told to leave as soon their properties had been signed over to Ugandans, ignoring time still in hand before the deadline. Harassment of the community as a whole went well beyond malicious verbal abuse. Drunken troops vented their anger on Asian families—bursting into homes, beating the physically fit and infirm alike, damaging furniture and helping themselves to anything they wanted.

Asians did not escape violent intimidation until they were safely out of Uganda.

The first group of several hundred bound for Karachi boarded the train at Kampala. The SS Karanja, berthed at Kenya's Mombasa port, would carry them away from Africa. The Asians left with what they could carry—mainly bundles of bedding and household goods which had survived rigorous searches by Kampala customs men. Little more than 50 miles along the line at Jinja a detachment of soldiers was awaiting the train. Brandishing rifles the soldiers clamoured through the train. 'All out. Bring all baggage out.'

Confused and alarmed, the passengers were herded onto the platform. There they were frisked individually and the baggage was searched again. What the Customs had left the soldiers took.

'Money? Where's your Uganda money? Where's your watch? Your radio? Your tape recorder?'

The soldiers butted the huddles of passengers with their rifles; they slapped their faces. Dazed Asians produced crumpled bank-notes and coins. Others stripped off their watches, handed over cheap Japanese transistor radios. The children were searched in case they were hiding valuables—and were hit whether they were or not. Aged Sikhs were ordered by jibing soldiers to take off their *pagris*, the sacred Sikh turban. Soldiers sneered at the Sikhs' humiliation.

Terrified girls and women were robbed of tiny items of gold jewelry worn as a part of their traditional costume.

The train was stopped another five times by bands of soldiers before reaching Tororo on the Kenya-Uganda border. Some of the soldiers staggered drunk, swigging from bottles of *waragi*; they fired shots into the air. They let the train pass when there was nothing left to steal.

Holding up the Kenya trains became a regular pastime.

On one occasion, the discovery of a 100 shilling note hidden in a Sikh's turban led to 30 Sikhs being stripped and made to crawl naked through the train.

Arriving in Kenya three young girls told how they had been abducted from another train weeks earlier. They had been kept at a military barracks where they had been sexually assaulted.

They escaped with the help of one kind-hearted Ugandan private. Soldiers had threatened to marry them. They did not know what had happened to four other girls taken to the barracks.

Asian girls pleaded with the soldiers to be allowed to remain on the trains, buying their safety with what money or jewelry they had. An Indian welfare group, The Brihad Bharatiys Samaj, reported some 20 Indian nationals missing from the special trains carrying the expelled Asians from Kampala to Mombasa. Letters from Asians after they had reached India gave more chilling details of misdeeds of Amin's rabble, including numerous instances of rape.

In Kampala Amin's soldiers were equally uncontrolled. Several Asians, including a young family of four, were shot dead in the city. On the streets Asians were stopped, in most cases they were manhandled— and left with varying degrees of injury. Soldiers cut Asians' hair and beards with broken beerbottles.

Understandably, many Asians hastened arrangements for their departure from Uganda. Police officials, powerless to curb the actions of Amin's Army, guessed that about five Asians were being shot each day by the military, mostly at the roadblocks which had sprung up everywhere.

Four checkpoints were manned over the first forty miles of the main east-bound route to the Kenya border from the capital. At each, the story was the same: The travellers were roughed up, their personal belongings plundered.

Affluent Asians tried other ways of getting money out. Some were able to buy extravagantly planned air travel—until the Government announced that no-one could buy an air ticket to more than one destination. By then a reported £200,000 had been spent on tickets refundable by airlines abroad. The possibility of safely driving an expensive car over the border to Kenya was eminently doubtful from the very beginning of the expulsion period. Those who did get away with their cars, generally, had asked friends in Kenya to register them there and send number plates for the border crossing.

News spread to Kampala from country districts that individuals had been kidnapped, only to be returned to their families on payment of large sums in ransom. Traders winding up their businesses were accused of hoarding money by soldiers who then snatched any money they could find on the premises. The most unfortunate of these traders would be thrown into the boot of an army car and driven off into the bush for severe beatings... or to be shot.

In some cases, an exception rather than a rule, low ranking troops seen looting Asian property were shot by their officers. Such executions, reasoned the Asians who witnessed them, were not carried out from any sense of discipline or justice—but rather in the understanding that it would be the Army brass who eventually share out the most valuable spoils. By shooting their subordinates officers were merely safeguarding their own future interests when they put Asians property under close guard.

Such was the intensity of racial witch-hunting it was no surprise that Asians still fulfilling provisions of

Amin's erratic decrees enabling them to stay in Uganda now turned their thoughts to getting out too. Some tore up their own citizenship papers, choosing to throw themselves at the mercy of the British and United Nations, instead of facing an uncertain and possibly brief future in Amin's Uganda.

Amin's own tirades continued.

'You have milked the cow, but you did not feed it.'

He directed the Uganda security forces to ensure Asians cleared for departure by the Bank of Uganda did not remain in the country for more than 2 days after clearance. Amin visited army training camps, the Uganda Argus newspaper ominously reported, 'to examine possible areas where camps could be set up to accommodate non-citizen Asians who without specific exemption from the Government would not have removed themselves from Uganda by the deadline of 8 November, 1972.'

Then another Amin decree ordered Asians staying in the country to leave the towns and 'go to the villages and mix up with other Ugandans.' No wonder that when November 8 came only a few hundred Asians remained in Uganda.

General Idi Amin's treatment of his country's Asian community was overtly racist by any standards. And yet to many in independent Africa it was a popular move. In neighbouring Kenya alone some members of parliament publicly approved Amin's actions, hinting the same could be done in their country.

The expulsions also shed more light on Amin the man . . . and the ease with which he could launch into clumsy but effective bullying tactics.

At the point he felt British officials were not processing the displaced Asians fast enough—the High Commission kept to its normal office hours, open to the public for five hours a day—Amin ordered the Army to go out and arrest the first 100 white British citizens they could find. As soon as the High Commission was working a 12 hour day and promised to bring in the extra staff and hire bigger premises Amin released his prisoners.

Throughout the Asian exercise the ill-educated General proved to many of his detractors that they had underestimated his brute cunning. He had a fundamental understanding of what he wanted and knew—however crudely—how to get it. And as usual, he was to make full use of diversionary tactics to turn attention from one thing to another.

Tanzania, Britain, Zambia, India, Rwanda, Sudan and 'some countries in NATO' were conspiring with Algeria, Czechoslovakia, Cuba, Malawi and Guyana to invade Uganda, he said.

Zaire's President Mobutu made a second visit to Kampala in an attempt to persuade Amin to talk to their common neighbour Rwanda over increasing border tensions, and extend the Asian deadline. As it turned out, Amin did neither, saying he was 'busy commanding the armed forces.' But he did present Mobutu with Uganda's highest honour, the Order of the Source of the Nile and declared that Lake Edward and Lake Albert, on the Uganda-Zaire border, would henceforth be renamed after himself and his Zairean counterpart.

At a stroke Amin created nine new provinces and sacked most of his top police officers. Quirksome Amin eulogised on the death of a leading Asian businessman just a few days before the expulsion deadline. Although he had refused Ugandan citizenship to Jayant Madhvani, head of the biggest Asian industrial and commercial group in East Africa, worth an estimated £50 million in 1970, who died on a business trip to India, Amin described Madhvani as 'a great son of Uganda whose activities and ways of life will always be remembered.'

Amin offered to help Britain settle the Northern Ireland issue and went on to say the United States had asked for his help in concluding the Vietnam War.

The big bluff extrovert soldier, whose coup had been welcomed by most political and non-political observers abroad as a man of action and sense, was now becoming a topical satire—a lampoon for articles in Punch and in special books depicting him as a genial buffoon. Uganda's departing Asians knew differently.

Idi Amin was no joke. He was ruthless—and adroit.

CHAPTER VII

*'I am the greatest politician in the world. I have
shaken the British so much I deserve a degree in
Philosophy.'*

Idi Amin Dada

By its very scale the Asian exodus was exceptional—but
it was by no means the only vivid event in Amin's
Uganda in 1972. Early in the year Amin had ditched his
Israeli 'friends' with a vigour that surprised even those
who entertained the least liking for Israel. His red carpet
visit a few months before, his oft-repeated 'love' for
Israel together with the widely-held belief that the
Israelis had been whispering in his ear the whole time,
counted for nothing.

Amin's praises changed to abuse, he accused Israel of
engineering an invasion plan—and gave the remaining
Israeli representatives in Uganda three days in which to
leave the country.

Over the following months the pitch of Amin's verbal
attacks on Israel became markedly paranoiac, and in
September—after Palestinian commandos killed Israeli
athletes competing in the Munich Olympics—he
despatched a telegram to UN secretary General Kurt
Waldheim, with a copy sent to Golda Meir. 'Germany is

the right place where, when Hitler was Prime Minister and Supreme Commander, he burnt over six million Jews. This is because Hitler and all German people knew that the Israelis are not people who are working in the interest of the people of the world and that is why they burnt the Israelis alive with gas in the soil of Germany. The world should remember that the Palestinians, with the assistance of Germany, made that operation possible in the Olympic Village.'

That Amin was an ignorant but devout Muslim—and that he surrounded himself with more loyal Muslim troops—perhaps had always made the ultimate break with Israel inevitable. As an opportunist, Amin was not above using anyone to his advantage—until, that is, their enemies offered a richer prize. For him the switch to the oil-rich Arab bloc was an easy one. The Arabs had a plethora of reasons for being sympathetic—and were able to turn a blind eye to what normally would have been an awkward diplomatic gaffe: for one of his first begging shuttles Amin used his Israeli jet.

In terms of hard cash, the Arab countries of north Africa did not respond to Amin's overtures as quickly as the Uganda president might have wished. To start with even radical Libya later an important backer of Amin was chary. Libyan leader Muammar Gaddafi lavishly commended Amin for his anti-Zionist stand. Congratulations, after all, cost nothing and the initial reaction of the Arabs hastened the demise of the Asians.

Only by the end of the year was Arab aid coming in. The first big cheque, for about £2.6 million, was handed to Amin on behalf of King Faisal of Saudi Arabia by the Chief Khadi of Uganda Sheikh Abdulrazaq Matovu in November. King Faisal had promised to buy Ugandan coffee, tea, timber and ginger, and would energetically support the Uganda Muslim Council.

The Chief Khadi reported to Amin that Egypt was recruiting English-speaking teachers for Uganda and Kuwait intended to give money to the Muslim council too. Amin replied that he had had another dream two nights before which showed 'in the next 100 years

Uganda will be very rich.' The Chief Khadi listened patiently as Amin recalled his Moroto dream dictating the action against Asians.

'My dreams always come true,' Amin boomed, adding as an evangelical afterthought: 'If the people of Uganda work very hard they will not pay school fees for their children, nor taxes.'

A fortnight later Amin announced that his Military Government had injected £65 million into the new Uganda Development Bank. The money would be channeled into modernisation and expansion of agriculture, housing, tourism and industry generally. The bank would provide finance to Ugandans who seriously wanted to establish or expand businesses, now that the 'saboteurs' were gone. Uganda's economy would go from strength to strength...

At the inaugural board meeting certain of the bank's directors had grave doubts. Stable and growing economies were not founded on bluster and the random dishing out of loans. Prosperity grew on firmer ground.

The board members may have suppressed shudders—but their apprehensions were confirmed when Amin returned to the mystical. 'Every 100 years God appoints one person to be very powerful in the world to follow what the Prophet directed. When I dream, then things are put into practice,' Amin told the board.

Not a very practical approach to banking. But Amin enjoyed playing in the heady world of finance—a world he did not understand but now had to power manipulate. He also knew how political capital could be gained.

Opening the grandly-named Libyan-Arab Uganda Bank for Foreign Trade and Development at the former Bank of India premises on Kampala Road Amin hailed it as an 'African achievement' indicating his 'determination to wage the economic war to ultimate victory.' In the past, Ugandan banks were 'controlled by imperialists' and 'the tools of imperialism.'

'The people of Libya join their Ugandan brothers

91

and sisters in the war against political domination and economic exploitation,' Amin said, beaming at the Libyans present at the ceremony. 'Africa has tremendous natural resources which could be harnessed for the benefit of the people of Africa, making it a modern and industrialised continent. African countries must cooperate to achieve their common objectives.'

The Libyan bank, Amin said, was not a foreign bank but a bank 'providing African solutions to African problems.' It would begin in assisting Ugandans acquiring vacant Asian businesses.

Amin's own solutions to his own problems were more pragmatic—shoot first before they ask questions. Chief Justice Benedicto Kiwanuka, it could be said, had indeed become 'a problem.' Released from detention by Amin in 1971 and appointed head of the judiciary, the former leader of the Democratic Party and Uganda's first prime minister was (in the words of his son Fulgensio Kiwanuka) 'a man of strong principles who would not yield to pressure—even if it meant imprisonment.'

In a habeas corpus case on September 8, 1972, Chief Justice Kiwanuka issued a judgement in favour of a British businessman, Donald Stewart, detained in Makindye Military prison. Ordering the detaining authorities to attend a further hearing the Chief Justice said there was a prima facie case of wrongful detention to be answered. He went on to point out that Stewart had been arrested by the military which, at the time, did not possess full powers of arrest.

The judgement annoyed Amin. Kiwanuka himself confided in friends that it was only a matter of time before he was arrested—more so because, on previous occasions he had given a number of stern warnings aimed at authorities exceeding legal powers. In what was believed to be an oblique reference to the Chief Justice, Amin earlier spoke out against a top civil official in whom the Government had 'lost confidence.'

On September 21 Kiwanuka was working quietly on

92

legal papers in his chambers at the High Court when soldiers burst in.

His abduction was accompanied at first by the Government's usual silence. However Amin, prompted by widespread accusations of complicity in Kiwanuka's disappearance, eventually saw fit to give an 'official' account of it. This account was proved patently untrue by the later testimonies of prison survivors and top Amin officials who defected from the regime.

In its statement the Government claimed it had carried out investigations into the kidnapping of the Chief Justice. The investigations revealed that Kiwanuka had been 'arrested' by three unidentified men masquerading as government security officers. The three had used a Peugeot car fitted with stolen Uganda Government number plates.

'It is clear that the planners of this plot wanted to confuse the country that the people who arrested Ben Kiwanuka were members of the security forces using an official vehicle. The Government investigated this matter thoroughly and so far no evidence has come to light as to who arrested the chief justice and where he is.'

The independent testimonies said Kiwanuka was driven away from the High Court in an Army vehicle. His immediate destination remains unknown. One account has it that he was recognised, bound at the wrists and ankles, in a military jeep heading from Kampala to Entebbe. Certainly, some days elapsed before Kiwanuka, strained, unshaven, barefoot and clad in tattered and stained denims, was taken to Kampala's Makindye prison.

One Makindye prisoner recounted how Kiwanuka was quickly recognised, despite his dishevelled appearance, as he shuffled into the communal cell. The inmates crowded to talk to him but his responses were barely articulate.

How Kiwanuka died has never been fully established. One prisoner believed the Chief Justice was hammered to death by an Army sergeant watched by a group of senior officers.

Ben Kiwanuka's abduction took place four days after a force of about 1,000 Obote guerrillas staged an abortive invasion into Uganda from northern Tanzania.

The invasion was a tragic disaster from beginning to end. The Obote forces were ill-trained and ill-equipped. Many guerrillas had spent several idle months at a forward camp near the Uganda border. As their training had tailed off, so had their zeal. As they waited to march inertia set in.

Morale was seriously undermined—a state of affairs not helped by reports, from recruits crossing the border from Uganda to join them that scores of youths heading for Tanzania had been caught and killed.

Once Milton Obote, with President Nyerere's agreement, signalled the operation to go ahead it was dogged by inefficiency and misfortune.

A commandeered East African Airways DC9 was to have flown commando units directly to Entebbe to coincide with ground attacks at Mbarara and Masaka in the south. The DC9 in the hands of an inexperienced Ugandan East African Airways trainee pilot was flown from Dar es Salaam to Kilimanjaro airport in north eastern Tanzania on the first leg of its mission. Due to the pilot's failure to complete flight checks he bumped heavily when landing at Kilimanjaro, bursting all the DC9's tyres.

So the Entebbe strike didn't get off the ground. That Amin's 'heart', Kampala itself, was saved from attack immediately put Obote's ground forces in a near-hopeless predicament. Amin was able to devote all his attention to crushing the invaders with all the firepower at his disposal without having to contend with the prospect of a military or civil uprising in the capital should Obote's men have succeeded in capturing the radio station. The invasion, therefore, was a localised operation which Amin's better equipped and numerically superior forces had little difficulty in heading off.

Yet another factor in Amin's favour, if he needed one, was that Obote's convoys crossed into Uganda well behind schedule. A number of the poorly maintained

Tanzanian-supplied trucks broke down on their way to the invaders' forward camp and those that arrived did so virtually empty of fuel—causing futher delays to get more.

Initially, Obote's forces met little opposition—they received a welcome deserving of liberators from village folk. But Amin knew in advance their plan was in the offing. The difficulty in concealing their movement in Tanzania, then their bungling gave him time to prepare.

Amin was ready for them.

Determined as they were the Obote Loyalists were no match for Amin's crack Simba (Lion) Battalion. To add emphasis to his victory Amin ordered his Air Force to bomb northern Tanzanian towns.

The grizzly consequences of invasion reverberated through Uganda for months. The invaders' casualties were extremely heavy: Amin's soldiers were not in the habit of taking prisoners. For isolated groups seized alive their capture was but a brief reprieve. One group held at the Kifaru Mechanised Regiment barracks at Bondo was wiped out after killing their guards during violent rioting in their prison block, Amin's government claimed.

Obote's cousin, and a commander in the invasion, Captain Oyile, and his former Information, Broadcasting and Tourism minister Alex Ojera were among eight captured invaders who escaped from Uganda Army custody, Amin further claimed. He said the eight had been detained for their part in the attempt against him and suggested that out of 'protective detention' the Government could not be held responsible for their safety. Few Obote sympathisers were fooled. It wasn't long before such escape stories were commonly taken to mean that the 'escapees' in fact had been murdered.

African diplomats attending a formal state house function in Kampala were among the last to see Ojera alive. Ojera was ignominiously led into the party wearing only a pair of khaki trousers. His hands were trussed behind his back. Amin personally interrogated him in front of the diplomats. Before being taken away

95

to his death Ojera was displayed on Uganda television.

The diplomats returned to their after-dinner brandies.

In the aftermath of the invasion Amin's revenge against Obote's former associates in Uganda was unbridled. Since the early months of Amin's rule Obote's Internal Affairs minister Basil Bataringaya had been left more or less unmolested. He was living quietly at his home near Mbarara when the invasion occurred.

Bataringaya, one-time teacher and an astute politician, must have known the dangers ahead that September and may have been planning to go into hiding until an opportunity arose for him to escape with his family to Tanzania.

Amin's soldiers got to him first. He was dragged from his home, tortured and then decapitated. In an extreme display of savagery, Bataringaya's head was impaled on a stake and paraded through Mbarara town to the Army barracks.

Bataringaya's wife later died in what was officially claimed to be one of the increasingly frequent 'car crashes' involving prominent people.

Joshua Wakholi, former minister of public service and cabinet affairs, was dragged from his Jinja home never to be seen again. He was peremptorily shot. The government claimed Wakholi was wounded taking part in the invasion and died as troops were taking him to the hospital.

The military did not explain why Wakholi's relatives were not allowed to recover his body for burial.

John Kakonge, former Minister of Agriculture, a founder member of Obote's Uganda People's Congress Party and once UPC's secretary general, was picked up in the middle of the day as he checked invoices in the wineshop he owned in central Kampala. He was probably killed at the barracks of Amin's favoured Malire Mechanised Regiment.

Frank Kalimuzo, formerly a senior civil servant, held the post of vice chancellor at Makerere University at the time of his death. He had spent a brief spell in jail, having been accused by Amin of spying for the government of neighbouring Rwanda. After his release Uganda Radio announced that the vice chancellor had disappeared with other 'enemies of the state'. Incredibly, the announcement came over the air as Kalimuzo attended a University wedding ceremony, along with more than 100 other guests.

The following day his wife went through final labour prior to giving birth. Kalimuzo went to answer the door bell . . . and it was then he vanished.

James Ochola, former minister of Local Administration also disappeared without trace—as did former secretary for defence Michael Rubanga, former Governor of the Bank of Uganda Joseph Mubiru and assistant commissioner of prisons Peter Oketta. In Acholi and Langi districts, long-time Obote strongholds, local council officials and regional administrators were rounded up.

Soldiers easily found Francis Walugembe, former Mayor of Masaka, south-west of Kampala. In charge of the arresting party was Amin's chief executioner and hatchet man, Lt Col Maliyamungu. In a public market place Walugembe was beaten, hacked down and castrated. Maliyamungu, thrashing at Walugembe with a panga, took a psychotic delight in the atrocity, horrified witnesses said.

How many Ugandans died in this wave of killing will never be known. Even Amin's 'security committee' admitted it had investigated the disappearance of 85 prominent citizens. Needless to say, the committee exonerated the Government, stating that perennial enemies of the state in general, and Obote supporters in particular, had begun a campaign of kidnappings in order to cause 'discontent and confusion.'

'In some cases some of the agents of Obote and other Imperialists and Zionists went to the extent of murdering some prominent Ugandans so that the blame would be put on the government.'

The security committee's figure must be regarded as a conservative one. Nor does it take into account the indiscriminate kidnappings of ordinary citizens and low-ranking soldiers. A group of 13 Western journalists detained briefly in Kampala at the end of September reported prison cells packed with up to 90 prisoners and daily clubbing and whipping rituals by hysterical, sadistic soldiers.

'You filthy British,' a drunk Uganda Army major slurred at one of the journalists. 'You come here to take our sisters. You come here to fight us. You stay here now, you sit on the floor and you die.'

Amin's extempore stream of consciousness remarks now began to seriously erode his image both abroad and nearer home in East Africa.

Though possessed of a kind of animal logic, they lacked consistency or strategy. They were rambling tirades distinguished only by their sense of hatred and brute contempt.

IN an astounding telegram to Tanzania's Nyerere attempting to excuse the expulsion of Uganda Asians Amin ranted: 'I love you very much and if you were a woman I would even consider marrying you although you have grey hairs on your head.'

Accusing Rwanda of harbouring anti-Uganda Israeli agents Amin bawled: 'I will destroy Kigali in one minute' (Kigale is the Rwandian capital.)

During the state visit of general Jean Bokassa, the president of the Central African Republic whose international reputation was based principally on his country's prison atrocities, Amin described Bokassa as his lifelong friend and the man who had 'put the Central African Republic on the world map.'

He promised to Africanise Uganda's Asian cricket team, liberate South Africa and learn French. He didn't like Capitalism, Socialism or Communism but believed in complete freedom instead. He vowed to erect a memorial to Queen Victoria and a statue of Hitler in Kampala—after expressing surprise that he had seen no such statues in West Germany.

Amin bestowed upon himself eight First Class medals in an effort to outclank Bokassa. He told visitors all he had ever wanted to be was a farmer—and the people had given him so many gifts of cattle and land that he would one day retire to the land . . . although with the Asians leaving he was wondering whether to become a merchant as well.

Amin proudly boasted of having fathered the children of twelve women from different tribes.

Amin denied that Miria Obote and the deposed President's three children had been assaulted by soldiers. The family spent nearly 18 months under virtual house arrest until, travelling under an assumed name, Mrs Obote managed to escape to Kenya. She was handed back across the border by the Kenya police. No explanation was given by the Kenyans for their action and what makes the matter even more curious is that the Kenyans apparently ignored an offer by Nyerere to fly Mrs Obote from Nairobi to join her husband in Dar es Salaam.

Back in Uganda the Obotes were taken first to a police hostel in Kampala. When President Nyerere telephoned President Kenyatta to protest over reports that the family had been mistreated Kenyatta—who may have received assurances on their safety before handing the family back—rang Amin.

Amin convened a press conference in Kampala to show the family was unharmed. Oddly enough, Amin urged Mrs Obote to leave Uganda—but did not dismiss the guards detailed to watch her.

Eventually the Obotes slipped across the border again. This time they were allowed to pass unhindered through Kenya to Tanzania.

Kenya later handed three other Ugandans over to the authorities across the border. Uganda claimed that Captain Sam Aswa, the man who read the coup broadcast in 1971, had stolen foreign currency intended for bicycle spare parts. After the expulsion of Uganda's Asians Aswa had been rewarded for his loyalty by being allocated the Sultan Bicycle Mart, Uganda's biggest bicycle importer. No specific charges were levelled against another soldier, Captain Kenneth Onzima, or veteran politician—journalist 'Jolly Joe' Kiwanuka. Amin again may have given Kenya assurances that the three men would not be harmed. But all three were killed shortly after their return to Uganda.

At times when Amin appeared to be contending with troubles aplenty he could be found, surrounded by bodyguards, officers and lissome Ugandan girls, at the swimming pool of one of Kampala's hotels. Sandwiches and soft drinks were laid out for the President and his entourage. They were left untouched until Amin gave his approval.

Fawning officers joined Amin in the water, answering his challenges for a race. Invariably, they were careful to let Amin win.

Amin snorted and splashed his whale-like bulk through the water.

Chiefly a result of Amin's treatment of Uganda Asians; Britain stopped its £12 million loan to Kampala.

The United States, angered by Amin's Hitler telegram, had cancelled a $10 million Uganda loan.

Amin hit back at the British by recalling Uganda's ambassador in London and expelling the British high commissioner from Kampala. He announced that all foreign owned businesses—more than 40 of them British—would be redistributed among black Ugandans and, he threw in, his Information Ministry was taking control of the country's only English language newspaper, the *Uganda Argus*. Britons, Amin erroneously stated, owned a majority share in the newspaper, which under the Government would be renamed the *Voice of Uganda*. Amin ommitted to say the paper had been critical of his government . . . although he once said he might take action against the paper because of a report published on sugar shortages in Uganda.

When Whitehall also confirmed the phasing out of a British technical assistance programme Amin threatened 'drastic' measures against British nationals.

Anyway, many of the estimated 3,000 British families in Uganda had begun planning their departure in anticipation of an Amin backlash and some—mistrusting the unpredictable and vindictive general—had already packed up and gone.

The seizure of British firms, a Cabinet statement said should be seen as 'the second phase of the economic war.' Aware of what had happened to Asians in the so-called first phase Uganda Britons had reason to be tense.

A flag raising ceremony commemorating the first raising of the Union Jack in Uganda was called off. Britons living in remote parts of the country moved to Kampala, hotels or to the homes of friends.

'We have not nationalised British firms and property. What we have actually done is to take over these from foreigners so that we ourselves can sell them to Uganda citizens at fair and just prices. The Uganda government and people have no time for Communism. All we want is to transfer the economy of Uganda into the hands of the Uganda people.'

Troops surrounded British-owned premises. Units of soldiers stood guard over the Kampala Club—a favoured meeting place of Whites long before independence now renamed the Government Club.

As if by diversion, Amin expelled 60 White missionaries—55 being Catholics. His explanation: The missionaries were in fact mercenaries who concealed weapons and military uniforms under their cassocks. Among those expelled were a 92-year-old French missionary who had spent more than 60 years in Uganda and an Italian-born former archbishop of Kampala, aged 80. Amin alleged the missionary-mercenaries were in the pay of 'Zionist and South African imperialists' and advised Uganda Catholics to pray for forgiveness.

The British Government—like Israel before it—at last acknowledged there was very little it could do about the vagaries of the irascible general's rule. It had to admit its grave miscalculation in welcoming Amin's 1971 take-over. Amin clearly had no intention of paying compensation for his latest seizures. The grandeur of his state visit to London was forgotten. All that remained was acid, if ineffective, condemnation.

Amin's actions, Foreign and Commonwealth secretary Sir Alec Douglas Home told the House of Commons, were 'outrageous by any standard of civilised behaviour and certainly incompatible with the behaviour expected within the Commonwealth partnership.'

Britain was to bring Amin's 'deplorable inhumanity' to the notice of the United Nations General Assembly.

Sir Alec concluded: 'We shall retain our present representation in Uganda in order to look after British interests and in the hope that one day more reasonable counsels will prevail there.'

Amin offered his own conclusion to the affair. He would pay compensation valued at about £20 million for British property as long as Queen Elizabeth and Prime Minister Heath came to Kampala to discuss it. He subsequently asked Heath for a loan to pay off the claims 'under similar terms as a previous British Government bought out White British Settlers in Kenya.'

He said he was willing to take over responsibility from Queen Elizabeth as head of the Commonwealth. 'The British,' Amin repeated an oft-stated phrase, 'are my best friends.'

A year later—while the compensation issue was still deadlocked and Asians estimated their unpaid assets were worth £150 million—Amin launched what he called the 'Save Britain Fund.'

Amin said he started the fund with a contribution of 10,000 shillings from his own pocket 'to help Britain survive its economic crisis.'

'I am appealing to all the people of Uganda who have all along been the traditional friends of the British people to come forward and help their former colonial masters.'

He fired off a telegram to Heath saying Britain's economic plight was an embarrassment to other members of the Commonwealth—but he was able to offer his advice to help cure Britain's ills.

'Feel free to ask me. If you will let me know officially the exact position of the mess into which Britain has been plunged I will do my best in asking some of Uganda's friends to join us in giving assistance to Britain.'

Amin did not attend that year's Commonwealth Conference in Ottawa because Britain did not fulfil his conditions—that Queen Elizabeth send an aircraft for him, complete with a company of Scots Guards, and that the Commonwealth Secretary General should provide him with a pair of size 13 shoes.

Amin went further: he could give Britain 'a radical military solution to the Ulster situation.' A speech read on his behalf to the Ottawa meeting accused Britain of racialism and of not having guts enough to stand up to Rhodesia's Ian Smith. Southern Africa was moving towards 'the most explosive racial war that man may ever witness.'

'Instead of rectifying colonial wrongs of her own making Britain has found fit to wage a dirty press war on Uganda, merely because we did what is internationally acknowledged as our legitimate right to exercise. Certainly we cannot help thinking racism is the motivating factor in this situation.'

British companies had given up any hope of fair compensation by the time Amin stated that Israel would receive compensation for its interests in Uganda . . . as soon as a specially appointed team of Soviet experts had completed their valuation!

It was a wet, over-cast Saturday nearly five months after the September invasion. At Mbale in eastern Uganda Tom Masaba, former captain in the Uganda Army, and a youth, Sebastiano Namirundu, squirmed uneasily off the back of an open Army Land Rover: They were manacled tightly at the ankles and wrists. The two were made to sit on the soft ground. They were blindfolded. They waited. It was not yet time. The rain started again.

At last, they stood. They were stripped naked, covered with white aprons crossed by a black 'target' band in the centre; black bags were pulled over their heads after they had been lashed to the trees. They did not struggle.

An officer's command, the report of shots. The two Ugandans slumped lifeless. Tom Masaba's apron was stripped from his body. Blood ran down his naked thighs. Blood spattered the trees.

Cut down, their bodies fell into the mud. A crowd of 20,000 people—men women and children—began to disperse.

At exactly 2:00 p.m. East African time that day a total of 12 men—all but one alleged Obote guerrillas—were publicly executed by firing squad in different parts of Uganda.

Amin ordered the spectacle for obvious effect. Speaking to the crowds at Fort Portal after the execution of two guerrillas from Toro district, Pharase Kasoro, a policeman, and Abwoli Malibo, the commanding officer of Amin's Second Paratrooper Battalion Major Onaah declared that more public executions would take place if subversion continued in Uganda. 'The family of anyone proved to be a guerrilla or anyone giving shelter to terrorists will be destroyed. The Armed Forces will not hesitate to take further action against terrorists.'

Subversives, Major Onaah said, had infiltrated every district of Uganda. 'The chiefs have not reported them. Chiefs will face the same fate if they do not alert us. Some people are trying to sabotage the re-organisation of our country's administration by His Excellency the President, General Idi Amin Dada.'

'Anyone disturbing the stability of Uganda will be crushed,' echoed Lt Col Ali, the officer presiding over the execution of three Kigezi men at Kabale sports stadium.

In West Acholi John Labeja and Amos Obwona were executed on Gulu Golf Course. More than 10,000 people watched them die. Golf tournaments at Gulu had never drawn so large a crowd.

James Karuhange, a 24-year-old mathematics teacher at Kyambogo College, was shot near the District Commissioner's offices at Mbarara. Responding to taunts by the soldiers the crowds chanted: 'Kill him. Kill him. We don't want guerrillas' as Karuhanga was blindfolded.

At Jinja police formed cordons to hold back crowds streaming into Bugembe Stadium to watch the killing of William Nkoko.

The twelfth man to die was Badru Semakula, sentenced to death for robbery. He faced a 12-man firing squad in Kampala. Three priests—a Catholic, a Protestant and a Muslim—were allowed to approach the trussed-up prisoner and conduct prayers. Among senior military personnel in the crowd: Amin's Air Force commander Col Toko.

The last public executions in Uganda had been carried out by the British colonial administration 50 years before. Three men were publicly hanged at Malongwe village near Kampala after being convicted of murdering a young girl and dismembering her body for witchcraft rites.

Amin's condemned men were convicted at secret hearings by a military tribunal. The tribunal's methods of procedure were not made known and can be considered, at best, to have been arbitrary. Other than that eleven had been 'involved in guerrilla activity' specified crimes were not given. Uganda Radio simply stated that Dr Obote and his Tanzania-based 'hench-men' had masterminded plans 'to cause trouble in Uganda.'

Obote had used supporters from his own Langi region to create dissent. 'Today the executions that have taken place have not involved a single Langi. In the end the master brains have escaped while people of other tribes who were misled by Obote's plans have suffered,' the official radio said.

CHAPTER VIII

'Some soldiers who talk a lot say they will kill
me or others. I do not want the shedding of
anyone's blood. I do not fear anybody.'

Amin

Idi Amin Dada, to whom the nickname 'Big Daddy' now
stuck, proved himself incapable of providing Uganda
with a workable, rational government. Uganda slid
further into anarchy. Forgotten were Amin's promises
of a new constitution leading to the resumption of multi-
party political activities and civilian rule. The caretaker
had become master of the house—and had run amok.
He could not give up without having to answer for
misdeeds. Big Daddy was in too deep.

Originally elections had been proposed for early
1973. The invasion attempt, and its consequences, gave
Amin an ample excuse to let time pass by. Keeping up
appearances, however, he did welcome interim suggestions for a re-styled administrative set-up headed by an
executive president, a Supreme State Council, a prime
minister, his deputy and cabinet and what was termed a
'National Forum.'

The suggestions were put forward by Amin's existing
cabinet. The reorganisation would be carried out in four
stages. The head of state and commander of the armed
forces would be appointed president; and the prime
minister, the deputy prime minister and commanders
and quartermasters-general from the three services
would make up the State Council, a policymaking body

106

advised by the cabinet; the prime minister and deputy would be military appointments. They would oversee a total shake-up of 21 government ministries under each cabinet minister and be responsible for provincial administration through 'administrators' ('Governors' has a colonial connection that makes people irritated'), district commissioners, country chiefs, sub-county chiefs, parish chiefs and village chiefs. The chairman of the National Forum would be picked by the president. He would not be a civil servant and his deputy would be elected by Forum members, themselves democratically elected from regional counties. The National Forum— 'acting as the eyes and ears of the Government'—would meet four times a year unless there was a need to call an extraordinary session to debate immediately important issues. Senior cabinet ministers, police, military and prisons commanders would be *ex officio* Forum members. All debate—copying parliamentary privilege—would be 'immune to the laws of the country' unless national security was affected.

Ordering the plan to be publicly aired on radio and television, and telling Ugandans unable to participate in broadcast discussions to write directly to the Cabinet secretary, Amin hinted that, once accepted, it would be permanently adopted.

In the climate of fear created by Amin, any national consensus had evaporated. The deliberations were stilted from the outset. The well-intentioned step back to democracy did not get beyond being a plan. It never stood a chance.

As he had done since the coup Amin governed by decree. Early on, he had pronounced himself president, banned political meetings (the ban was still in force) and restricted the movements of politicians. He forbade the honorific 'president' in any connection other than in reference to himself as head of state. The wording of his decrees—endorsed by the Defence Council (the military government's top decision-making body)—carefully nullified provisions in the Uganda Constitution.

The collapse of law and order had been attributable

107

to decrees giving the Forces, in or out of uniform sweeping powers of arrest, search, interrogation and seizure of property.

Out of the National Forum plan, Amin salvaged the Supreme State Council, allocating its posts to members of the Defence Council. Public discussion, he said, had judged a new Cabinet superfluous. A forum of people's representatives was not consistent with Government thinking. He proceeded to apportion the task of regional administration to ten senior army, police and prison officers. This dovetailed with a scheme called 'mass mobilisation' which had been in progress for several weeks 'to create national consciousness and increasing discipline.'

The scheme involved basing troops throughout the country: the soldiers were to receive crash-courses in rural administration and development before being called upon to select administrators and chiefs in the districts.

Those selected were also receiving 'intensive training' to help them work effectively in their new position. 'This is the year of co-operation, of discipline and of speaking the truth,' was how Amin heralded it. 'If this is done the country will move forward and if anyone did a bad thing during the past year it must be forgotten altogether.'

'Mass mobilisation' stirred little enthusiasm among Uganda's rural people. Stoic coldness awaited the troops and it was not long before many new appointees, accused of corruption and inefficiency (a usual fallback), were fired. Thus, some 800 poorly-educated junior servicemen were delegated to act as local chiefs.

The effect: real inefficiency and corruption; murders and other unchecked abuses.

The sending of ten service heads to the provinces rubber-stamped Uganda's return to police state conditions—just the conditions for which Amin denigrated Obote and Akena Odoko. The accompanying turmoil made mockery of Amin's flamboyant revocation of his predecessor's State of Emergency laws.

Having given the military unprecedented powers

Amin soon alienated civilians in the government. The Defence Council met several times a week. At most sessions Cabinet guidance was negligently cast aside and the civilians vilified. The Cabinet's meetings were infrequent, its composition subject to Amin's caprice. In a moment Amin dismissed Labour minister Abu Mayanja, Culture minister Yekosofati Engur, Tourism minister Apollo Kironde and Animal Resources minister Professor William Banage, branding them as "inefficient". Not surprisingly, some ministers were nervous to get down to any government business at all lest they incurred Amin's vicious wrath.

During a visit to Kenya, Education minister Edward Rugumayo cabled his resignation to Amin. 'After very careful consideration of the situation in our country I have decided to resign my office,' he said. 'The reasons for my resignation are purely personal and moral and are based on the fact that I have found it increasingly difficult to fulfill my duties in the atmosphere that prevails in our country.'

Amin hastily replied that he was unperturbed by Rugumayo's decision and accepted the resignation without hesitation, adding that the Education minister had been under strain because of the death of his wife and 'threats made by anti-government guerrillas to assassinate him and other ministers.'

Rugumayo approached European and African diplomatic missions in Nairobi before travelling on to Tanzania and Europe.

A few days later Kampala security men scurried to Nairobi, where Kenyans were enjoying a spate of vivid rumours of more impending defections. Amin's 31-year-old brother-in-law Foreign Minister Wanume Kibedi had apparently booked rooms 301, 302 and 303 at the Panafric Hotel. The rooms were suddenly vacated. Hearsay put Kibedi, a talented lawyer, among 20 senior Uganda Government representatives determined to leave the administration.

According to Kenya, Kibedi arrived with a special message from Amin for President Kenyatta and intended to discuss matters relating to the position of Kenyan and Ugandan nationals under each other's jurisdiction. Although no formal extradition procedures existed between the two countries, Amin wanted to be sure Kenya would not give sanctuary to his potential victims. In return, Amin promised Kenyatta: 'The Uganda armed forces will do everything possible to ensure that Kenya citizens and all our brothers and sisters from the African continent will not be molested or mishandled. The lives and property of all people living in Uganda will be protected."

Silence.

Kibedi turned up in Nairobi Hospital and was said to be under constant care and sedation. It transpired that he had been touring Kenya's up-country farming areas—Nakuru, Kericho and Eldoret. News slowly filtered back to Nairobi that a private party held for the minister at Kericho had been brought to a premature end when the Ugandan security men travelling with him began brawling drunkenly amongst themselves.

From his hospital bed, however, Kibedi dispatched a letter to Amin in Kampala. The letter (according to a version released by Amin) refuted press reports that he had resigned and reaffirmed Kibedi's 'total support and loyalty as Minister of Foreign Affairs.'

'The imperialist newspapers have been writing up their own false stories...suggesting that I am not in hospital at all here, in order to cause confusion between you and me.

'You know that I have been your strongest supporter since we came to power, indeed even before you became President. Not on one occasion have I done anything without consulting you.'

Kibedi, said Amin, told how he had been admitted to hospital suffering from severe headaches, chest pains and exhaustion. He was taking drugs hourly and hoped to return home as soon as his condition improved.

'I hope to be out of hospital within the next few days. Greetings to the family and to the cabinet,' the letter supposedly ended.

Amin said he advised his brother-in-law to take three months recuperation leave. When Kibedi did resign, shortly afterwards, Amin claimed that was his advice too. The minister could no longer continue because of failing health. Amin thanked him for his work for the Second Republic over the two years he spent in high office.

Big Daddy's familial generosity did not last. He berated Kibedi for not returning home (where he could get lasting treatment for his sickness) and accused him of planning a military attack against Uganda from abroad.

Kibedi gave his version of his resignation. Like Rugumayo, he had given the decision careful thought. He had not taken advice, least of all from Amin.

'There were many adverse and retrogressive developments in Uganda over which I had no control or influence whatsoever, despite my office,' he said, adding reference to 'the continual disappearance of innocent people without any adequate investigation by the people concerned. Many of the victims were in fact supporters of the Government or indifferent to politics.' He denied he was joining Obote's foreign minister Sam Odaka in Europe to recruit Ugandan guerrillas.

Wanume Kibedi played on Amin's mind for a long time. At a press conference in Paris in June the following year the exiled Ugandan released a lengthy open letter to Amin which began: 'Ever since I resigned from the office of Foreign Minister . . . you have not ceased to broadcast slanders, calumnies and other fabrications about me. Hitherto I have not bothered to answer back, because I found it unnecessary to deny statements whose falsehood was obvious even to a three year old Ugandan. Furthermore, I wanted to give you plenty of time to wallow in the mire of your own lies, contradictions and other inconsistencies, the more so to expose your true character to the people of Uganda and to the world at large.'

The letter mentioned Kibedi's personal experiences as a cabinet minister. It recalled Amin saying to him on the day Chief Justice Kiwanuka 'disappeared': 'The boys have got Kiwanuka. They had to pick him up at the High Court because he knew he was being followed, and he was very careful about his movements.'

Replied Kibedi: 'Oh! My God! This is terrible. He is the Chief Justice. Whatever he has done, his arrest will be disastrous for the country in terms of the rule of law and for the international image.' The foreign minister believed Kiwanuka would be tried on criminal charges.

Later, as acting Justice minister, Kibedi was compelled to defend Amin's official denial of involvement in the murder.

Kibedi's letter recalled the time Amin casually admitted that Makerere vice chancellor Kalimuzo had been killed at Makindye (again, at variance with official denials) and that the head of Uganda Television James Bwogi disappeared at about the same time.

Separate accounts said Bwogi had been abducted while driving to work—his crime being that he had shaken his head in dismay during a television discussion.

'I could go on page after page quoting denunciations by you of specific individuals who were shortly afterwards murdered. Not in one single case did you produce a shred of evidence to support your allegations against the victims. You simply made denunciations, which then amounted to a death sentence without trial. In such cases you have been the accuser, the judge and the executioner all rolled into one,' Kibedi wrote.

'Even while I was serving in your Government as Minister some of my very best friends, people who had been my closest associates in the pre-coup political campaigns, were liquidated.'

Among those were Kagulire Kasadha, a Czech-trained engineer at Makerere, Henry Kasigwa, town treasurer of Jinja Municipal council, Lume Kisadha, personnel manager at Nyanza Textiles, Jinja, Ndaruzi, a Jinja trader, Mrs Ogwang, a Jinja businesswoman, Ruhesi, the Jinja council's town engineer and Haji Balunywa, administrative secretary of Busoga district.

'Kasadha, for example, was working at his office at

112

Makerere University when the assassins came for him. They were driving two cars, one of them a Peugeot. On being told that he was being taken for questioning, Kasadha told his abductors: 'Take me to Kibedi or at least inform Kibedi that you have arrested me. Thereupon the abductors set upon Kasadha, beating him up severely. They bundled him into the boot of one of the cars and drove off.'

Kibedi heard of his friend's kidnapping within 15 minutes and, with a description of one of the cars, telephoned security departments in Kampala: the Military Police, the State Research Unit, the Public Safety Unit and the Ministries of Defence and Internal Affairs.

'I also telephoned you personally, asking you to help trace Kasadha. This was the pattern that I followed whenever an abduction was reported to me. You gave me your standard answer whenever I made such reports to you, namely that the individual concerned was probably a guerrilla and that was why he had been arrested.'

Kibedi's uncle, Shaban Nkutu, was seized from his Jinja home in January, 1973 when the Foreign Minister was in Ghana heading Uganda's delegation to the Organisation of African Unity's Liberation Committee meeting there. He was the Committee's outgoing chairman.

'Local citizens put up a determined fight to try and save him, but they were overwhelmed by the gang of assassins. The following day you ordered a statement to be put out saying that Nkutu had run away, and that anybody who saw him should inform the police.

'A few days after I returned from the Ghana conference, Nkutu's body was discovered on the bank of the Nile, badly disfigured by several bayonet wounds. The local police took the body to the mortuary at Jinja hospital. Soldiers mounted guard over the mortuary and refused to surrender Nkutu's body to relatives.'

Challenged by Kibedi on his uncle's death Amin claimed Nkutu, a minister in Obote's government, had

113

been recruiting guerrillas. 'I protested that in that case he could have been tried and punished according to the law rather than being murdered secretly. You did not wish to discuss the matter. I then asked if the body could be handed over to the relatives for burial. You said you would think about it. For three days you would not give me an answer.'

Amin finally agreed—but by the time quick arrangements had been made to collect the body it had been unceremoniously buried by soldiers in a mass grave at Masese public cemetary outside Jinja.

'Your personal involvement in the liquidation of thousands of innocent Ugandans is beyond dispute or contradiction,' Kibedi said. Amin ordered the deaths of men whose wives or girlfriends he wanted. By killing for personal reasons soldiers emulated Amin.

Stephen Epunau, Kibedi's classmate at school, managed a branch of Barclays Bank at Kabale. He turned down a soldier's loan because as branch manager he was not empowered to grant it. 'He was dragged away from the bank in full view of bank employees to be murdered in cold blood. Later the assassins took his trousers and shoes back to his family to show that he had been 'finished'.' (The official explanation said Epunau had gone on holiday to Rwanda and failed to return.)

Kibedi corroborated the occurrence of tribal killing directed especially against the Langi and Acholi. But no ethnic group, except Amin's Kakwa tribe, had been safe. Amin had surrounded himself with his own Nubian Kakwas, giving them unlimited powers in the State Research Bureau, the Public Safety Unit, the Military police and the army.

'You have . . . at various times ordered the liquidation of tribal groups in the army and in civilian life, largely as a result of your paranoiac hatred arising from your deep-seated fear of all ethnic groups other than your own small one.

'The lawless elements that you have licensed to kill are certainly not the Uganda armed forces as a whole, who have suffered at the hands of the assassins as bitterly as the civilians. The assassins are a small cabal of men owing direct loyalty to you personally.

'In order to entrench your brutal, erratic and factional rule in Uganda, you have without any shame, extensively employed mercenary soldiers clandestinely recruited from the southern Sudan. Since you yourself come from the Uganda-Sudan border you have ruthlessly exploited the ethnic loyalties of the people on both sides of the border. The mercenaries...have debased the standards of the Uganda armed forces since the pre-occupation of the mercenaries is to kill, maim and loot.'

On the 'Economic War' Kibedi said the expulsion of Asians from Uganda was not intended to place the economy in the hands of the common people but to transfer wealth to individuals and foreigners favoured by Amin. 'Your ehtnic kith and kin, as every Ugandan knows, have done extremely well out of the allocations of the businesses and other assets left behind by the expellees. You have yourself shared the booty.

'The scandalous fact is that you have used the economic war to buy support from sections of the community (civilian and military), and sometimes from foreigners, by giving individual men gifts of factories, farms, mansions etc. formerly owned by Asians or other foreigners, as if it were your own property. The Speke Hotel, Kampala, for example, was given away in this way. In the same way you have awarded individual lucrative export or import contracts in order to secure their personal loyalty to you.

'Your economic war has not improved the condition of the masses in any way.'

Uganda's rejoinder was predictable. Amin's mouth-piece *The Voice of Uganda* newspaper, published the full text of a speech made by Foreign Minister Kibedi at the 'good neighbours' summit of East and Central African countries in Dar es Salaam during the Asian expulsion period.

Kibedi had argued the economic war hurt imperialists exploiting the Uganda economy. Firm measures were justifiable wherever a government put the interests of its own nationals first. The speech cited previous mass expulsions from Ghana (Prime Minister Dr Kofi Busia chased 250,000 non-Ghanaians home to neighbour countries such as Mali, Upper Volta and Nigeria), from Sierra Leone and from Uganda itself.

Milton Obote had given thousands of Kenyans, Tanzanians and Zairois two weeks notice to leave. Kibedi swiped at Britain for planting racialism in many parts of the world . . . at British news media for heading 'every manner of abuse and blasphemy' on Amin . . . and at 'anti-Uganda filth spewing out the mouths of British cabinet ministers' over the Asian question.

A point *The Voice* ignored was that while he vindicated the theory behind the economic war nowhere in the Dar es Salaam speech did Kibedi defend the way the so-called war was being waged in practice.

Amin's next attack on Kibedi was equally predictable and ineffective. He tried to paint his brother-in-law with the bloodied brush . . .

Before a commission of inquiry a Uganda army sergeant testified that Kibedi offered him 50,000 shillings to murder Chief Justice Ben Kiwanuka. Sergeant Stephen Kintu alleged that he had been invited to the Foreign Minister's official residence where Kibedi urged his fellow tribesman from Busoga province to kill Kiwanuka because President Amin had implied the Chief Justice would become Uganda president when the country returned to civilian rule. Kibedi sought the presidency for himself.

'I refused to carry out the murder. Mr Kibedi asked me to think it over,' Kintu said. A few days later, he claimed, Kibedi offered the bribe. 'I still refused.'

In an affidavit sworn before a London solicitor Kibedi questioned Kintu's evidence in detail.

'The man's testimony clearly shows that he himself does not know me at all. He gets my father's name wrong, my home village wrong, my *muluka* (parish) wrong, my *gombolola* (sub-county) wrong, my county wrong.

'During my tenure of office I never had for my personal use as much as £2,500 on me or to my credit anywhere in or outside Uganda. The Ministry of Foreign Affairs knows this.

'If Kintu is reported correctly, he has perjured himself before the commission. I do not know the man at all and I have certainly never met anybody by the name of Sergeant Stephen Kintu.'

And the next episode *was* both unpredictable and bizarre. Amin declared his brother-in-law had reformed ...and supplied Kampala with damning information on the activities of exiles abroad.

'I have alerted all our contacts overseas and asked them not to chase Mr Kibedi because he has written letters informing me all about some Ugandans in exile who are conducting subversive activities against Uganda,' said General Amin. 'He is also keeping me informed about the attitude of the British and Americans towards us.'

In the same breath Amin asserted that Rugumayo Banage, Obote's attorney general Godfrey Binaisa and lawyer John Kazora—now all living in exile—were not bad people.

'They were among my best friends and performed their duties efficiently. But they were confused by bad elements and decided to run away.'

Amin added impudently: 'I am happy they are all employed. Nobody will harm them if they decide to return to their motherland.'

SIMULTANEOUS to Kibedi's resignation from the Uganda government a course of events took place which made the prospect of any cohesive public service even more remote. Amin insisted that civilians in the government were not functioning as well as they could because of the fear of guerrillas, affairs of state therefore being left in the hands of his more resolute supporters.

His way of dealing with the deepening political crisis was to send all his remaining ministers and their assistants on compulsory leave—so that he could concentrate on improving the military side of things. He sacked Minister of Works and Housing J M N Zikusooka, saying the minister's 'early retirement' had become a necessity. Most of the roads in Uganda were not being supervised properly because Zikusooka devoted much of his time to running private business—a jaggery farm and maize mill at Bukoboli Estate, cattle and poultry farms at Wanyange, a dairy farm at Njeru near Jinja and a sugar cane estate.

Inconsistent as ever, Amin said Zikusooka would not forfeit his government pension or benefits.

'I have retired him but not because he is a bad minister. Any business which a minister, Army officer or public officer has must not interfere with his official duties and if it does he will be retired in the same way. As long as Mr Zikusooka concentrates on his business without breaking any laws of Uganda the Government will not interfere with his affairs.

'The Government is even willing to assist by giving him a loan through the Uganda Development Bank so as to expand his business.'

Amin continued: 'If he needs any assistance he should make an appointment to see me.'

But Big Daddy did not retire, let alone reprimand, favoured Army officers to whom he had given the vast expropriated Asian estates.

'The only governments that can manage the continent of Africa are military governments. Politicians keep on talking and do not work for the interest of the public. Until we started the Second Republic the black people in Uganda towns were like slaves.'

He found at least one criticism for his Army, however. 'Most of the Armed Forces Jazz Bands are left to roam around with girls. Looking at the faces of the Entebbe Air Force Jazz Band I know straight away they are drunkards . . . Some people look as though they are painted with cosmetics just because of too much drinking of alcohol. The Simba Battalion Jazz Band is the best band because if they are taken to the battlefield they can do anything a soldier should do.'

On April 27, 1973, the Uganda chairman of the joint Uganda-Kenya-Tanzania East African Railways Corporation, Dan Nabudere, resigned; again on moral grounds. He protested the abduction of four senior railway employees by plainclothes agents in Kampala. No subsequent investigation had commenced.

On May 1 John Barigye, Amin's ambassador to West Germany and the Holy See, resigned. Earlier, Barigye, learning that his brother Ruhinda had 'disappeared', telephoned Amin from Bonn. The call sent Amin into a rage; Amin rang Foreign minister Kibedi, demanding Barigye's immediate recall. In the conversation, (Kibedi recounted), Amin wanted Barigye to be told that the president was not a policeman, it was not his job to inquire about missing persons and an ambassador had no right to speak to the president on such matters.

Barigye couched his letter of resignation in by-now familiar terms. 'While innocent people continue to be brutally and savagely eliminated your regime has failed to bring justice to the perpetrators of these crimes. Indeed, eyewitness reports and circumstantial evidence tend to implicate you and your henchmen in these barbarous acts which show complete disregard and contempt for human life.'

Amin's doctor Professor John Kibukamusoke fled Kampala at two hours notice, having received a private warning that he was to be killed. Kibukamusoke, head of the Department of Medicine at Makerere University, treated Amin for gout before the coup. In power, Amin asked him to lead his personal medical team—a surgeon, a pathologist, an ear, nose and throat specialist, a haematologist and a biochemist.

Dr Kibukamusoke gave some revealing observations on Amin's personality. He confirmed what many considered obvious. The general suffered from hypomania, a condition bringing about a rapid succession of often contradicting ideas expressed in confused verbal outbursts and fits of anger alternating with spells of extreme optimism and a sense of the grandiose.

Clinically defined, hypomania also causes periods of

restless activity leading to exhaustion and the need to rest.

Kibukamusoke's team treated Amin for minor complaints, including gout. 'Our tests on him for syphilis proved negative. But such negative tests could have been accounted for by a late stage of the disease's advance or as a result of partial treatment ... We had no opportunity of investigating the complaint by immuno-logical tests since he denied any previous infection.'

The doctor said he found out some time later that an Israeli psychiatrist, Dr Marcel Assaed, had in fact treated Amin for syphilis in the period leading up to the coup. 'This would help explain the syndrome of grandiose paranoia which is not unknown in syphilis sufferers. General Paralysis of the Insane (GPI), as it is known in its advanced state, is relentless.'

Amin's hypomania had become increasingly more pronounced since he became head of state. 'We felt this could be a trend to schizophrenia, but it was impossible to be absolutely sure.'

Physicians tried to calm Amin down by prescribing anti-schizophrenic drugs, only to find he would not take the drugs regularly. 'He was very suspicious of treatment. For example his suspicions were thoroughly aroused when we suggested that he should have a simple tonsillectomy under anaesthesia.'

It was during this time that Michael Kagwa, president of Uganda's Industrial Court, was seized from the swimming pool at the International Hotel, Kampa-la, and brutally murdered. His body was so badly mutilated no proper autopsy could be carried out. Later, Dr Sembeguya, a leading medical practitioner and former MP, was killed and his body mutilated.

'Amin was subject to attacks of frenzy. He would go through periods of extreme agitation and indecisive-ness. These bouts would come and go, but as one wasn't with him all the time it was difficult to say how frequently these moods occurred,' Dr Kibukamusoke said.

'At the same time he would appear in public and

behave as an amiable gentleman...This behaviour is typical of the double personality—the Jekyll and Hyde syndrome, a state of schizophrenia with paranoid reactions.

'Another feature of the killings in Uganda that can be associated with hypomania is shooting victims in the mouth. This has happened on numerous occasions in the case of Amin. Psychologically, this kind of action is to stop an argument you cannot otherwise stop by reasoning.

'I...have good reason to suppose that this was the fate of the former chief justice of Uganda Benedicto Kiwanuka...When the Chief Justice spoke up in defence of his judicial role—as Kiwanuka would do—he was shot in the mouth. Another variation of shutting up opponents by killing them was the case of the Roman Catholic priest Father Musoke, of Kitovu mission. He was dragged away by security officials while he was reciting Mass.'

Exiled Education Minister Edward Rugumayo made his views on Amin known in a memorandum after his resignation addressing African Heads of State and Government. He described Amin as an illiterate soldier of very low intelligence from the minority Nubian/Kakwa tribe and an adherent of the minority Islam religion.

'He is medically unfit; he suffers from a hormonal defect. He is racist and a fascist; a murderer and a blasphemer; a tribalist and a dictator. General Amin has no principles, no moral standards and scruples. He will kill, or cause to kill, anyone without hesitation as long as it serves his interests, such as prolonging his stay in power or getting what he wants, such as a woman or money. He is an incorrigible liar, both locally and internationally; his word in international dealings should never be relied on. He possesses no moral or political standards. He sets his own 'standards', writes his own 'rules' and changes them as he moves along. It therefore becomes very difficult for anyone to predict his moves. The only prediction which one can make is that he is highly unpredictable.

'If we take the aspect of illiteracy for a President of a modern state, the problem takes on fantastic dimensions. For instance, Amin finds it well nigh impossible to sit in an office for a day. He cannot concentrate on any serious topic for half a morning. He does not read. He cannot write. The sum total of all these disabilities makes it impossible for him either to sit in the regular cabinet, to follow up the Cabinet minutes, or to comprehend the briefs written to him by his ministers. In short, he is out of touch with the daily running of the country, not because he likes it but because of illiteracy. He rarely attends Cabinet, and even then it is only when he is giving directives about problems concerning defence or 'security' of the country, or when he is sacking some civil servant. So the only means of getting information about the country which he rules is by the ear from various sources. In other words he relies solely on listening and perhaps seeing.

'Since most of his ministers are what one might term technocrats, he finds them too complicated and uninteresting, although they are the people who should actually give him correct information. Instead he has to have recourse to people of his own level of intelligence and calibre. In effect, these are the people who rule the country: the illiterate and semi-literate army officers who have been over promoted, the illiterate and semi-literate intelligence officers who have recently been drafted into the service. Practically all of them get their information by word of mouth, and get directives from their superiors verbally. Since little is ever written down, and once said, there is little or no follow up to change the plan or check the facts. This type of government can lead to disastrous results, especially where security is concerned.'

Illiteracy led to the overloading of Amin's memory. In one instance he deported three expatriate doctors he had been told were British spies, bombastically accusing them of spreading 'political gonorrhoea'. Two of the men were members of Amin's personal medical team—

when he next wanted a medical check up he demanded to know why they were not available.

'We are presented with a picture of a man who cannot fathom the complex problems of a modern society . . . he oversimplifies the problems as well as their solutions, to the detriment of the entire nation's future. He thinks that governing a country means talking to and entertaining big crowds of people. He does not possess the slightest rudiments about economics. For instance, he was urging his Finance Minister to print more paper money if there was not enough money in Government coffers. The country is bankrupt. A lot of the money is spent on spying, the army and on his personal projects. He has literally millions of shillings, in USA dollars, which he keeps at his house in case of trouble. He has deposited millions in Libya, to which he will retire in the event of trouble. In fact, he has bought three big villas in Tripoli for his personal use.

'His abysmal ignorance has made him hate education, educated people and educational institutions. He brags that if he could rule the country well, then there is no need for highly educated people.'

Amin fired an experienced, fully-qualified public servant from the job of Permanent Secretary to the President's Office, replacing him with an assistant district commissioner educated only to School Certificate level. Chairmanship of the Public Service Commission went to the town clerk of a small town in Karamoja region, Moroto. Both the new appointees came from Amin's West Nile home region.

Rugumayo verified that on his first trip to Libya Amin assured Col Gadaffi that 80 percent of Uganda's population was Muslim and this majority had long been dominated by the Christian or 'heathen' minority.

In truth—Muslims—mainly the Nubians, accounted for not more than 10 percent of the population.

Both Libya and Saudi Arabia donated money from the Jihad (Holy War) Fund to be used, in the words of a visiting Libyan diplomat recalled by Rugumayo, 'to eliminate the few remaining Christians and turn Uganda into a Moslem state.'

Amin's first campaign had been against Catholics. Chief Justice Kiwanuka was a Catholic; Father Kiggundu, editor of the Catholic daily newspaper *Munno*, had been abducted and burnt to death.

Munno reported a Women's Council resolution calling for investigations into 'disappearances'. Amin 'went on to liquidate many of the important Catholics in the civil service and the business world...many Catholic prison officers, administrative secretaries and others. He went on further to attack the nuns and priests in the press for allegedly acting as spies. He also turned against Protestants.'

Among leading Protestants killed: Michael Kaggwa. Amin was also known to have been interested in Kaggwa's girlfriend.

Rugumayo said a death list had been drawn up, containing more than 2,000 names. At least ten 'assassination squads' roamed the country with impunity, seeking their victims.

'The pattern is a familiar one: They enter an office, call their victim out, put him in the boot of the car or just inside the car. And that is his end...On some occasions, they ambush their victim along a motorway, or along the road leading to his home. Earlier on, most of the victims were men, but now women have fallen victims of his (Amin's) deadly plans.'

While the assassination squads came under Amin's overall control they were directly accountable to Nubian officers—Towilli of the police, Marella of the military police and Maliyamungu of the army.

'He (Amin) considers himself first and foremost as a Nubian/Kakwa, secondly as a Moslem, thirdly as a West Niler, and fourthly as a Ugandan. Consequently the closest people around him come in this order...

'...and others who are former Anyanya guerillas and who therefore have no loyalty to Uganda.'

One aspect of Amin's character about which Rugumayo also remarked was the general's deep-rooted superstition. 'He is surrounded by witch doctors, fortunetellers, soothsayers and all manner of bogus persons. He relies more on these men than on the actual facts as they exist. Hence his reliance on 'dreams', apparitions and other occult practices, and his inability to realise the importance of pertinent information relating to his government.'

A bush 'prophet' much trusted by Amin was Zambian 'Dr' Ngombe Francis, whose big break had come early in January 1971: he predicted Milton Obote's overthrow. Amin could not resist inviting the diminutive seer to Kampala, where he was paraded in front of the television cameras to perform various psychic feats.

Big Daddy was impressed and admitted 'Dr' Ngombe to his close entourage. Boosted by Amin's generosity the Zambian opened consulting rooms in Nairobi, reportedly became a dollar millionaire and bought a luxury mansion in Zambia, two houses in Kenya, a villa on the Cote D'Azur, three Mercedes Benz, a British sports car and part ownership of a four seater helicopter. On one occasion 'Dr' Francis freely admitted his gambling losses exceeded £25,000—despite his frequent boast: 'I can predict anything.'

Rugumayo's denunciation was lengthy, explicit and detailed.

'The methods of killing during the first months of the coup included straight-forward shooting or beating; with the disposal of dead bodies becoming a problem, the soldiers resorted to throwing bodies of their victims either in rivers,, swamps or even water reservoirs. This was found to be unsatisfactory, as human bodies tend to float and to attract vultures. Later on, they were simply thrown into the bush and left there to rot or be eaten by wild beasts, or were burnt in petrol fires.'

Amin's principal killers were to devise harrowing tortures.

'The victims would line up, and the first one would be ordered to lie down while the prisoner next to him would be ordered to smash his head with a huge hammer. And

125

he would be the one who had just smashed the dead man's skull. Then the third person would be ordered to demolish his brains and so on until the last man, who would be either shot by Towilli himself or be killed in the same brutal manner by a police officer.'

'The victim's heads would be smashed beyond recognition by one of the appointed executioners.'

'Slow killing is a common practice. Towilli would shoot into a man's arm, leg or chest and let him bleed to death.'

'Another method is to cut off any of the man's organs, such as an arm, leg, genitals, and let him die in agony. Sometimes these organs would be stuck into the victim's mouth.'

'There is a technique of cutting a victim's flesh, and forcing him to feed on it raw, until he would bleed to death while living on his own flesh.

'The other despicable method is to cut a man's flesh, have it roasted and let him feed on it until he dies. . . . There is a constant fire in which human flesh is roasted, and a man is fed on his own flesh until he dies of sepsis and bleeding.

'There are in Makindye Prison very deep and dark holes in which certain prisoners are kept. These holes are filled with ice-cold water in which prisoners are kept and are fed once a day on some form of diet, and are at the same time tortured until they die.'

'There are other horrible methods of torture which are too terrible to describe, such as sticking bayonets through prisoners' anuses or genitals; or women being raped and afterwards having their reproductive organs set on fire while they are alive.'

'The instruments of murder, torture and human degradation have been perfected by Amin. Most of the bodies of important people are put in incinerators and those who cannot be burnt for one reason or another are buried, while wrapped in a cloth, by prisoners who would not live to tell the tale. In some towns the Army, after their killing sprees, carry the dead bodies into the nearest town or hospital mortuary. Nobody can venture to ask any questions. The following day the town or city cemetery workers are told to bury the dead without asking any questions.'

Evidence collated from other separate sources added further to the Uganda list of institutionalised torture:

Electric shocks were used in Towilli's torture cells at Naguru Police College by fastening power terminals to the genitals, nipples, neck, head or face.

Victims' eyes were gouged out and left hanging from their sockets.

Beatings with hammers, iron bars, car axles, wooden mallets to smash joints and limbs, prolonged beatings with stout Rhinoceros whips; the wheel torture and sexual assault on women prisoners was commonplace.

Women's breasts were hacked off with bayonets; in other cases hands and feet were chopped off; prisoners were made to bury the dead and clear up the remains of victims' corpses.

Victims' bellies were slashed open and their intestines pulled out. Prisoners were made to walk over upturned nails and were subjected to physical exertion until they collapsed or were beaten down.

Burial squads were fed on human flesh. Weakened by beatings prisoners were 'finished off' by decapitation; others were forced to dig their own mass graves, trenches along which they were lined and shot.

Bodies that did not fall into the trench were pushed in by the next group to prisoners lining up to die.

IN THE aftermath of Chief Justice Kiwanuka's death Uganda's judiciary made a largely ineffectual grumble to Amin which blamed the armed forces for impeding the course of justice. A resolution drawn up at a judicial conference in Kampala complained of widespread interference by soldiers, district commissioners and chiefs in court procedures.

'Members of the security forces turn up in court and demand that someone be released, or that someone be sent to jail, or that someone be prosecuted. Very often members of the security forces, when called to give

127

evidence, fail to turn up and no explanation is given. At times when they do turn up they refuse to answer questions put to them.'

Before the resolutions were submitted to Amin, Kampala businessman, Samson Ddungu, appeared in court on allegations of theft. Defence lawyer Enos Ssebunnya showed there was no conclusive evidence as alleged that Ddungu had stolen cash from the Asian-owned business which had been allocated to him and an Army officer.

But as soon as the magistrate pronounced Ddungu's acquittal men of the Public Safety Unit attempted to re-arrest him in the courthouse. Once outside the court, they chased Ddungu, eventually opening fire. The businessman took refuge in a nearby building—but was dragged out and killed. Ssebunnya was arrested, beaten up and tortured.

This incident and others like it put the judiciary in an invidious spot; judges and magistrates themselves were not exempt from violent threats although the conference resolution mildly concluded the forces behaviour may have been due to their lack of adequate knowledge of the court system. It proposed courses for soldiers to teach them judicial procedures. Amin agreed—but the courses never started.

The resolution was published in the Government-owned press . . . hard on the heels of an assurance by Amin that the judiciary would always be allowed to retain its 'absolute independence.' Amin also openly criticised a number of his own security officers for random arrests. For public consumption, the government said Amin had been disturbed by his discovery that 41 people were being held without charge on the sole instructions of Army officers at Kampala central police station. What was left unsaid was that jails were crammed full anyway, the Forces, given a *carte blanche* to shoot on sight any individual suspected of Kondoism (violent robbery), were immune from any civil prosecution, and Military Tribunals had usurped the powers of the High Court.

The tribunals' expanded jurisdiction empowered it to deal in secret with all capital offences. Presiding officers had no legal training and the presentation of evidence bore no relation to recognised judicial practices.

Military Tribunals eventually spread throughout the country, replacing local courts and meting out the death penalty without surcease.

By mid-1973 4000 formerly Asian owned businesses had been handed over to black Ugandans. The Government took over the Madhvani and Mehta companies and other larger concerns, leaving the allocation of smaller businesses to committees comprising mainly of military personnel. The committees travelled throughout the country interviewing queues of business aspirants. Consideration was supposed to be based on sensible criteria—business assets and experience, educational qualifications and the like. In practice, the process was extremely haphazard, with preference being given to Nubians, Muslims (many hopefuls faked Islamic faith), tenderors of the largest bribes and Amin's Army clique.

The names of re-allocated proprietaries became suitably jingoistic: The Exodus restaurant, the New Transelectric Economic Independence Co. The sublime nature of the giveaways also had its ridiculous aspect. The roof of Uganda's main cement plant collapsed when thick layers of production dust which should have been swept away daily turned to concrete in the rain.

All industrial production fell. Essential commodities—like sugar, salt, soap, matches and milk —were in short supply, a situation aggravated by hoarding and overcharging. The deteriorating foreign exchange position led to a big drop in imports of building materials, manufactured goods, vehicle spares, and other luxury items. Exports increased slightly— largely as a result of bumper cotton, coffee and tea crops. Exports were affected by transport difficulties.

Kenyan East African Railways staff left the country after 40 Kenyan workers were reported missing in Uganda.

Then Amin himself had to admit: 'A very disturbing factor arising out of the declaration of the Economic War is that some of the people to whom the Government and the entire people of Uganda entrusted the businesses left behind by exploiters have now formed themselves into a notorious racket of cheats and exploiters. They have inflated prices at their will so as to enrich themselves overnight. They are creating artificial shortages of certain essential goods through hoarding them. This is economic sabotage which the government cannot allow to continue. We are committed to ensure that these evil practices are put to an end at once.'

Later, abolishing the Special Business Levy tax, Amin blustered: 'I want all my countrymen to be millionaires, to expand their businesses and be free of hatred of those who are doing well and are rich.'

Among other choice judgement on his country's economic well-being:

'Uganda is a paradise in Africa. If you have a shirt and trousers you can live in Uganda for years—even without working...

'Even if I am killed my operation is already a success. No single Ugandan will ever allow non-citizens to come back and control our economy. I am the hero of Africa.'

AT LEAST The Congress of Racial Equality (CORE) took the effusive Amin at his word. Roy Innis, executive director of the radical Afro-American organisation declared: 'This is the truth, quiet as its kept: The Ugandans are happy under General Amin's rule of Africa for Black Africans.'

Innis had been invited to Uganda by Amin and saw, he said, 'an unprecedented thing in recent history— black people owning the businesses and running the government of their own country.' Leaving Uganda Innis' delegation received Ugandan passports and offers of land, jobs and dual-citizenship for black Americans. CORE replied by promising Amin a first batch of 40 teachers and technicians to come home and be part of this great era of African pioneering. Uganda offered government employees almost rent-free housing, free medical treatment and some types of free dental care—all at government facilities. CORE's Ugandan lands would be used to develop pioneer settlement stations, which might be farms, African style kibbutzim or industrial centers.

Uganda offered Blacks the unique experience of belonging at last, of contributing where their effort was valued, of making a commitment according to enlightened self-interest to the world-wide Black community.

After more than 45 hours of talking with Amin, Innis came away convinced: 'Uganda's top foreign policy priorities are to solidify links with Black African nations, normalise relations with Tanzania and re-connect the kidnapped citizens of Africa from the Western Hemisphere. To really fuse the Africans and Blacks of the United States is a very critical element in African development. Amin's really tuned into it, more than anyone I've ever seen. He believes more than we do in the US. He sees the massive resources we squander.'

Innis was equally convinced that Uganda's political and economic outlook was promising. 'The first thing he has done is to give people confidence. The next good thing he did for the first time in the modern history of black folk was to give us political and economic liberation. The next thing he has done is to set up a programme that fights against tribalism. It is an active, working programme to diffuse tribalism from being a factor in Uganda political life.'

Amin rewarded Roy Innis by including him in Uganda's official delegation to the Organisation of African Unity's 1973 summit meeting in the Ethiopian capital, Addis Ababa. The black American was the first non-Ugandan ever to attend such a gathering as a delegate.

The summit was a significant one for Big Daddy. He had accused Tanzania, in league with Zambia and Zaire, of breaking the conditions of the peace accord drawn up by Somali mediators after the abortive 1972 invasion. According to Uganda, Tanzania broke the terms of the

131

Mogadishu Agreement by aiming a campaign of hostile propaganda at Kampala (among other charges Dar es Salaam claimed seven young Tanzanians had unaccountably disappeared in Uganda) and by persistently supporting anti-Amin guerrillas. Matters came to a head when Tanzanian authorities arrested about 50 Ugandans, working for the East African Harbours Corporation, on spying charges. Amin put the Uganda Army on standby, claiming that a force of 3,500 Tanzanian troops was poised to attack Uganda. Somali mediators who went to the border area, however, reported no unusual troop movements. The dispute cooled down when President Nyerere deported most of the arrested Ugandans. Amin in return proposed an amnesty allowing Dr Obote, 'the guerrillas in Tanzania' and all exiles to return home and 'join other Ugandans in building the nation.'

In Addis Ababa the two countries attempted a rapprochement. Amin shook hands with Nyerere for the first time as Ugandan head of state and made two major concessions to the Tanzanians. He admitted responsibility for the deaths of 24 Tanzanians in Uganda, subsequently paying compensation; he dropped his hitherto unflinching demand that if Obote and his colleagues in exile did not choose to return home they should at any rate leave Tanzania.

But The OAU summit conference was not all plain sailing for the Ugandans. Milton Obote broke 28 months of silence and accused Amin's government of having killed 80,000 people, many of them having been disembowelled. Appealing to African leaders not to support Amin, Obote said that while the OAU celebrated ten years of existence 10 million Ugandans mourned their dead. Obote's letter to the African leaders detailed 3,500 killings—including the deaths of seven of his former Cabinet ministers—and recapped massacres and methods of torture. He quoted Edward Rugumayo's memorandum: 'Amin's ex-minister states that at a conservative estimate the death toll in Uganda in Amin's first two years of terror was 80,000 to 90,000 people.'

Obote described Amin as 'the greatest brute an African mother has ever brought to life.' He said that in one instance Amin's troops surrounded the Eastern town of Mbale, sealing it off for three weeks and massacring 300 people. Massacres also took place in Kibedi's home district of Busoga in revenge for the foreign minister's escape into exile.

'Too many nations regard what is happening in Uganda as an internal matter. Is the systematic genocide an internal matter or a matter for all mankind? The Sharpeville Massacre was condemned by the entire civilised world but nobody has yet condemned the wholesale killings and disappearances of innocent people in Uganda. I plead that even if as Africans you cannot materially and morally support Ugandans in their determination to overthrow Amin, do not materially and morally support him and do not arm him; for to support him and to arm him is to give him an international certificate to massacre the people of Uganda at will and on his whims.'

CORE jumped to Amin's defence. The letter, it said, contained wild and reckless accusations against Amin. Imperialists, colonialists, their agents and their stooges used the letter as a 'dirty trick' to discredit and sully Gen Amin and thus to discourage the thawing in relations between Tanzania's Julius Nyerere and the general.

Uganda was the symbol of the most important tenets of Pan-Africanism and black self-determination. Roy Innis telephoned CORE's national headquarters in the US from Addis Ababa to commend Amin's speech before the OAU. He called it: "powerful and impressive.'

CORE might have been Amin's most enthusiastic champion, but the international community as a whole was skeptical about the extent of the bloodshed in Uganda. The number of dead was generally felt exaggerated—although many leading Ugandans who had fled Amin's rule actually thought Rugumayo's figure was too low. Obote's letter, and its attendant

133

publicity, pricked the conscience of foreign governments and rattled Amin. But international complacency was not significantly altered.

AMIN turned back to domestic affairs. He enacted the Customary Marriage (Registration) Decree allowing Ugandan men to marry as many wives as they wished. Husbands who failed to register customary marriages within 6 months of them taking place would face a possible 500 shilling fine. The decree stipulated that district commissioners chosen to officiate at marriages would not be allowed to marry a man to more than one woman at the same time. The decree, Amin said, would not interfere with established Christian or Muslim marriage rites. It would help orientate Ugandans 'towards our cultural heritage and regain our self respect and dignity.'

He banned mini-skirts, saying that while Ugandans should be free to wear what they liked all people should ensure dress was 'decent'. There followed a rush of prosecutions: A 15-year-old girl was fined 100 shillings for wearing a dress with its hemline 3½ inches above the knee; a teenage boy whose shorts were too short—six inches above the knee—received a year's probation.

Amin's mini-skirt ban was succeeded by a more elaborate decree which forbade women of 14 or more to wear wigs, trousers and skirts with a deep slit. Wigs, said the official announcement, were made by callous imperialists from human hair mainly collected from the unfortunate black victims of the miserable Vietnam war, thus turning human tragedy into lucrative commercial enterprises.

Amin provided an additional rider: 'I do not want Ugandans to wear the hair of dead imperialists or of Africans killed by imperialists.' The Government could not stop Ugandans wearing wigs in private but: 'No member of my own family is to wear a wig or she will cease to be my family member.'

The new decree made clear that the prohibition did not apply to women whose occupation, profession or official, cultural and sporting activities obliged them to wear trousers or wigs. 'In this category are women lawyers who have to wear wigs in court, women who wear trousers while taking part in sporting activities like gymnastics, women hunters while in the bush and police, prisons and military officers.'

Mini-skirt devotees had apparently circumvented the decency law by putting on outfits with plunging necklines, open backs nad provocative thigh slits. The decree had been prompted by 'heaps of letters and oral demands to Amin by Ugandans from all walks of life.'

The decrees did nothing to hide Ugandans deteriorating public services. Hospitals and schools were kept open by skeleton staffs; remote facilities were closed altogether. Ghana sent 82 teachers to Uganda, and Rugumayo's replacement, Brigadier Barnabas Kili, stated that educational policies were under review. No innovations materialised. The first 20 Soviet doctors arrived in Kampala as Amin stopped Ugandan doctors travelling abroad unless they were going for specialist courses. This restruction was because of grave problems left behind by colleagues who had run away from the medical service, Amin said.

Amin undertook to set up a National Organisation of Trade Unions to look after the welfare of all Ugandan employees and review salary scales. But in another rambling utterance the General said salaries would be frozen until further notice, the Defence Council would not tolerate industrial disputes, would-be strikers should respect their bosses, love one another and have discipline. If workers still had grievances they could seek expert advice from the President himself...

Women, Amin told Air Force officers one of whose number had been killed in a quarrel, were not worth dying for. 'It is shameful to hear that Ugandan officers are dying because of women.'

Black Americans taken to the United States as slaves should take over the US and elect a Black President and Secretary of State; 'Kissinger is not so clever because he always goes only to weak leaders'; British Foreign

135

Secretary Sir Alec Douglas Home did not visit Uganda because he was scared of the country's tough leadership.

"I like the Scots because they are the best fighters in Britain and do not practice discrimination. The English are the most hopeless. I don't know why Scotland does not decide to become independent and leave the English to suffer.'

Israel, Amin said, planned to poison the waters of the Nile River in Uganda during the 1967 Middle East war to weaken the Sudan and Egypt. 'What the Zionists planned in Uganda was nastier than what Hitler did to the Jews.'

Uganda had forged contacts with the Palestinian Black September group and the Irish Republican Army (IRA).

'Black September should make suicide attacks on Tel Aviv and Haifa.'

Amin's sagacity and magnanimity did not stop there. He cabled London asking Prime Minister Edward Heath to send an aircraft to collect a consignment of Uganda vegetables and wheat. The produce had been donated to the Save Britain Fund by farmers of Kigezi district.

'I am now requesting you to send an aircraft to collect this donation before it goes bad. I could have sent the donation direct but as we do not have facilities for doing so I hope you will react quickly so as not to discourage Ugandans from donating more.'

To Heath's successor at Number 10 Downing Street, Harold Wilson, Amin again offered to mediate between the warring Catholics and Protestants in Northern Ireland. Irish religious leaders—could come to Uganda to negotiate peace 'far away from the site of battle and antagonism.' 'Regrettable developments in Ulster call for Britain's best friends to come to her assistance.' Amin also offered to ask arms merchants supplying both sides in Northern Ireland to impose arms embargoes.

To the new American president, Gerald Ford, Amin suggested a black man should be nominated as vice-president. 'I wish to address you on a burning issue of our time and to alert you to a situation fraught with dangers, namely the position of black people in your country.

'You are aware Africans were kidnapped from Africa by whites and forced against their will to leave their motherland and to go in chains to the United States. The black people are hardworking, sincere and indeed have many other talents. They have contributed a lot to the development of America. Their important role in society must be recognised.

'As a fellow President and a fellow commander in chief I wish to advise you that for the smooth running of the administration in your country you must not discriminate against black people. Not only should you appoint them to high offices in your White House staff but you should also appoint them as secretaries of state. Your vice president should be a black man. They are entitled to their rightful share in the running of the country. You know that a general talks less but does more action, and I trust you will take my advice very seriously.'

Amin signed off: 'I wish you a happy time in the office of the President of the United States of America.'

By now Amin's black American supporters in CORE had every reason to be puzzled. Amin had cold shouldered them and inexplicably scrapped the plan to bring CORE workers to Uganda.

Amin's cocky telegrams to world leaders were given extensive publicity in Uganda by the government media. And if Amin's image at home was tarnished in his fourth year of bloody, ruinous rule, his propagandists were not letting on.

Waxed *The Voice of Uganda* newspaper:

Oh! Idi Amin Dada, thou great African of our time,
Yours have been words and deeds in their sacred prime,
For the fates of great nations have hung on your words
And how very shrewdly you have always played your
    cards
No matter what the prophets of doom may say,

137

Idi Amin, you have paved the clearest and safest way
For the African people to feel for the first time really free
And see their socio-economic life boom like an
   evergreen tree.
Before, the life of your people was a complete bore,
And they were poor, oppressed, exploited and economi-
   cally sore.
And then you came and opened new, dynamic economic
   pages
And showered progress on the people in huge realistic
   stages,
In such expert moves that have baffled even the great
   sages.
Your electric personality pronounced the imperialists'
   doom,
And your pragmatism has given Ugandans their
   economic boom.
O Amin, you the volcano that has erupted truth out to
   pass,
You the bulldozer that has given the African special
   class.
You are the hopes and aspirations of the youth of
   tomorrow
And also the fear and object of every oppressor's
   sorrow.
Ah, see African women, men and children, how they
   dance,
All rejoicing at such precious and rare lifetime chance.
In the field of diplomacy you have excelled them all,
For you always know just where to pass your diplomatic
   ball.
How you forged solid solidarity with our rich Arab
   friends
And how with foes you sought peace and made firm
   amends.
At the OAU you stood and spoke firmly in one piece,
And you spoke of unity, true independence and peace,
And you have made the African to be respected more
And made our destiny more sure with real hope in store.
Ah, where are the blind ones who do not know

How fast and truthfully you made Africa's fame grow?
Ah, let the wicked ones lament in their disappointed sobs,
While the Africans do their dignified, justified jobs.
Wasn't it you who gave them their beautiful economic notions,
That has given all the people satisfactory business options?
Oh, how Africa does greatly honour thee
For your noble efforts to make her truly free.
Surely, your unswerving dedication to the African cause
Shall drive us all to ultimate victory in due course.
And how loudly all the freedom fighters extol you
Since you have proved yourself sincerely true.
Now your people enjoy their coffee, tea sugar and bananas
And their abundant citrus, oranges, mango, guava and ananas.
While here a textile mill and there a sugar mill rolls
As vast hydro-electric power flows from the Jinja Falls
To weld and strengthen the people's socio-economic recovery
Following your economic war—a unique social discovery.
Now you champion the federation of EA's men and women,
Something which has been lauded in these past ten years,
To have common trade, tariffs, laws and free flow of money
To enjoy our meat, fish, tea, coffee, grains, milk and honey,
For all East Africans to feel one people once again,
For socio-cultural cohesion, political unity, economic progress and mutual gain!!
LONG LIVE IDI AMIN!
LONG LIVE THE GREAT AFRICAN REVOLUTION!
LONG LIVE AFRICA AND ALL HER PEOPLES!

CHAPTER IX

*'Don't disturb the people of Uganda at night by
running about shooting. Uganda is going at
supersonic speed and the peole must not
unnecessarily be made to panic.'*

Idi Amin Dada

Sunday, March 24, 1974.

A Tennessee Ernie Ford recording of *Onward
Christian Soldiers* would be played on the radio early in
the morning. It would mean the first part of the uprising
had succeeded—and Amin was dead, Towilli and
Marella were under arrest. The plotters would be
holding key installations in the capital, others would
mobilise in the districts to secure the coup d'etat.

The telephone rang at Kampala radio station. A
voice asked for the special request. The hymn blared out
over the air. But the plan had gone wrong. Idi Amin
Dada was alive and kicking...

Mortar and machine-gun fire continued erratically
throughout the morning. Tanks and armoured personnel carriers had surrounded Entebbe airport, the
Command Post and State House. The radio went briefly
silent, then repeated Saturday's news bulletins. More
church music.

During the night 70 Lugbara soldiers had commandeered a tank and shot their way into the Malire Mechanised Regiment armouries. Instead of moving straight to strategic points in the city the rebels went first to Makindye to free fellow Lugbara. The Malire Regiment rallied behind Amin: The gun battles lasted until dawn.

As Amin himself liked to brag afterwards he had just climbed into his pyjamas when a group of the conspirators came. The officers appeared at his house asking to see the President. Amin braced a sub-machine gun against his hip and went out to meet them...

The night left about 100 soldiers dead. The coup leader Brigadier Charles Arube was shot twice in the stomach.

On Sunday afternoon Amin visited loyal troops of the Malire Regiment at their barracks. Radio Uganda took up the story. 'Gen Amin was told someone had confused the troops of the Malire Regiment that there was an invading force which was going to kill him and capture Kampala.

'On hearing this, they explained, the troops jumped into their tanks and APCs and drove to defend the city.'

Addressing the men, the broadcast went on, Amin 'thanked all officers and men of the Uganda Armed Forces who have been working with him since midnight last night up to 2:00 p.m. this afternoon. . . . a total of 14 hours. The President also thanked the officers and men who have kept him well informed and told him all the truth behind the confusion.

"President Amin told the officers and men that whoever will be found involved in the matter will be dealt with according to the laws of Uganda. The General, however informs all countrymen that the situation is completely under control and there is no cause for alarm.'

Amin said: 'If you are not happy with me, then kill me or make me resign and don't disturb the people of Uganda at night by running about shooting. Uganda is

141

going at supersonic speed and the people must not unnecessarily be made to panic.

'What happened showed how powerful we are and how loyal the troops are to me. We are happy and there is no reason why we should worry at all. The situation was saved because all the commanders know my voice. Even if I died anytime now I would be happy because I have made Uganda a revolutionary African country. Nobody should feed on rumours. I am free, I have no problem.'

Late in the afternoon most of the troops had withdrawn from the streets. A heavy guard was maintained at the Ministry of Information, the radio station and Makindye prison.

Amin got into his open jeep and drove from the Malire barracks through the city—Katwa, the bus park, Kampala Road, Wandegeya, Mulago and Kamwoja—to the Presidential Lodge.

That night Entebbe airport was reopened and the official radio concluded the day with a report that Brig Arube, the officer who caused the 'confusion', had shot himself in the head with his pistol. Arube, lately returned from military training in the Soviet Union, had died during an operation at Mulago Hospital to save his life. Hospital records not subsequently contested by Amin's government corroborated the independent versions that Arube had been shot in the stomach.

Other officers involved in the coup attempt had fled into the bush, the radio said.

Brigadier Arube's revolt had sinister undertones. The previous month Amin's Lugbara Foreign Minister Lieutenant Colonel Michael Ondonga had been 'assigned to other duties' as the cabinet announcement put it. Ondonga's relationship with Amin was known to have been an uneasy one. Lugbaras in the Forces had been loyal to Amin from the beginning ... to the extent they shared much of the blame for Army executions with their neighbours from Western Uganda, Amin's Kakwa. But the Lugbaras were mainly Christians—and they were to find the Muslim Kakwa more richly rewarded for their services to Amin. Kakwas were getting the promotions; the Lugbaras were moved sideways, demoted or completely removed—Ondonga being the most notable example.

At the beginning of March Ondonga's bullet-riddled body was discovered floating in the Nile near Jinja. Like many other Amin victims, Ondonga must have known his 'disappearance' was close.

It is possible Ondonga was warned of an intention to seize him at one of his favorite haunts, the Nile Hotel. But it was at 8:00 o'clock in the morning on a street corner near Nakasero Primary School—where he had delivered his young son. Crying hysterically: "You are going to kill me for nothing. I have done nothing wrong to your governemnt,' Ondonga was bundled into the boot of a waiting car. Amin claimed Ondonga, a former Ugandan ambassador to Moscow, had been abducted by 'imperialist agents'.

Recovered from the Nile Ondonga's body showed that death had come as a merciful end to the last terrible hours of his life.

For Lugbara officers Ondonga's treatment at the hands of Amin's men confirmed that they too were now dispensible. More Lugbaras were accused of conspiracy and thrown into Makindye prison.

Just what happened prior to Ondonga's murder is difficult to establish. It was no secret the Lugbaras were disillusioned and desperate and getting more so. Rumours of an imminent uprising circulated in Kampala, and could not have escaped Amin's attention. In all likelihood Amin ordered the killing of Ondonga to bring forward the dissentors action. He would be able to crush them and purge the Army of Lugbaras once and for all.

Brigadier Arube returned from Russia to learn the former Sudanese Anyanya commander Marella had replaced him as acting Chief of Staff. Although himself Kakwa, Arube was a Christian and already felt deeply

143

aggrieved by the extent of killings among Acholi, Langi and Lugbara Christians by the Nubians. In Lieutenant Colonel Elly Aseni, another Christian Kakwa, Arube found a sympathiser who possessed considerable support in the Malire Regiment. Aseni was arrested after the uprising, tried by a military tribunal and released—but only because of his following in the Army.

Wtih the rebellion quelled Kampala rapidly reverted to apparent normality. But Amin's purge was only beginning. At the month's end 400 Lugbara had died—executed by firing squad, shot in the knee caps and left to bleed, thrown alive to Nile crocodiles, drenched in petrol and burned. Reprisals against the Army's 2000 Lugbara carried on for weeks, spreading to other military units, especially the Mbale garrison. So ferociously were imaginary plotters hunted down that even *The Voice of Uganda* was moved to comment: 'Where is all this bloodshed taking the nation? Heartbreaking disappearances of people—from the eminent to the humble—continue to cause misery.' The comment seemed to have been overlooked by the paper's overseers. One of the latest disappearances was that of a High Court judge, Mr Justice Opu. Amin again said the missing man was 'confused' and had 'run away to join his imperialist masters.' Only one loyal serviceman had died in the entire period, Amin claimed. And he had been a guard at Makindye on the night Arube's men attacked.

Amin was quick to point out that he did not believe the Soviet Union had in any way influenced Brig Arube, or encouraged him to try and snatch power in Uganda. 'I want to assure you that nobody should accuse the Soviet Union of brainwashing Brig Arube,' he emphasised.

Uganda certainly did not wish to fall out with the Kremlin at this juncture, despite Big Daddy's professed aversion to Communism.

Several provocations had led the US to close down its Kampala embassy: Amin took the American charge d'affaires Robert Keeley, along with the Russian and

Chinese ambassadors, to a house in Kampala's Kololo district. In front of the ambassadors he launched into a lengthy diatribe, charging that the Americans equipped the house with 'Watergate type machinery' used for bugging the homes and embassies of not only the Chinese and Russian in Kampala. Recording tapes were handed over to the ambassadors, Amin adding: 'When the Israelis were in Uganda the Americans and Israelis made Uganda the headquarters of the CIA for Africa.'

'It is also well known that you introduced into Uganda several religious organisations which were causing confusion,' Amin jabbed at Keeley. 'We still have 200 missionaries in schools and missions. The government is watching carefully the activities of these people and if they are found to be carrying out any activities not connected with religion I will take immediate steps. Some years back there were 2000 Americans in Uganda but since the declaration of the Economic War you have found it extremely difficult to carry out your spying activities.'

Amin followed this up by summoning the American diplomat and Britain's acting High Commissioner James Hennessey for another telling off, this time about intelligence reports he'd received saying British, Israeli and American commandos—at the instigation of the CIA—were about to parachute into Uganda. That was why any Britons or Americans on Ugandan streets without identity papers would be jailed forthwith.

Amin had also expelled the six Marine Guards assigned normal security duties at the Kampala embassy on the grounds that they were subversives. That happened before Odonga's death too. It was left to the ill-fated Foreign Minister to protest to Keeley about harassment of Ugandan representatives in the US, including two burglaries at the official residence of the Permanent Representative to the United Nations, Elizabeth Bagaya, in New York. Ondonga said to Keeley the Ugandans had been the victims of 'great and various kinds of harassment culminating in complete

145

acts of barbarism.' US authorities had failed to honour the Vienna convention obliging them to protect government officials. But the Uganda government, however, was confident the US security forces were capable of doing so.

Earlier, Amin threatened to arrest all US nationals in Uganda because of US 'meddling' in the Middle East.

He regaled Washington thus: 'The Uganda Government will continue to condemn the USA interference in internal matters of other states. The United States of America has now realised that the many peace loving countries of the world have condemned its policy of direct military involvement in the Middle East and that is why the United States Government had decided to send Dr Kissinger, a great enemy of the Arab world, to negotiate a peace agreement with the Arab states. This same man was the one who directed the supply of arms to Israel for destruction of thousands of innocent lives. All peace loving people in the world will always continue to condemn such confusing agents . . . and understand the USA policy of interference . . . The problems brought about by this policy in South East Asia are well known in the world. Many innocent people have been killed through bombing and military involvement in South East Asia.'

Many countries were scared of the US, Amin said, but not Uganda.

As Washington's seven-strong embassy staff packed up to leave Kampala, trusting the welfare of remaining Americans to the West German embassy, Amin announced the Defence Council was thinking of drastically reducing its diplomatic representation in the US, perhaps keeping only one person in the Washington embassy—and he would probably be a private soldier. If necessary, Uganda might ask another African country to caretake the embassy.

'Uganda gets nothing from the US,' Amin recalled US aid cuts. 'What we have in Uganda is through the people's sweat.' But it was not sweat alone.

What Amin got from the Russians in 1974 was substantial: Arms, training for his favoured personnel in Eastern Europe, Communist bloc military and technical advisors (mainly Russians and Czechs).

Two hundred Uganda Air Force trainees—all of them Kakwas and Southern Sudanese handpicked by Amin—went for pilot training in Czechoslovakia, enabling them to operate three squadrons of MIG fighters for Amin from Gulu Air Base. Following habit, Amin had steadily boosted the Nubians in the Air Force. At least ten non-Nubian senior officers had been eliminated.

A Soviet cargo vessel, the *Klim Voroshilov,* docked at Kenya's Mombasa port carrying an unspecified number of light tanks and armoured personnel carriers, seven dismantled helicopters, explosives and 750 cases of small arms. Amin indignantly blasted off at Kenya's *Daily Nation* newspaper for reporting the arrival of the consignment. 'The disclosure to the imperialists of armaments sent to East African countries indicates the paper is owned by Zionists.' (The Nation Group, in fact, is owned by the leader of the Ismaili sect of the Muslim faith, the Aga Khan.) He went on to say that every independent African state had the right to equip its forces to modern standards so they could be 'effective in the liberation of Africa.'

Two more ships, MV *Mir* and the *Korosho*, arrived with cargo for Uganda listed as dangerous. This consignment was held up by Kenya Harbour authorities alerted to its nature by curious Kenyan dockers herded away from the ships by Soviet seamen. Kenya would not release any cargo until both Uganda and Tanzania returned railway wagons to the port. The standstill, which held up sugar and salted fish bound for Tanzania, gave Kenya time to ponder Amin's designs.

The 'dangerous' Uganda cargo included crated MiG fighters, tanks, APCs, trucks and anti-aircraft guns. Amin profusely thanked the Soviet Ambassador to Uganda, Mr Zakharov, at a meeting at Makindye

Lodge. 'I am very grateful for the free gifts such as tanks, mobile trucks, guns and fighter planes that the Soviet Union has given us. I am happy the Soviet Union has supplied my Mechanised and Artillery regiments with new weapons.' He would commission the weapons at Mbarara Mechanised Regiment; the MiGs, together with others recently handed over by Libya's Gaddafi, would 'make the balance of power good in East Africa.'

'This will make Uganda defend herself properly and make Uganda provide help to our brothers in Angola, Mozambique, Rhodesia and South Africa in case of need.'

Neither outsiders, nor Ugandans bearing the brunt of Amin's purges, saw it quite that way. Kenya, Tanzania, Zaire, Rwanda and Sudan began worriedly monitoring the flow of gifts. Amin's expanded military muscle helped him put down fresh mutinies in the Services, one of which involved Lt Col Baker Tretre, a Lugbara who had enjoyed Amin's closest confidence.

Amin once made Tretre, then a major, head of a military delegation to France which paid cash for 80 armoured personnel carriers fitted with surface-to-surface missiles. Tretre earned notoriety and promotion as one of Amin's most vicious torturers. Tretre fell from favour, tried to get back on top...and disappeared.

Russian strategy at the time was probably not designed to keep the rapacious Amin in power. More likely, its aim was to secure Soviet influence over his army in case it overthrew him. The Kremlim had close military and political relations in East and Central Africa only with Somalia. To the north, the Russians had been thrown out of Egypt and the Sudan (after the abortive communist coup d'etat there in 1972). For the time being, Amin satisfied the wider requirements of the Soviets' African strategic interests...and for the first time young Ugandan officers returning from training in the Soviet Union and Czechoslovakia brought with them, so the Russians thought, a sincere commitment to Soviet ideology. Implicit in this were strong anti-

Chinese and anti-Western feelings . . . a foundation the Russians dearly cherished.

'Uganda's relations with the USSR have improved very much since the birth of the Second Republic,' *The Voice of Uganda* reported the Soviet Charge D'affairs Valentin Kasatkin as saying. 'Ways and means are being probed to further strengthen these relations.'

But Amin was not as mute or as malleable as the USSR hoped.

Gushed Amin to Gaddafi during an official visit by the Libyan: 'You are not in the pockets of any super power and I want to assure you that we in Uganda are not controlled by any super power. That is why when I learnt of your policies I became one of your best friends.'

Amin thanked the Chinese for small arms and a rice development scheme at Kibemba. He glowingly commended the Italian Agusta helicopter company for extending the unquestionable benefits of its pilot training programme to Ugandans—and sent off another military shopping list to the French.

He still wanted spare parts for the Fougar jets originally supplied by the Israelis and wondered why France had not yet taken up his offer of a site in Uganda for a car factory.

Amin again met British High Commissioner Hennessy. He demanded Britain resume sales of spare parts for British-manufactured cars and guns in use in Uganda because 'when members of the same family quarrel they are always ready to forgive and forget.' The diplomat tactfully replied he hoped he would succeed in interpreting British Government policy to President Amin and the policies of President Amin to the British Government. Amin later confided to junior Army staff that he had found Hennessy 'a brilliant and intelligent officer' in whom he had full confidence. Britain turned down Amin's request.

Big Daddy was at pains to make out the Kremlin was not his sole supplier of military hardware—and that *he* wasn't in anyone's pocket either.

"I approached various countries such as the United States to supply arms to Uganda but they refused, saying their policy did not allow it. Therefore we had to get from those countries who accepted our request, the Soviet Union being only one of them.'

If only forgetting Tretre's spree in Paris, Amin vehemently denied the regime was squandering money on arms at the expense of civil development. All the hardware was *gratis*. 'These donations are from friendly countries which are ready to arm Uganda to the teeth because of her stand against the imperialists and Zionists. More planes, weapons and ammunition will be pouring in for the defence of Uganda. Some of our friends want to arm us up to international combat level.'

For his part, Soviet *chargè* Kasatkin had little difficulty convincing Amin that Uganda should not be troubled by propaganda disseminated by reactionaries and the Chinese saying that the Kremlin desired to manipulate Ugandans for strategic advantage. Suspicions to that effect were unwarranted because Moscow strove to safeguard the political integrity of all independent African nations. Kasatkin presented Amin with lesser gifts: six copies of the journal, *The Soviet Military Review*, and two copies of magazines dealing with the sporting activities of the Warsaw Pact armies.

Not that Amin cared much, or even understood the implications of the Russian ties—as long as his own insatiable greed was fed. The General was tantalised by an invitation to pay a state visit to the Soviet Union and hints the Russians might give him some SAM ground to air missiles—a weapon no other African army then possessed. Amin was also toying with the idea of buying a navy.

'The Pioneers of the Uganda Navy' returned from an intensive seamanship course in Libya. The only trouble: landlocked Uganda had no ships for them. Amin placated the disappointed mariners by telling them arrangements to buy a fleet were well in hand, and the problems of transporting gunboats and larger vessels across Kenya to Lake Victoria were not insurmountable. As a stopgap, Amin seconded the sailors to Army units engaged in muddled ground manoevres.

'I ask you to maintain a high standard of discipline, keep physically fit and cooperate with all members of the armed forces and civilians. Do not do stupid things which tarnish your good name as pioneers of the Uganda Navy. Your names will go down in the history of Uganda but it will be very bad if you spoil your record as pioneers of the service. It is very awkward if someone starts something good and later becomes the one who spoils it. I ask you to uphold the good name Uganda has earned in the world ... Every country in the world today wants to build and control its economy and this has been achieved in Uganda because of the soldiers. Do not indulge in excessive drinking and getting involved in affairs with wives of other men ... Col Gaddafi loves the people of Uganda. If your training was done in another country it would have cost Uganda a lot of money ...'

Much as he wanted a navy Amin never got one. Much as Gaddafi might have loved Ugandans, warships were out of his range. Uganda, like neighbours Kenya and Tanzania sharing the Lake Victoria shoreline, maintained a motley collection of steamers, official launches, pleasure cruisers and fishing boats on Africa's largest (35,000 square miles) lake.

Among the land exercises to which navy pioneers were assigned was a three day shindig codenamed 'Liberation of Guinea-Bissau Operation'. The operation had a number of connotations: in one of his periodic meetings with Kasatkin Amin said the guerrilla war waged by PAIGG nationalists against the Portuguese in Guinea-Bissau had been a symbol of Africa's determination to rid itself of colonial domination. Portugal, however, had amassed a mercenary force to fight the PAIGG and Russia should think twice about having any dealings whatsoever with the Portuguese.

Amin commanded the exercise himself, saying at a prior briefing he had selected terrain for it more or less similar to the Golan Heights in Syria. The most modern of Uganda's recently acquired weapons would be used. The 'very important and historic training exercise' got off to a shaky start. By the end a child had died in a bombing sortie which accidentally spilled over into Tanzania, five Ugandans had been killed and 119 injured, five of them seriously. Several new vehicles had been written off.

Amin wasn't fazed in the least. The exercise, he said, had been a great success. "If we are attacked we shall win the battle as God will be on our side because the Uganda army will then have a cause to fight. All battalion workers should know how to handle guns, even those working in the hospital, because an enemy cannot be selective; he will kill everyone . . . Uganda will attack and crush the enemy in case of any provocation. There is no need to wait for permission from me to go and fight. I only want progressive reports on the enemy."

Russian military attache Col Rubanov and senior advisor Col Novikov, invited to a lunch winding up the liberation of Guinea-Bissau, kept their comments to themselves, merely nodding to acknowledge the First Simba Mechanised Battalion commander Major Adek praising Soviet instructors for bothering to learn a workable vocabulary in the local language, Kiswahili and Kinyankole.

Amin continued to badger the Soviet Union for more armaments. Now he wanted long-range bombers because White South Africa had infiltrated 'immigrants with sophisticated weapons' into Mozambique Angola and Guinea. South Africa felt threatened by Portugal's scheduled withdrawal from its African territories and was drawing up plans of attack. 'We are all too well aware of the White racist masterplan to recruit these white immigrants to entrench their hold on the African continent. If we are called upon by the Organisation of African Unity to defend any African country Uganda must be able to discharge her duties.' Russia huffily reminded Big Daddy it was well acquainted with the situation in Southern Africa and suggested his time might be better spent concentrating on the affairs of East Africa.

Amin did not take offence to the mild rebuke, said he was pleased to hear young Muscovites were learning Kiswahili—'a big weapon in uniting the people of this eastern region' and announced the establishment of formal diplomatic relations at ambassadorial level with Cuba.

Amin's son Shaban, given a Soviet scholarship to study aviation technology, left for Moscow.

CHAPTER X

'There is a tide in the affairs of men,
Which, taken at the flood, leads on to fortune;
Omitted, all the voyage of their life
Is bound in shallows and in miseries.
On such a full sea are we now afloat;
And we must take the current when it serves,
Or lose our ventures.'
William Shakespeare, *Julius Caesar*

She quoted Shakespeare's Caesar to the United Nations General Assembly.

She held forth on African nationalism at a lunch hosted by Henry Kissinger—and told the US Secretary of State to go to Africa and see for himself.

Wearing braided hairstyles, heavy gold necklaces and flowing dresses she was constantly escorted by a large retinue of admirers.

She hoped France would reconsider its unfortunate decision to build a 1,000 Megawatt nuclear power station in South Africa.

She charged that Black Americans still lived in conditions of slavery.

She called for the formation of a powerful international body to formalise maritime law.

Chairing a special OAU sub-committee at the United Nations she advocated the UN's expulsion of South Africa and military intervention to end apartheid.

The United States, she said, created and perpetuated world tension by interfering in the affairs of other countries.

She blamed Middle East tension, in part, on a British vendetta devised to frustrate Arab aspirations.

Americans, she argued, persuaded the World Bank and the International Monetary Fund to block aid to certain developing countries.

She said Idi Amin seized power to restore freedom and human rights in Uganda.

"I have no time to answer silly questions," she snapped, challenged on General Amin's praise of Adolf Hitler.

Elizabeth Bagaya had replaced murder victim Lt Col Ondonga as Uganda Foreign Minister.

Born Princess Elizabeth Edith Christobel of Toro, daughter of Ruhiidi III, the Omukama, or ruler, of Toro, one of Uganda's seven ancient Kingdoms, the strikingly attractive, willowy six-footer had been educated at a school reserved exclusively for the children of Uganda kings and chiefs and at Britain's snob Sherborne School for Girls. She qualified with honours in law at Cambridge University and became East Africa's first practising woman barrister. The Omukama died in 1965 a year before Milton Obote's abolition of the Kingdoms and Princess Elizabeth's first escape into exile.

In London her patrician beauty soon caught the imagination of the fashion world. Soon she was modelling elegant designs for leading couturiers; her picture appeared in top magazines, *Vogue*, *Queen* and *Harper's Bazaar*; she took the so-called international jet set by storm. Liz, as friends knew her, landed the female lead role in the Hollywood film version of Ghanaian author Chinua Achebe's book *Bullfrog in the Sun*. Barely a month after filming had been completed Obote was ousted ... Princess Elizabeth gave up the glamour of society life to accept an appointment first as Amin's Roving Ambassador and accredited representative to the UN General Assembly. Amin had not restored the Kingdoms and required the Princess to drop her royal titles. Miss Bagaya adapted to her new job with flair, soft-spoken charm and urbanity. Elizabeth Bagaya lasted 10 months at Amin's Foreign Ministry. She was put under house arrest in Kampala. Accounts reaching the Kenya capital of Nairobi said she had been interrogated at Kampala Central Police Station, where her inquisitors threatened to shave off her hair with broken glass. Persistent rumours that Amin had sealed the same fate for the princess as befell her predecessor Lt Col Ondonga may well have saved her. President Kenyatta again cautioned his impetuous Western neighbour. The Kenya statesman had been an old friend of the princess's father; he had stayed with her family during Uganda's independence celebrations. Miss Bagaya's wide circle of friends abroad had also canvassed for Kenyatta's weighty intervention.

Amin chose to reassure Kenyatta through two visiting representatives of the Palestinian Liberation Organisation. Amin's media reported him telling the Palestinians of his willingness to release the princess from house arrest.

'I have nothing against her. She must feel free to go anywhere. Miss Bagaya has been treated in the best way during police investigations.' The fact that she had been kept at her home and not taken to Luzira prison emphasised his sincerity, he said.

'She is free to go out and start making malicious propaganda. I am immune now about such propaganda. I don't care.'

This last admission was anything but the case. In an unguarded moment Amin warned of reprisals against the families of Ugandans who left the country and engaged in 'opposition and subversion'. 'Uganda is already fed up with problems and no Ugandan should be

156

ready to lose relatives as was the case when Uganda was invaded.'

Just before Elizabeth Bagaya fled Uganda another exasperated cabinet colleague, Finance Minister Emmanuel Wakhweya, had made good his escape. Representing Uganda at an East African Legislative Assembly meeting in Tanzania the minister flew to London and cabled his resignation to Amin from there. His earliest disclosures naturally dealt with fiscal affairs. Uganda's inflation was running at 85 per cent, the currency was virtually worthless and many staples were almost unobtainable. 'To live in Uganda today is hell. The country is facing economic catastrophe. I cannot imagine how the ordinary people are able to carry on because of the shortages of the simplest essentials for life and the soaring cost of living. It is hard even to get soap—children are developing scabies—something that hasn't happened for years.'

Wakhweya became Finance Minister after the 1971 takeover. He had been sent on compulsory leave with the other civilian ministers, then served on a valuation committee dealing with sequestrated British assets until Amin restored him to the finance ministry.

'As the months went by it became increasingly clear that any advice tendered by the Minister of Finance was either completely ignored or countermanded.' Uganda's economic situation worsened, credit facilities for imports and essential services were withdrawn. The government became a 'one-man show' with Amin making impossible decisions bearing no relationship to the country's resources. Despite falling revenue Amin increased government expenditure by expanding administrative departments and existing parastatal organisations.

'Whatever advice one tried to give Amin to alleviate the situation he brushed aside and refused to listen. One can't get through to him. He still seems to think everything in the garden is lovely.

'It is obviously worrying to be in a Government where you can't explain what is happening to the people. I have naturally also been worried about the lack of value of human life which is a terrifying aspect of the situation.

'You survived by keeping your head down and trying to keep out of trouble. I simply used to go from my office to my home. But how long can you go on living in this way?'

Wakhweya described how Amin ruled 'via radio.' 'Every minister has a radio in his office. We switch on at five o'clock in the afternoon to hear what has been decided, who has been appointed and who has been dismissed. For example, at five o'clock I learned from the radio that I had been directed to import colour television sets into Uganda. Because such a small country as Zanzibar had colour television we also had to have it. Whoever fails to carry out these directives is an economic saboteur—and you know what that means.'

Amin had been infatuated with colour T.V. during a visit to the spice-rich island of Zanzibar.

Amin accepted Wakhweya's resignation in his usual way. Uganda radio said the minister wanted to reveal Government secrets to his imperialist masters. 'His flight to London will not help at all since Britain is in economic chaos. Uganda's economy is much better than that of many other countries. The economy of Britain is worse than that of Uganda... Nothing will stop Gen Amin and the Ugandan people from their political and economic revolutionary activities.'

For customary effect the radio levelled corruption charges at the Finance Minister. He had, it said, delayed foreign exchange allocations to businessmen and had been engaged in a currency swindle involving supplies to Army shops.

Wakhweya, a gifted financier who was snapped up by the World Bank, had no difficulty in showing that the methods by which he was accused of defrauding the Government, in fact, were impossible for him to have carried out.

Spots of blood led under the garage door. Inside the house at Kampala's Rubaga suburb Dr Peter Mbalu-Mukasa, his wife and young children lay unconscious from barbiturate poisoning. The baby had been suffocated in a cupboard. Amin's police, called by a neighbour alerted by the family's maid, smashed into the house.

At Mulago Hospital—where he had been a senior surgeon—Dr Mbalu-Mukasa died. His wife and three of the children regained consciousness.

Police forced open the boot of the doctor's car. It was awash with blood. A gunny sack contained a woman's torso wrapped in a nightdress. Her arms and legs, cut off at the hips and shoulder joints, were in cardboard boxes. Separate boxes in the car contained surgical instruments, pads of blood-soaked lint.

A post mortem was carried out. 'The external wounds were consistent with the dismemberment of the body which was done after the person had died. The woman had been three to four months pregnant and the foetus had been removed with the use of instruments. Pieces of membranes had remained inside the womb and caused severe bleeding. There was also haemorrhage, bleeding of the bowels. Cause of death was bleeding because of an incomplete abortion.'

The dismembered body was that of Kay Adroa Amin, estranged wife of Idi Amin Dada.

The circumstances of Kay's death have remained a mystery. In a single announcement—the day before the uprising led by Brigadier Charles Arube—Amin divorced three of the four wives his Muslim religion allowed him. He said he had found Kay was related to him and that Mama Maliyamu sister of exiled former Foreign Minister Wanume Kibedi, and Nora—who was related to a cousin of Milton Obote—had acquired businesses in a way 'contrary to national policy.' Mama Maliyamu and Nora had actually been given Asian businesses by their husband.

Two months after the divorce Kay Adroa was

arrested, apparently in possession of 15 rounds of sub-machine gun ammunition. The pretty university graduate was jailed overnight for interrogation, then escorted to Amin in Parliament Building.

'Do not involve yourself in dirty activities or allow yourself to be deceived or confused by the wrong people,' Amin bawled, slapping her hard. 'You are an educated woman who Uganda should be proud of. Never fear to contact me any time for any kind of assistance.'

Releasing Kay from custody Amin told her to go home to Arua and ask her brother, Wilson Adroa, to come and see him. 'He is too young. Whatever he is doing is childish and needs advice.' Wilson Adroa had just been fined 16,000 shillings for possessing a pistol and ammunition. A member of Amin's presidential body-guard later spoke of a belief among his close clique that Amin suspected Kay and her family of having links with the Lugbara revolt, and that Kay specifically informed the plotters of his less changeable routines and habits. Kay's acquaintances in Kampala believed Amin still summoned her to him after the divorce and did not conceal his jealous traits. Amin would have been angered to learn Kay and Dr Mbalu-Mukasa were lovers. He would have been particularly embittered to learn Kay was expecting a child by the doctor.

The last time relatives saw Kay was when she returned to her Kampala home with Dr Mbalu-Mukasa in the early hours of one morning to collect a night gown. It was assumed that Kay, constantly tailed by Amin's police, had seized an opportunity to slip away to spend the week-end with the doctor. Four days later she was dead.

According to one informant Amin was indeed enraged by Kay's affair, and had been heard threatening her at least once. Kay told Dr Mbalu-Mukasa of her fears—and he knew at once that both their lives were in danger. The next part is conjecture:

The doctor decided on his first action—to get rid of

Kay's incriminating baby. He took her to his private clinic, Basirika Clinic at Buganda Road, and conducted the abortion himself. It would have been a desparate decision; normally, doctors would have considered it unsafe to terminate Kay's advanced pregnancy. The operation went horribly wrong. Mbalu-Mukasa, demented and in a state of shock, could have dissected the body for disposal...

However Kay Adroa died, blame for her death lay with Amin. One of his staff officers was to recall Amin once saying to his men: 'Take her and do with her as you wish.' If Amin's men did not wield the surgical knives or force Mbalu Mukasa to do so—leading to subsequent mental collapse—it was Amin's command of fear that crazed the doctor.

Amin claimed the surgeon had a long history of mental disturbance and had carried out other illegal abortions.

An alarming but revealing episode followed Kay's death. Amin ordered her body to be sewn together again—but with the limbs sewn to the wrong joints—and took their children, Kide, Masters, Lumumba, Adam and Mao Mozambi, Kay's parents and a group of friends to view it. Present at the mortuary was Amin's Health Minister at the time Henry Kyemba, the Army chaplain general, the commander of the loyal Malire Regiment and Nubian security men. After his own escape from Uganda Kyemba recalled that Amin addressed the children: 'Your mother was a bad woman. See what has happened to her.'

It was about this that time details of an autopsy carried out on the body of murdered Foreign Minister Lt Col Michael Ondonga began to emerge. Ondonga's liver had been removed—giving rise to accounts that Amin required it brought to him, whereupon he ate it in accordance with a Kakwa superstition that this killed the soul of the victim and absolved the murderer.

An attempt was made on the life of Amin's senior divorced wife, Mama Maliyamu Mutesi,—but only after she had been arrested, jailed, given bond and fined

161

for allegedly smuggling five rolls of textile fabric to Kenya.

Maliyamu was arrested with seven others near the Kenya border. For a fortnight she was refused bond expressly on Amin's orders. At the final Tororo court hearing Mama Maliyamu and two of the co-accused were cleared of smuggling but fined for 'acting as travelling wholesalers without travelling wholesalers' licences.' Maliyamu's arrest and imprisonment was probably ordered by Amin in the first place. He suspected she wanted to leave the country, intending to cross the border into Kenya from Tororo.

Later Maliyamu was on her way to visit relatives just outside the capital. She was alone in the car. In Gaba road a heavy army truck pulled out in front of her; the car was rammed off the carriageway by an oncoming saloon. The attackers left her for dead, slumped in the wreckage.

But Maliyamu was lucky. Passers-by took her to Mulago Hospital with serious injuries. Amin's police promptly announced she had been involved in a car accident while drunk. Amin visited his ex-wife at Mulago.

'You are getting into trouble because you changed to Islam not as a true Muslim, but because you wanted to stay married to me,' he started in a confused lecture on Islam. Maliyamu had accompanied him on a pilgrimage to Mecca, but she had never been a true Muslim and reverted to Christianity.

'I did not force you to become a Muslim. In Islam people are severely punished if they do things which are against the commandments of God. If you are not blessed by a special sheikh from Mecca you will continue to suffer until you die.'

Amin took along two of his children, Maliyamu's daughters Kadara and Alima, while he delivered the lecture.

But Maliyamu eventually managed to leave Uganda for further treatment and she did not return.

Out of Mulago Big Daddy also had words for the

300-or-so members of Uganda's Supreme Muslim Council. He would sack the lot and replace them with non-Muslims—Catholics, Protestants and Orthodox Christians. 'Muslims in Uganda should not blame me at all because the present Muslim officials have failed to fulfill their obligations. The council's executive is only interested in riches such as luxurious cars, building houses for girl friends and earning fat salaries instead of carrying out the services of God.' He criticised the council for wanting to build a 35 million shilling mosque on Old Kampala Hill when the existing mosque was adequate, but in need of repair.

Amin's digs at the Muslims did not save the Christians from his preaching: the Catholic Church had been the original Christian religion and it was only the issue of the marriage of clergy that caused the protestants to break away. Concerned by Amin's ignorance of theology Anglican bishops sent him a terse memorandum. 'In matters of our faith in Jesus Christ we would appreciate it if you would consult us before making a national statement about our Church in Uganda, and if you have a desire to be informed about what we believe feel at liberty to summon us and get all the information you require.'

The Christian Church found Amin took little or no notice of its protests, either on spiritual doctrines, on his phobia about bible-brandishing spies and subverise sects or the continued disappearances.

'BOOTS of cars are designed for the transportation of luggage not people,' Amin's most recent chief justice Samuel Wako Wambuzi told the court session. 'Suspected criminals are entitled to human treatment.'

Army private Ayubu Aluma, charged with violent robbery, was acquitted after testifying he had been beaten, handcuffed and locked in the boot of a government car. 'This is not the first time this has happened,' said the Chief Justice. 'A stop must be put to it.'

As he walked down the High Court steps Aluma was

surrounded by plainclothed policemen. They barged him to their car, opened the boot and bundled him in. At the Central Police station Aluma was charged with rape.

The Chief Justice's remarks may have made Amin think for he ordered another commission of inquiry into disappearances. The investigations would cover all Ugandans reported missing regardless of the period which had expired since they disappeared, and those found to be involved would be dealt with according to the law. 'In my view there is no greater natural resource than human life.'

A legal notice signed by Amin appointed a High Court judge, Mr Justice Mohamed Saied, chairman of the four-man commission responsible to Chief Justice Wambuzi and Justice Minister Godfrey Lule and said the commission should give 'due consideration to the logical and natural events of the military take-over as well as the events pertaining to the defence of Uganda.'

No sooner had the commission begun proceedings than it was adjourned *sine die*—to enable evidence to be gathered and processed.

A leading Kenyan businessman Achando Weke, a Ugandan colleague and their two women companions were ordered out of Susanah's nightclub, Kampala, by soldiers. They were frisked and shot dead in the street.

Seven men were paraded in front of a 10,000 strong crowd at Masaka and were said to have been kidnappers. Henceforward, all kidnappers would be shot on sight, a local Army commander told the rally.

Ugandan forces would open fire if Tanzanians so much as stepped over the border delineation into Uganda. 'We must guard against African countries who always claimed they are brothers and sisters whereas, in fact, they are not.' Amin said.

Prince Ronald Mutebi, heir to the Buganda throne, paid another visit home—this time accompanying the body of his other parent, Lady Sarah Kisosonkire. Amin took the opportunity to reaffirm there was absolutely no question of a revival of Uganda's traditional kingdoms. Lady Sarah's burial was not as full blown as her husband, the Kabaka's—but Amin did provide a guard of honour and suggested to Prince Ronnie that he should spend vacations from his British university in the Uganda Army...an offer Prince Ronnie nimbly refused.

Clergymen were not the only people Amin had in mind as potential spies. Fourteen members of the British High Commission staff were expelled from Kampala. 'I have broken the backbone of the British spy ring in Uganda,' boasted Big Daddy, warning that other foreign embassies or companies which sheltered secret agents did so at their own risk. 'It will be their fault if they do not see such people again.' Of all spies Ugandans should be specially on the look-out for American and British agents, who dared offer bribes even to the president. Britain, Amin claimed, wanted to give him £12 million not to go ahead with the expulsion of the Asians and Americans tried to buy his silence about their East African espionage network with millions of shillings.

Another brainwave: Amin wanted to celebrate the Economic War by visiting Ugandan Asians resettled in Britain. He despatched a message to the Queen of England telling her so. He hoped Queen Elizabeth would arrange for him to meet Scottish, Irish and Welsh 'liberation movements' who were struggling for independence from the imperialism, racism and economic serfdom of her rule. 'I am sending this message early so that you may have ample time to arrange for what is required for my comfortable stay in your country. For example, I hope during my stay there will be a steady supply of essential commodities because I know that your economy is ailing in many fields.'

So confident was Big Daddy in the state of his own ailing economy that he offered immediate food relief to 32 Third World countries affected by drought. Crops such as maize, beans, simsim, groundnuts, peas and sorghum would be dried, bagged and stored until airlifts could be arranged. Farmers should stockpile cassava and sweet potatoes for their own needs while producing

165

the relief crops. The operation never began ... Ugandans could barely feed themselves and anyway Amin was off on another track: He outlawed begging. Offenders who exposed wounds or deformities to obtain alms would be liable to imprisonment, he said. Few of the beggars rounded up after this decree ever reached jail. A number of physically handicapped citizens were also picked up and killed. Amin drove through Kampala in his Citroen Maserati to see if the decree had been effective ...

Amin turned up at the Crested Crane Hotel, Jinja, for a reception honouring competitors in the All Africa Boxing Championships and entertained bemused guests on the accordion. When he visited Ugandan boxers in training at Lugogo indoor stadium he gave them one piece of simple advice. 'The only way you can be sure of beating your opponents is by knocking them out.'

He did not manage to knock out Uganda coach Grace Sseruwagi when he stepped into the ring with him to inaugurate the championships, but was conveniently awarded a points win. At a time when hardly an Acholi of Langi family had not lost one or more of its members Ugandans knew exactly what Amin meant by knocking out opponents.

Amin instructed the Ugandan High Commissioner in London to set about recruiting two six-foot Scotsmen as personal bodyguards. The successful candidates would have a military background with good service records and should be experienced in playing the Scottish bagpipes. The High Commission was also asked to find an experienced British office messenger to work in Uganda training office messengers. Next, Amin invited the United Nations to move its headquarters from New York to Kampala, lifted the ban on women wearing trousers (women tourists would thus be protected from snakes and thorns, he emphasised) and chided Makerere students for sexual promiscuity. 'I am told that venereal disease is very high with you ... You had better go to the hospital to make yourselves very clean, or you will infect the whole population. I don't want you spoiled by gonorrhea.'

'Our prisons,' he told prison officer recruits, 'are no longer places of terror or torture as during the colonial days. You will rehabilitate our prisoners in tailoring, carpentry, metalwork, handcrafts, shoe-making, leather tanning, printery, masonry, building and agricultural and livestock farming.'

At a time when Amin's military mainly controlled the prisons inmates who survived knew all about rehabilitation Amin-style.

THE FESTIVITIES marking the first four years of military rule were as bizarre as their sponsor. Ugandan soldiers parading at Nakivubo football stadium wore Royal Stuart tartan kilts, glengarries and regimental sporrans made of plastic, instead of badger skin, decorated with pied crow feathers. Complete with a strutting pipe major, a pipe band played a cacophonous rendition of 'Scotland the Brave.' In the march past: a corps of archers, a detachment of rubber suited frogmen, helmeted Air Force flight crews, khaki-clad infantrymen, jogging commandoes and paratroops in their camouflage battledress, formations of students, businessmen, schoolchildren, Boy Scouts, and a profusion of drum-bashing, rattle-shaking feather-plumed tribal dancers. Though Amin had promised to show off his new military equipment—including tanks none appeared—on Russian advice. The boisterous Nakivubo crowd had to make do with a tin model aircraft sputtering along, pulled by a car engine bolted into its nose.

Some of Amin's senior officers rose from their places to join the bare-breasted gyrating dancing girls.

Invited guests repaired to Nakasero Lodge for the garden party. Amin, chewing at chicken legs and pieces or roast beef served off silver trays, circulated among the guests. Beer, scarce elsewhere in Kampala, was plentiful. Amin—and his remaining wife, Madina—joined seated VIPs—the Somali vice president, the North Korean vice premier, a Pakistani senator and a Russian Lieutenant

General.

Big Daddy's anniversary address said it all.

'I am not able at this moment to hand back the reins of Government to politicians because corruption is still rampant among civilians and we ... cannot deliver the affairs of state into the hands of corrupt civilians. I have no intention of seeing Ugandans going through again what they have already suffered during the Obote regime. I am determined to wipe out all evils of corruption and all sorts of malpractices.'

Amin awarded 3,000 Republic medals to a cross-section of the people for their loyalty to Uganda, coined a new word (Ugandans had ended decades of *under-dogism*') and lied his way through the speech.

'The soldiers gave exactly eighteen reasons for the military take-over ... I find it important to report to you what we have done so far about those points ... The unwarranted detention without trial and for long periods of a large number of people, many of whom are totally innocent of any charges: Since the establishment of the Military Government there has not been any unwarranted detention without trial even for short periods, leave alone for long ones. We put an end to this type of practice and it will never be repeated as long as the Military Government has the mandate of rulership of this country ...

... The continuation of a state of emergency over the whole country for an indefinite period, which is meaningless to everybody: There is no more state of emergency in any part of the country. The Military did not believe there is any justification to have a state of emergency in this peaceful country of Uganda ...

... The lack of freedom in the airing of different views on political and social matters: We have encouraged the people to be free in airing their demands, grievances and wishes. We have always been very much ready to receive and digest criticism ...

... The frequent loss of life and property arising from daily cases of robbery with violence and kondoism: My Government has taken stern measures to wipe out

168

kondoism.

...Widespread corruption in high places: This is why I haven't returned rule to the civilians...

...Economic policies left many people unemployed, insecure and lacking needs of life, like food, clothing, medicine and shelter: My economic policies led to the declaration of economic war which we have at last won. I started cleaning the house until I succeeded in placing indigenous Ugandans in all important posts. Can you remember that even cooks in hotels were Whites? Insecurity prevailed before; new people are now free to move and talk without fear of being grabbed or manhandled by the General Service boys. Nobody now lives in fear of being arrested or detained when he is innocent...

...High taxes left the common man poorer than ever before: I have made sure the burden of the common man is lightened...'

Amin said he had got tough with racketeers. In a way, that was true. Shopkeepers rigging their prices, smugglers and cheats faced execution by firing squad. In another, it wasn't. Army men with businesses were above control.

Amin said he had eradicated tribalism and class consciousness in Uganda.

Amin said the Armed Forces no longer had anything to complain about. They did not lack accommodation, vehicles or equipment.

'In present day Uganda there is no tribe which is above the other. We all want only unity in Uganda. We do not want bloodshed. Everybody in Uganda knows that. I want to see unity everywhere...Obote failed to do in ten years what I succeeded in doing in only one day...I have united the people in accepting me and working with...My popularity is ever increasing not only in Uganda, East Africa, Africa but also in the whole world. I want peace. Fellow countrymen, what we have achieved during the four years we have been in power is indeed great.'

CHAPTER XI

'Because of Amin all prejudices against the blackman have risen again to the surface. He has done harm to his people and, from his tiny territory, to the cause of Africa as a whole in that governing like the village tyrant by fear he has reimposed on Ugandans old habits of submission and servility.'

Dennis Hills

It was an unprecedented move by the British monarch. Queen Elizabeth sent a personal message to Idi Amin carried by two British officers under whom the Ugandan served in the British Army—Lt Gen Sir Chandos Blair (commander of the 4th Kings African Rifles in Uganda from 1959 to 1961, a fluent Swahili speaker and the man who first recommended Amin for a commission) and Major Iain Grahame.

Amin was not at Entebbe to meet them. At the end of the welcoming red carpet was a military band, a guard of honour mounted by the Air and Seaborne Battalion and Chief of Staff Major-General Mustafa Adrisi. The Britons were perplexed.

Adrisi challenged Lt Gen Blair. 'Why have you come, and not the secretary for Foreign Affairs or

170

Defence?' Gen Blair replied it was considered easier to discuss sensitive matters 'among friends'. He could not talk of Queen Elizabeth's message until he had delivered it personally to President Amin.

'What hope of success have you come with since President Amin does not change his mind once he has made a decision?' Adrisi said.

'I don't know.'

The two British officers were taken to the National Museum, Makerere University and the Kampala Zoo. They saw lion, leopard, hippopotamus, Uganda cob and cheater. The Zoo had been improved, Gen Blair politely remarked. How glad he was to be back in Uganda.

Amin flew from Kampala to Arua by helicopter. Dennis Hills, he announced would be executed by firing squad at 11:00 a.m. the following Monday. 'The presence of British Foreign Secretary Mr Callaghan in Uganda is absolutely necessary before Monday if the life of Mr Hills is to be spared,' he said. 'I know that every Ugandan likes me. If you see me fierce I am only fierce to the British alone because I want these people to kneel down to my feet.'

Lt Gen Blair did kneel to Big Daddy. An especially low entranceway led into their meeting place, forcing all visitors to crouch down. A tempestuous argument developed, which ended with Lt Gen Blair storming out, shouting: 'I am not a politician.' Amin smashed his fist down on a balustrade and yelled: 'You can do that in your own country but not in Uganda.'

Amin called in waiting aides and told them Lt Gen Blair had arrived at the meeting drunk and had thrown Queen Elizabeth's message onto the floor. Blair still behaved as if he was a commanding officer, Amin bellowed.

'They (the British) still think they are the bosses in Uganda. They will think they can get Africans washing their bottoms and their feet.'

Queen Elizabeth's emissaries caught the next plane out. Amin, in military fatigues, stormed into Kampala's International Hotel to confront the bevy of British

171

journalists there. To speed up the reporters' departure from Uganda telex and telephone links with the outside world were cut.

Amin convened a meeting of the Defence Council, claiming that Lt Gen Blair had forewarned of British military intervention to free Hills. 'Get your regiments, move to the border, its a full alert. Tell Libya to send aircraft.' An invasion was to be launched from Kenya, but before it came the 700 British subjects living in Uganda would be taught a lesson Britain would never forget, Amin rattled. In a reply to Queen Elizabeth he added: 'I still want cordial relations with you. That is why the Defence Council has given another ten days for Mr Callaghan to come before the death sentence on Dennis Hills is carried out.

'Blair expected me to comply with all that he was saying. Had he not been a hot tempered person I assure you that his mission could have been successful. Mr Hills could have followed him back in a very short time...'

Hills would be executed by firing squad at 'Execution Valley'—the site where British troops shot 27 Muslim Sudanese soldiers after an Army mutiny in 1898.

The 61-year-old British author/lecturer Dennis Hills had been in jail for more than three months. The unpublished manuscript of his book *The White Pumpkin* put him there. Not only did the manuscript liken Amin to the village tyrant ruling by fear. It referred to 'the black Nero'. Hills commented 'How exhausting it is to be evil' and, said the government, confessed to spying in another passage: 'Amin is fond of calling us spies, and there is truth in it for we foreign residents whether we like it or not, are the eyes and ears of the outside world. Our presence in Uganda must have an inhibiting effect on the excess of the government. The African feels less isolated and less vulnerable while there are white faces around. For the information they gather reaches news media, and a Nairobi or a London newspaper will announce it.' All this and more, Internal

Affairs minister Charles Oboth Ofumbi maintained, was seditious and aimed at damaging Uganda's name.

Hills, who two years before had undergone major surgery for cancer of the bowel, was taken to Luzira Prison. In Uganda he had taught a decade at the National Teachers College and Makerere. Friends knew him as a self-reliant loner and adventurer. An accomplished linguist he first left Britain for Poland; at the outbreak of World War II he escaped the occupation and became a liaison officer with Polish forces in the middle east. Afterwards he taught languages in West Germany, where he married for the second time, and Turkey. Although he had written newspaper articles throughout his life in Turkey and Uganda he sat down to record more fully his experiences and observations as an inveterate traveller, climber and hiker. 'I have always liked sleeping out on the ground...There is the excitement of waking up in a strange landscape with the early morning sun on it.' Tramping through the African bush alone Hills paid scant regard to danger. He toured Uganda thoroughly, visiting trainee teachers in their remote schools.

First, Hills appeared at Mengo magistrate court, where he denied the spying and sedition charges. The hearing came to an abrupt end when the state prosecutor announced he was not proceeding with the case. The Briton was awarded 250 shillings costs. A little earlier, however, Amin had decreed the trial should be held before a military tribunal chaired by Major Juma Ali, second in command of the Malire Mechanised Regiment.

Amin had just gone out of his way to ensure a certificate of permanent residence was granted to Hills' German born wife Ruth Ingrid. Amin told Mrs Hills how much he admired Hitler—and that he was to rename a spot in southeastern Uganda after the Fuhrer because it was the site of a famous World War I battle. In fact, the clashes to which he referred, between the German forces of Gen Paul von Lettow Vorbeck and

Jan Smuts' allies took place hundreds of miles away in Tanzania.)

Hills was moved from Luzira to the headquarters of the Malire Mechanised Regiment. British officials were denied access to him and told no foreigners would be allowed to attend the tribunal. The charge was now treason.

The Bombo tribunal sat for three days. At 2:00 a.m. Police Special Branch had raided Hills' Elizabeth Avenue, Kololo home acting on a tip-off, prosecuting officer Captain Augustus Kania recounted. The Police wanted to know if Hills was writing a book. He replied he was working on an autobiography, and showed them his two previous books, *Man with a Lobelia Flute* and *My Travels in Turkey*. But the police found their clue— letters from a British publisher including an agreement to publish *The White Pumpkin*. Then the manuscript itself 'hidden with old examination papers in a cardboard box.' Among Capt Kania's exhibits was correspondence between author and publisher dealing with the inclusion of photographs of corpses and a swimming pool card purporting to bear a message by Hills to Ingrid asking her to hide *The White Pumpkin* manuscript.

Conviction was a foregone conclusion. 'Had the police not discovered the bad things Hills was intending to do in the country Uganda would have been in great danger as a result of his bad acts,' Major Juma summed up. Addressing the author he added: 'If you thought President Amin was doing something wrong you should have gone to the President to tell him. It was bad to write a malicious book.' Major Juma persisted: 'Hills had remained in Uganda after the expiry of a teaching contract two years before "to spy on the country and cause confusion on behalf of your country."

'According to the laws of Uganda anyone who commits an offence cannot be left free, and accordingly you cannot be left to go free. You will be shot by firing squad.'

In his own testimony Hills pointed out the first

174

chapters of *The White Pumpkin* dealt with times at school, in the British Army and as a teacher in Uganda (when he also climbed 15 Ugandan mountains). It was a continuation of *Man with a Lobelia Flute*, a copy of which he gave to Amin when the president visited Kyambogo Teachers college.

He wrote with a belief in the sanctity of truth. That an atmosphere of fear existed in Uganda at the time he finished the manuscript in 1973 (soon after the Tanzanian invasion) could not be refuted. Many of his friends had been robbed or injured and expatriate teachers at Kyambogo left the country after one of their number was badly beaten up. In any case, it was proposed initially to print only 1500 copies of *The White Pumpkin*.

Asked about the photographed corpses during the hearing Hills said bluntly they had lain in the open for several days. 'The police had not removed them. If there was no secrecy about their existence then there could be no objection to photographing them.'

Before being marched back to his cell Major Ali stammered Hills could appeal against the death sentence—either to the Defence Council or directly to the president. Hills had a cell to himself, measuring roughly 12 paces by 4. Armed soldiers guarded the door. Later, he was allowed into the courtyard—followed by extra guards—for an hour's exercise each day. He slept on the cell's concerete floor. He read the Bible: one of the guards suggested he read the sixth psalm...

Hills' arrest took up one of the periodic slacks in Britain's endless diplomatic tug-of-war with President Idi Amin Dada. Making matters more difficult for Whitehall was the arrest in Uganda of another British national, Stanley Smolen, a building contractor charged with hoarding several thousand tons of cooking oil. Hoarding—'economic sabotage'—was also a capital offence and Amin ordered Smolen to be tried by the same tribunal that had just despatched Dennis Hills to the death cell.

Big Daddy let it be known he was prepared to enter

into a deal with Britain. He listed a set of demands to be fulfilled by Britain if he was to reconsider either man's case. Britain would have sent him supplies of military spare parts, put a stop to hostile propaganda against him, repatriate Uganda emigres and pledge not to give sanctuary to exiles in future.

Britain found the terms both fanciful and impossible to implement. Prime Minister Harold Wilson sent a three page telex message to Amin, who told long-suffering James Hennessy he was not going to read any message from London unless it was signed by Queen Elizabeth, or Wilson, or both. Amin reminded Hennessy that Hills had nine days left to live.

For Britain the situation was not made any easier by the well publicised remarks of a former Royal Air Force pilot who thought the mother country had taken too much cheek from Amin. Harry Williams offered to take Hills' place in front of the firing squad—as long as his family collected the life insurance (it would have been deemed suicide) and the RAF mounted a reprisal raid against Uganda 'to show the flag.' The Foreign Office was trying not to irritate the mercurial Ugandan leader and swiftly disassociated itself from Harry Williams. 'What he is saying makes the position of the British Government and Dennis Cecil Hills even worse,' the FO flapped.

But another volunteer stepped out: English teacher Trevor Morrison worked at Makerere until he was deported from Uganda in 1973. 'Amin wants exiles back. I feel I fit that category. I am not suicidal and I still have a lot of friends there. I believe I understand President Amin, the country and the political scene well enough to be able to take the risk.'

The Foreign Office was not so tart about Morrison's slightly more reasoned approach. 'We have advised him of the intense diplomatic activity going on to secure clemency for Mr Hills and that we were hopeful it would succeed.'

Harold Wilson's signed letter duly arrived in Kampala—as did a flood of appeals from world leaders asking for clemency. Big Daddy was unimpressed. Why, he lamented, was the world in such a fuss over two Europeans who should have known better than to tangle with him? He had noticed no similar uproar when Ugandans were being shot down by invaders from Tanzania. 'Appeals on humanitarian grounds should not only apply to people of certain nationalities.' Piqued in particular by Harry Williams, Amin tightened the screw...

Now he wanted either the British Defence or Foreign minister to fly out to Kampala. Whoever came must be accompanied by a full-fledged military delegation to hammer out Uganda's spare parts requirements.

When Lt Gen Blair and Major Graham arrived Amin had turned the screw some more: he would only see Foreign Secretary James Callaghan. Callaghan should be well briefed so he did not behave stupidly. But he would be warmly welcomed and could take home the latest donations to the Save Britain Fund—money, cows, goats and many tons of food. On the eve of Hills scheduled execution Amin took the two British officers to see him in prison. On his own admission, Hills had not been ill-treated. Lt Gen Blair asked him to write a letter of apology to Amin. Before the day was over Hills had pen and paper and the ten day stay of execution.

Originally Callaghan stood his ground. He told the House of Commons he would not go to Kampala under duress—but intimated that he had left the door open. If Amin's two British hostages were treated humanely he might still be able to go to Uganda to discuss British relations as a whole. As Amin dressed down Lt Gen Blair, Callaghan was attending to the local affairs of his Cardiff constituency.

Amin's bluff was called—Smolen was acquitted and during a visit to Zaire, Amin announced he had commuted Hills death sentence.

Amin entrusted all future negotiations between Uganda and Britain to his intermediary, Zaire's President Mobuto Sese Seko. Callaghan flew from Rome to Kinshasa and thence to Kampala. The reception was chilly; the few hundred spectators at Entebbe airport watched the Foreign Secretary step down from the white Royal Air Force VC 10 in silence. A mild flurry of murmurs greeted Zaire Foreign Minister Bula Mandungu. Amin was not at the airport.

Big Daddy received Callaghan at the Command Post the next day. 'We had talked for half an hour without mentioning Mr Hills. Suddenly the president without further discussion gave an Army colonel an order. He saluted Amin,' the Foreign Secretary explained later. 'The President turned to me with a smile and said his colonel had gone to fetch Mr Hills.'

For a few days Hills noticed his prison guards had become decidedly lax, until they eventually stacked away their rifles and left the cell door unlocked. At last he was told he was to be driven to Kampala. Shabby and unkempt he was led to the Command Post. Amin, wearing the Glengarry cap of Scotland's Seaforth Highlanders, pointed to the British Foreign Secretary.

'Mr Callaghan, isn't it?' Hills said.

Amin's intriguing comment: 'This proves I'm not mad.' Amin picked up his son Mwanga (dressed in miniature camouflage fatigues) and posed for a group photograph.

Thousands of feet above night-dark Africa Dennis Hills drank champagne. 'I really believed I was going to die. I got over my initial fright and just accepted it. Facing death, when you get used to the prospect, is not so unusual. Having been in the war I know what death is all about.

'It was not until I saw all the cameras and Mr Callaghan that I realised something was happening and that I might be freed.

'I am very happy with the way things went,' Callaghan said. 'They could not have gone better.

'I was met with great courtesy and politeness. In fact when he (Amin) knew that I came from Wales he said our meeting was bound to be a success.'

Far from giving Callaghan the barracking he expected Amin said he guaranteed the security of British

178

Nationals in Uganda, promised James Hennessy would no longer be the butt of abuse in Ugandan broadcasts and agreed to meet British officials to discuss the long disputed issue of compensation for the impounded assetts of Ugandan Asians and British investors...

'Now I am free,' Hills said, 'I am just so sorry for all the trouble and expense I have caused. I have apologised to President Amin. I have genuinely loved Uganda. I am saddened I cannot go back. I'll never forget its beauty and the kindness of its people...'

As his release receded into the distance the erudite academic was less repentant. 'Amin spoiled a country that was learning to be free.' His had been a small protest against Amin's dictatorship...'just a mosquito bite' ...An African raising the same criticism would probably have disappeared.

Typically, Amin wanted the last word. If *The White Pumpkin* was published Britons would suffer. When it was, Hills came under safer fire. Amin called him a sex maniac and drunkard who mixed with prostitutes in Uganda. 'It is not surprising his marriage broke up,' Amin blasted. *The White Pumpkin*, he asserted, showed Hills kept the company of prostitutes and pimps in bars. 'Hills' comments should serve as a warning to the harlots of Kampala. They are a shame to Africa. We wonder what sort of influence this man had on our students.'

A copy of *The White Pumpkin* had been sent to him by 'Irish, Scottish and Welsh friends.'

CHAPTER XII

'Let's leave President Idi Amin severely alone to physically eliminate his opponents, to worry little about or be indifferent to the mysterious death or disappearance of Uganda citizens, to nationalise foreign investments without paying compensation, to use human beings as political bargaining counters, to discredit, humiliate and disgrace his Cabinet ministers, to insult or provoke foreign neighbours etc. If Ugandans choose to put up with his eccentricities, that is their own lookout. This continent will have none of him.'

Times International, Nigeria.

WITH the Hills saga fresh in their minds African Heads of State prepared for the annual Organisation of African Unity summit meeting with trepidation. It was Kampala's turn to host the summit—and throughout its eleven year history the OAU's practice had been to choose the host president as its chairman for the forthcoming year.

Amin's treatment of Dennis Hills had already embarrassed his colleagues. Several African countries indicated they would consider boycotting the summit if

Hills was executed. The outgoing OAU chairman, President Mohammed Siad Barre of Somalia, had cabled Amin urging him to spare Hills and not 'stain the OAU conference with blood'.

Many African leaders were dismayed by the prospect of having President Idi Amin Dada as their chairman. At the last count, five had discreetly said they would support a coup toppling Amin from power in Uganda and another three that they had no objection to such an idea.

President Barre was particularly uncomfortable about the Kampala conference, suspecting as he did that important business sessions would be in constant danger of boycotts and walk-outs. The questions were clear: Could delegates ignore Amin's domestic policies, his gun law, his trials by torture? Would the Kampala meeting jeopardise the principle of African unity? Would Africa's image be tarnished? Would Amin's chairmanship lend him Africa's approval in the eyes of the world at large? Independent Africa had fought the colonial powers for the freedom and dignity Amin had destroyed in Uganda. Could Africa's world status withstand Amin's perpetual ravings?

President Barre sought not to put the continent to test and quietly needled Amin to step down. The summit could go ahead in Kampala—but Samora Machel, president of newly independent Mozambique should take the chair. This solution, the Somali argued, would appropriately exalt Mozambique and the liberation movements of Southern Africa.

But Big Daddy was having none of it, and actively canvassed OAU members countries (especially in the Arab bloc) to elect him saying they should not be hoodwinked by smear campaigns...least of all a campaign by non-OAU member Britain. Amin claimed that Prime Minister Harold Wilson urged African Commonwealth heads not to attend the Kampala summit during a Commonwealth 'club' meeting in Kingston, Jamaica. Said Amin: 'I understand this was aimed at humiliating me personally. Britain's machinations were an imperialist manoevre designed to split the African ranks and involve itself in the affairs of the OAU through the back door.'

It was too late to change the venue of the OAU summit even if Wilson's friends—'the Quislings of the African continent'—had the power to do so, Amin said.

'I am very popular among OAU members and most of their heads of state are my personal friends.'

Botswana's President, Sir Seretse Khama, did not count himself among Amin's friends. Botswana was the first to say it would not go to Kampala under any circumstances. Sir Seretse condemned Amin's 'disregard for the sanctity of human life' and recalled that Amin had recently exhorted the armed forces of Botswana, Zambia and Tanzania to overthrow their respective goverments. Zambia and Tanzania followed suit, the latter delivering a swinging attack on the OAU in general. 'Tanzania cannot accept the responsibility of participating in the mockery of condemning colonialism, apartheid and fascism in the headquarters of a murderer, an oppressor, a black fascist and a self-confessed admirer of fascism.'

Mozambique decided not to attend Amin's summit either, and without Machel a still-worried Siad Barre realised Amin's chairmanship was more or less inevitable. No significant opposition to it had emerged ... many of the African politicians had skeletons in their own cupboards ... and Barre gently suggested another face-saving answer might be to make the chairmanship an honorary post.

Kampala geared itself up for the summit. The poinesettias, bougainvillea and hibiscus were out. Big Daddy, or rather the Saudi Arabians from whom he had secured an enormous special loan, spared no expense. Some 200 Mercedes Benz cars were imported for the brass, and scores of Peugeot 504s (the make favoured by the State Research Bureau car-boot kidnappers) and Datsuns arrived for lesser officials. The cars would be distributed evenly 'on a cooperative basis' throughout the country's ten provinces by the armed forces after the conference, Amin asserted.

For the first time in a very long time flour, eggs, salt, soap, chickens, butter, milk, sugar and liquor appeared—but only in the hotels and villas reserved for visitors. The government's guest accommodation had been refurnished and redecorated; hundreds of thousands of rolls of toilet paper, another scarcity, had been imported. Commissioning the colour television system he had ordered Wakhweya to buy Amin squealed: 'All this has been done by Ugandans. And you see, I have won the economic war.'

Kampalans would be required to wear special dresses and shirts during the summit emblazoned with President Amin's picture, the OAU symbol and a map of Africa. Information minister Juma Oris sternly warned Ugandan tailors making the garments to observe professional ethics. Out of either 'inexperience or sheer malice' some of the garments showed the map of Africa and President Amin's portrait upside-down or mutilated, cut into unrecognisable pieces . . . The tailors ought to show more respect for the dignity of Africa and the President, said the minister.

Amin himself prefaced the summit by telling OAU secretary general William Eteki Mboumoua he would appreciate it if proceedings stuck closely to an agenda and—so the conference could be wound up as quickly as possible—delegates kept their speeches brief and to-the-point. Delegates who had more to get off their chests were free to hold press conferences. If Eteki had further qualms about Amin's intentions they were confirmed when arrangements were made for an OAU motor rally covering some of the roughest roads in Uganda, Zaire, Rwanda, Sudan, Tanzania and Kenya in which the Ugandan president wished to take part. There were also plans for a 'Miss OAU' beauty contest.

An announcement said that in keeping with Amin's position as OAU host, and in recognition of his service to Uganda, the General had been promoted to Field Marshal. The vote by the Defence Council and 2000 men of the Armed Forces had been unanimous.

Another announcement said 37 of the OAU's 42 member states had assured Kampala of their presence at the summit meeting. Ultimately, only 19 heads of state turned up; 20 others sent deputies. Amin was not disappointed; purely speaking, his sums were nearly right.

'The long awaited OAU meeting is now with us. We must thank God. We must seriously consider ways and means of enhancing our cooperation and unity. I've got nothing against Nyerere. He has been confused by exiles. If he came he could see the true image of Uganda and be warmly welcomed.'

At Entebbe Honour Guards stood their ground, the gunners expended all the blank shells they could muster. The drums drummed, the dancers danced. CORE's Roy Innis arrived and asked for permanent observer status at the OAU. UN Secretary General Dr Kurt Waldheim commended the OAU's contribution to international peace and security. A message arrived from Chinese premier Chou En Lai saying the Kampala summit would advance the unity of the Third World 'against hegemonism.'

A business-like 41-item agenda was drawn up for the conference.

When the summit opened Arab African heads of state outnumbered the Black Africans. Of the total number of heads of state in Kampala 14 were army officers. Big Daddy got his prize—the chair.

'As brothers we must rally behind each other in overcoming Africa's common enemy—the colonialist, neo-colonialist and the Zionist,' Amin declared. 'We are totally committed to the liberation of our continent. If the whites in Rhodesia and South Africa cannot accept immediate majority rule, then we must get the solution militarily. We are capable of fighting those countries.'

Applause swelled through the hall.

'Political independence alone will remain meaningless unless we buttress it with economic independence ... I am not against the whites, but they must accept the Blacks as the majority and grant our brethren majority rule...The total liberation of Africa must be put into practice, we must act militarily...and I Field Marshal Idi Amin will, for one, lead a volunteers force into the impending liberation onslaught...I was born on the site of this conference centre. My father was a police staff sergeant and this was the police barracks.'

Nigerian head of state General Yakubu Gowon spoke. 'Time is on the side of Africans. The struggle will continue and Africa will not flinch.' Addressing himself to the four OAU newcomers, the Cape Verde Islands, Sao Tome and Principe, the Comoro Islands and Mozambique, the Nigerian offered: 'My little advice to you is to give your people good government and to uplift Africa and mankind.'

Listening attentively were PLO leader Yasser Arafat, seated near Algerian president Houari Boumedienne; Jonas Savimbi, bearded and dressed in fading bush denims, the leader of UNITA, one of the three black nationalist groups fighting a civil war in Angola.

Moods changed on the second day during the starting plenary session. News came from Nigeria that the army had moved. A coup d'etat had ousted Gen Gowon. He left the conference hall briefly, then returned to his place for a further half-hour. Gowon sat unruffled, cameramen bustled to capture his every movement, whispers hissed between delegations. Speakers gamely carried on...lost to their audience.

Amin reprimanded the photographers and finally suspended the session.

And so, before Amin's summit went behind closed doors to debate the agenda's thornier issues, an exodus began. Not that Egypt's Anwar Sadat, Congo's Marien Ngouabi, Gabon's Omar Bongo, Niger's Seyni Kountche and Cameroon's Ahmadou Ahidjo necessarily felt unsafe in Kampala—but they headed for home anyway. Of course, it was only a coincidental reminder that their new chairman had used an international conference to get where he was.

Gen Gowon closeted himself in his hotel room with aides, emerging finally in good humour and with calmness to say he had accepted his ouster and would support the new Nigerian government.

'My dear Field Marshal, as I leave Kampala at the end of a visit that has been marked with quite unexpected and unusual developments I am writing to thank you most sincerely for your genuine demonstration of kindness to me, for your hospitality and for all the courtesies and consideration that have been extended to me since I arrived in Kampala. I feel very deeply touched by your kindness and I am confident that these acts of generosity and friendship are a mark of your genuine friendship not only for me as a person but for Nigeria, in whose name I arrived here in the first instance.'

Not only did Gen Gowon's bowing out make the Kampala meeting an eventful one. Amin provided other *divertissements*. At a reception the band struck up the old British marching song, Colonel Bogey. Amin, in a home-made sedan chair, was carried into view by four British businessmen—followed by a Swedish engineer waving a small, spotted parasol. Amin called the jovial demonstration the 'white man's burden.'

'It was the Field Marshal's idea,' justified Anthony Coe, one of the chair-bearers. 'He asked us if we wanted to take part in a joke. We had lunch with the President earlier in the day. We decided to do it because if we British can't laugh at ourselves then that's the finish, isn't it? It was a heavy responsibility. The president is 18 stone (250 pounds). And it was all we could do to prevent ourselves from singing the bawdy British words to Colonel Bogey.' (Lyrics referring to the testicles of Hitler and other Nazis.)

For the occasion he wore his blue field uniform and that Seaforth glengarry. Gleed the Ugandan information ministry: 'The British explorers and colonialists at the beginning of this century travelled on the continent in comfort. They would ride in chariots—rickshaws pushed by Africans who toiled and earned little presents in return. For their toil and sweat they did not reap anything much. Isn't the President setting up a chapter that balances history?'

Not all delegates found the strange breach in conference decorum as amusing as their host seemed to. Laughing and waving Amin climbed down from the chair, swept up his piano accordion and puffed out a batch of simple tunes.

More was in store. At parades in the capital thousands of children bandied placards proclaiming 'We are happy under the care of Marshal Amin'; soldiers drilled to snatches from Franz Lehar operettas. Big Daddy flagged off the motor rally, jumped into his Citroen Maserati and chased the leading cars. He had as co-driver a beautiful girl soldier from the Army's impressively named 'Suicide Regiment', 19-year-old Sarah Kyolaba. Before the week was out Amin had married Sarah in a impromptu ceremony attended by a handful of dignitaries, including Siad Barre, Yasser Arafat and Mauritania's president Moktar Daddah. The simple Muslim marriage ceremony took everyone by surprise...Amin's cabinet knew nothing of it. Swathed in her white bride's garb Amin produced Sarah at a reception for a small group of journalists, bundled her back into the Maserati and sped off—overtaking, with a roar, his own escort and the motorcade of state guests—to watch a military exercise. Summit gossip had it that Amin had ordered the killing of Sarah's boyfriend—and that the former singer/dancer with the Suicide Regiment jazz band had absolutely no say in choosing her new partner.

Two days later summiteers were treated to a piece of stage-managed umbrage. Amin's latest wedding would be held again, under the glare of the colour TV lights, because the Armed Forces and the Defence Council had not seen the first ceremony. 'It is fitting that the marriage is held with full military honours for all the members of the Armed Forces to see and enjoy since both the bride and bridegroom are soldiers. The President's new bride is being referred to by people, and especially delegates attending the summit conference, as Mrs Africa.'

The exercise to which the newlyweds drove was none

other than an attack on the South African port city and
seaside resort, Cape Town. Actually, Amin substituted a
tiny, barren Lake Victoria island just offshore for his
target. A South African flag had been hoisted on the
island. The Uganda Air Force Migs swooped again and
again—missing their target again and again. Onlookers
looked askance. A few of the bombs showered up the
sand. Commandoes crawled up to the intact flagpole,
pulled down the intact South African flag and hauled up
the OAU flag in its place.

The display was anything but impressive. Big Daddy
gave an awkward lecture on military tactics, before
going off for a cooling swim. 'Military might will
eventually dislodge the racists from southern Africa,' he
concluded despite his flop. 'Imperialists will face fire.'

In session, however, the conference rejected immediate, all-out war in southern Africa, voting in favour of
pursuing contacts with South Africa agreed at an earlier
ministerial meeting in the Tanzanian capital, Dar es
Salaam. Total war would be waged if peace efforts
collapsed irrevocably; the conference did support
economic boycotts of South Africa.

Amin persisted: 'A truly volunteer African army is
already being raised to fight...unless Pretoria and
Rhodesia give immeidate majority rule to their black
populations. A division of thousands of South African
exiles have been trained and are ready to fight at a
moment's notice. Some of these people are already there
(in South Africa) and are awaiting the green light from
me.'

Far to the south, Pretoria, at least, was listening.
Cautioned South Africa foreign minister Hilgaard
Muller: 'Although Amin is the laughing stock of many
parts of the world we cannot afford to ignore his threats
or take them lightly. We must assume he is voicing the
sentiments of the militants in Africa.' Pretoria was also
peeved by Dr Waldheim's address in Kampala attacking
South Africa's inhuman policy of apartheid. 'There was
not a word about the inhuman policies of General Amin
in the very country in which he was speaking.'

Big Daddy focussed on smaller fry—the miniscule French territory of Djibouti, sweltering on Africa's Red Sea coast. He proposed a joint African-Arab invasion to dislodge French foreign legionnaires defending the desert colony. Neighbouring Somalia could provide a base for the invaders.

On the Middle East the summit also moderated—to the bitter disappointment of Amin's main Arab patron, Libyan leader Col Gaddafi. The radicals wanted the OAU to lobby for Israel's expulsion from the United Nations.

Arafat helped argue the case. In both Southern African and the Middle East (not apparently, in Uganda) indigenous peoples were being slaughtered by oppressive regimes. Israel and South Africa, strategically and integrally tied together, were becoming increasingly isolated. 'They call our just struggle and resistance against their crimes in Africa and Palestine terrorism, but they themselves are the real terrorists, the enemies of the people,' he said. Palestine was Africa's gate to Asia. 'We are not fighting for the sake of war or revenge. Our cause is that of an occupied homeland and a people that has been uprooted. We are fighting to liberate the Palestinian Arab citizen from humiliation, suffering and alienation...from racism, oppression, fascism and hatred.'

President Idi Amin Dada was a foremost champion of the cause.

Col Gaddafi twice postponed his departure from Kampala to hear the Middle East debate through. For all his pro-Arab platitudes chairman Amin, having difficulty keeping up with quick-fire arguments, was unable to soothe the confrontation between Libya and Egypt. Nor could he steer the summit's resolution his benefactor's way.

The compromise resolution simply asked OAU members to take adequate measures to reinforce pressure on Israel at the UN ... 'including the possibility of eventually depriving it of its membership.' To Gaddafi's chagrin, and Amin's shrugging embarrass-

189

ment, even the watered-down wording had trouble. Zaire said it was totally opposed to the original resolutions and the amended one, and Ghana, Sierra Leone, Senegal and Liberai said they had no mandate from their absent heads of state to accept it. Gaddafi flew into a temper and stormed out of the closing session threatening to revise Libyan aid to African countries. Chairman Amin smarted as Gaddafi accused the OAU as a whole of coming under the domination of the United States, and said he would probably boycott its future meetings. Egypt complained of what it termed Gaddafi's gravely offensive behaviour in Kampala and noted the Arab world had witnessed 'regrettable theatrical acts by this whimsical, sick man.'

Big Daddy cleared his throat. There were those who saw another candidate allusion. Formally closing the meeting Amin said the 12th OAU summit had been a great success. 'We have had very good, friendly and frank discussions which have strengthened the oneness and unity of the Organisation of African Unity. I believe in frankness and I like tough people like you to participate in a crucial meeting like the one we have just had. If you see something wrong you should not say: "Yes Sir!" We are not slaves.'

The delegates had finally agreed to send a conciliation commission under Big Daddy's auspices to troubled Angola . . . and hold their next gathering at an altogether less explosive venue—the Indian ocean island of Mauritius.

For four nights the bombs shattered the Kampala quiet. An explosion keeled over an electricity pylon eight miles from the city centre: the idea had been to plunge the late-sitting conference into darkness, but the wrong pylon was blown up.

No-one was hurt in the other blasts, and damage was slight. The Army defused an inexpertly-made device at Kampala Municipal city hall, a professionally-made one at Nakivubo taxi and bus terminal. Soldiers unobtrusively ringed the conference complex and security officers, wearing OAU lapel badges, mingled with the bona-fide representatives inside. Radio Uganda announced the explosions were part of a military exercise by the Jajja Battalion—although African visitors' own security men reported no such exercise under way.

The Tanzania-based Uganda guerrilla group, FRONASA, had threatened to sabotage the OAU summit but an unknown group calling itself the Uganda Liberation Movement claimed responsibility for the explosion in a telephone call to a Kenya newspaper. It wasn't until a week after summit guests had safely left Kampala that Amin conceded an underground resistance group was at work within Uganda. He said the attempt to disrupt the summit had been foiled by the vigilance of loyal soldiers and a number of the saboteurs had been caught. They would be tried according to the law. (No such trial was recorded as having ever taken place.)

'If anyone is thinking of staging a coup it will never succeed,' Amin declared, saying at the same time that the countries which boycotted the summit had inveigled exiles into smuggling the explosives in from Tanzania.

The explosions brought attention to the constant, albeit ineffective, opposition to the rule of Idi Amin. The previous year had seen half a dozen carefully hushed-up attempts to overthrow him. Early in 1975 Amin was wounded in a machine-gun ambush just outside the capital. Amin's cortege had set out after dark for Gulu, the Air Force base north of Kampala. Along a deserted stretch of road the President's official Mercedes came under fire from thick bush on both sides. The car, and another police car preceding it, slewed off the road, overturned and exploded—killing all the seven occupants. Amin had switched to another car lagging slightly behind and hit only by stray shots which smashed one side window. Amin received a flesh wound on his left arm, caused by a richochet or flying glass. Shortly after the incident Amin's wife Medina was treated at Mulago for injuries consistent with a severe beating-up— including a broken jaw. Amin may have suspected

Medina, a former dancer, of warning his would-be assassins—but the connection was easily disputable. It was well known among his retinue that Amin flailed fists at his women as the mood took him.

Palestinian commandoes and Libyan marines were among Amin bodyguards killed or injured in the ambush staged by disaffected Army officers.

Over the preceding months Big Daddy had shown an uncanny instinct for survival; changing cars, changing plans at the last minute, sending out decoy motorcades and decoy presidents—anyone unfortunate enough to be of roughly the same enormous build. A western diplomat arriving late at Entebbe for a ceremony welcoming Amin back from a tour of Arab capitals found himself on the blind side of the reception committee. But he saw Amin climb into the presidential limousine, slide across the back seat and get out the other door. The motorcade squealed away and Amin raced off in the opposite direction driving a covered military jeep.

'God is on my side. Even the most powerful witchdoctor cannot hurt me. I am 50 years ahead of my time. I am not thinking of today or the day after tomorrow. I am thinking 50 or 100 years ahead. That's the problem. Some people are 10 years behind the times. They cannot keep up with my speed. When I was in the British Army I could not read my name or write my name. I completed the Cambridge School certificate in the armed forces. That's why you see I am better than anybody who has got a doctorate of political philosophy because nobody can easily put what I am putting in to action in Africa today. Nobody can challenge me.'

To convince traditionally patriarchal Ugandans of his invincibility Amin proclaimed that he had taken on women bodyguards—but just in case anyone still had mischievous ideas the four policewomen and a prison wardress had beaten the combined Ghana-Uganda army teams in a marksmanship contest.

Another coup attempt occurred soon after the

An early picture of Amin from his private album, recovered after the fall of Kampala, April 1979.

a) *The first picture of Amin as President. January 25th, 1971.*

b) *Amin plays with one of his 35 children.*

The many faces of Idi Amin.

Amin and his friends: (from top to bottom) PLO's Arafat; Soviet Military advisers; Gaddafi of Libya; Castro of Cuba.

a) *Amin with Kenyan President Jomo Kenyatta*

b) *Amin at Kenyatta's funeral, August 1978. Prince Charles is seated second from left.*

a) *Amin's Command Post.*

b) *Two of Amin's 35 children—sons Moses and Mwanga.*

Bob Astles—Amin's British-born adviser.

'The White Man's Burden': Astles (arrowed top) arranged the spectacle;
Scanlon (arrowed bottom) was later to die at the hands of Astles' torturers.

Top left: Amin's Vice-President, Mustafa Adrisi.
Top right: Amin's feared strongman, Colonel Isaac Maliyamungu.
Bottom: Archbishop Janani Luwum and Lt. Col. Oryema, assassinated.
16th February 1977.

Execution by firing squad in Uganda.

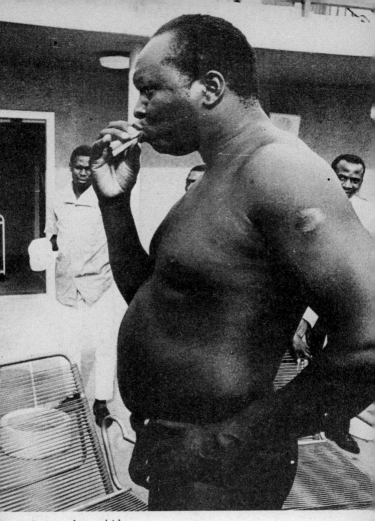

Amin at the poolside.

Amin the showman.

a) *In the basement of the State Research Centre, the door of the main death cell where thousands of Ugandans and others met their death at the hands of Idi Amin's henchmen.*

b) *These men were killed when Amin's SRB men fled, after throwing a hand grenade in the cell.*

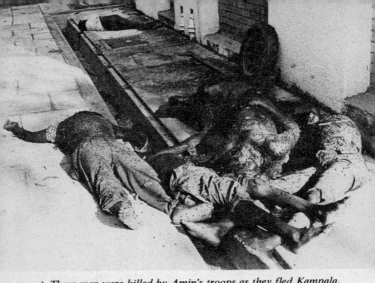

a) *These men were killed by Amin's troops as they fled Kampala.*

b) *A Tanzanian soldier waves his gun with joy after shooting three Libyans near Kampala.*

a) *The new President of Uganda, Yusufu Lule, arrives at Entebbe. He is met by new commanders of the Ugandan Army and Tanzanian military officials.*

b) *The swearing in of the new Head of State: (l to r) Tanzania Defence Minister, Rashidi Kawawa; Commander of the Ugandan Army, Col Tito Okelo; President Lule; Uganda Chief of Staff, Lt Col David Oyite-Ojok.*

a) *Tanzanian tanks and infantry march on Jinja, Amin's last stronghold. April 22nd, 1979.*

b) *The capture of Jinja airport. April 22nd, 1979.*

summit, when chairman Amin was visiting the OAU headquarters in Addis Ababa. This revolt was led by Lt Col Gori from Masaka, in the south west, and a young major in the Malire Regiment at Bombo, a cousin of murdered foreign minister Lt Col Michael Ondonga. The major had prepared to mobilise the regiment's tank units, but before he could do so a frightened lieutenant betrayed the plotters by telephoning army chief of staff Gen Mustafa. Military police units sent to Masaka to arrest Lt Col Gori were met by hails of gunfire—but Gori's followers were overpowered and the colonel fled.

Grievances spread among soldiers. Recent pay increases—sometimes more than doubling the pay—had been given to only favoured troops. Others had not been paid at all. Once favoured officers now found their families being evicted from homes given to them after Amin's expulsion of the Asians—to make way for Amin's influx of Pakistani teachers, technicians, doctors and artisans. The homes and belongings of exiles, and of the families of men who had disappeared, were also commandeered.

Evictees included the widows of Ben Kiwanuka and Alex Ojera.

Amin's adjourned inquiry into the disappearances at last completed its work. Not unexpectedly, the government said Mr Justice Saied's report had not made 'the remotest suggestion that President Amin had directed the disappearance of any person or the annihilation of any ethnic group.'

A clandestinely-reproduced circular letter had appeared in Kampala. 'We're tired of Amin. We workers, peasants and soldiers of Uganda want an end to killings, beatings and kidnappings. We are tired of Amin's lies, his murders and his government of scarcity. We want a country where our children can grow up as human beings. We are tired of fearing you Amin. We want sugar, hoes and soap. We want good transport and not tanks and jets. People of Uganda rise up and stop this oppression.'

Big Daddy was getting the feed-back—but he didn't

show it. Instead, he offered to lead Egyptian troops against Israel—and to emphasise how seriously he took Middle East problems he would swim the Suez Canal. In Addis Ababa he emerged from his suite wearing black and gold striped trunks and belly-flopped into the hotel pool. His main concern as he dived again, wallowed, backstroked and snorted was for his physical prowess. 'You know, I have 25 children,' he told startled onlookers. 'I am very good at it.'

Amin went home to reaffirm that his ban on Ugandans wearing wigs still stood—"They can be used to conceal dangerous weapons.'—and to take the kneeling oath of allegiance from 14 longtime British Uganda residents who joined the Uganda army as volunteer reserves. He readied himself for longer trips abroad, ending up at the United Nations General Assembly in New York, where he wanted to see President Ford for a private chat. 'If America respects the views and decisions of the African continent Ford will receive me. If he ignores my presence I will make my speech and go home. Then I will call for the transfer of the UN to another country,' presaged Big Daddy.

Amin dropped in on his Muslim Arab allies on his way to the Vatican. At a lavish party thrown by the Ugandans at Rome's Grand Rumor. 'Why, I can go away and leave Uganda for ten months a year and nothing will happen. I'm not afraid. The forces all support me.' Amin was 18 minutes late for a private audience with Pope Paul VI—the first head of state in the recollection of Vatican officials to have kept the Pontiff waiting. The audience lasted a further hour, with Amin explaining what he liked best about Italian missionaries was their frankness. He had already assured Pope Paul by letter that "foreign religious personnel' would always be welcome in Uganda—without mentioning the expuslion of 12 Italian priests a few weeks earlier because of the 'imbalance' between Uganda's Catholic majority and its 10 per cent of Muslims.

Pope Paul saw Amin off with a brief, non-committal

speech which recalled his own visit to Obote's Uganda. 'Special bonds of affection join us to the Ugandan people . . . We intend to give another attestation of our respect, esteem and love for Uganda.'

In New York Big Daddy put on a show the likes of which had never been seen before. For starters, an advance party of 47 tribal dancers and four kilted bagpipers were flown to Kennedy airport to welcome the Field Marshal, his family and personal entourage of 20. But Amin ducked out of a big arrival reception—as it was the Islamic month of fasting. At the UN building, however, he showed no constraints.

For his bizarre debut at the General Assembly, Amin arrived 40 minutes late resplendent in his medal-bedecked blue, red and gold uniform, thwacking his thigh with a field marshal's baton. He called a greeting to the assemblage in crude Swahili and handed a copy of his English speech to Uganda's chief representative, Ambassador Khalid Kinene, for reading out. UN officials couldn't remember that happening before either.

The speech lasted nearly 100 minutes, and Amin added an extempore epilogue for another 10 in a mixture of faltering English, Swahili and his own Kakwa dialect. And by the end the British, French and Israelis had walked out.

Amin accused the French of delaying the independence of the Comoro islands and warned they had better rethink their African policies 'before our patience is exhausted.'

Britain came under the Amin hammer for suppression of Catholic minority rights in Northern Ireland. The Israelis stuck it out as long as they could. They heard Amin echoing Gaddafi's stand at the Kampala summit—*almost*. 'I call for the expulsion of Israel from the UN Organisation. *I like the Jews*. But I don't approve of Zionism.' The US was merely a colony of Israel. Israelis had infiltrated CIA murder squads, Israel had received missiles from the US capable of carrying nuclear warheads.

'We condemn any perpetuation of illegalities and sustenance of the bogus state of Israel . . . We call for the extinction of Israel as a state . . ."

The Israelis could take no more.

Amin leapt onto more of his favourite hobby horses, including southern Africa, the subjugation of Black Americans and Uganda's tourist attractions . . ." the unforgettable *waragi* . . . Rare, huge and extremely shy gorillas.'

Amin's appearance at the UN had resounding repercussions chiefly because of the reaction of US ambassador to the UN Daniel 'Pat' Moynihan. In a speech prepared on the plane from New York to San Francisco and delivered to a union convention there, Moynihan called Amin a racist murderer.

'It is no accident, I fear, that this racist murderer is head of the Organisation of African Unity . . . Israel is a democracy and it is simply a fact that despotisms will seek whatever opportunities come to hand to destroy that which destroys them most, which is democracy. I hope and trust that members of the Organisation of African Unity will disavow Amin and all he stands for.'

If there were moderate voices on both sides perhaps the most frightening aspect of Amin and his regime was the extremes of passion which he aroused. Even at this time Amin was to the average African in the street, perhaps the most popular figure of the century.

He articulated, in a language that most of them could understand—simple, direct, without sophistication—their most treasured dreams. Dreams which had come about through the years of colonial suppression and the catalytic effect of freedom.

Similarly, he outraged many moderate thinkers on the other side who saw him for what he was; who saw him, indeed, as Moynihan saw him.

It was Moynihan's aspersions against OAU that rankled Africans the most. OAU secretary general Eteki lashed at Moynihan's wild and frenzied attack on Amin. 'We cannot but wonder about the sincerity of the American government in their so-called quest and desire for improved relations with African countries. The attack, supported by President Ford, had slurred the whole OAU by association.'

The White House nervously parried that while Ford did feel several of Amin's references uncalled for and Moynihan had said what needed to be said—his high regard and respect for the OAU had not changed.

But the damage had been done. African and Arab UN members—56 in all—were deeply wounded. And salt was rubbed in when Clarence Mitchell, a black US General Assembly delegate, observed that Moynihan's remarks occasioned pride not apologies from the US.

Big Daddy left New York (without having seen President Ford) as the clamour was in full swing. Amin's mouthpiece, radio Uganda, broadcast he was as surprised as anyone by the American response to his address. 'Everyone he met in the US, including Jews, commended President Amin because nobody had ever before told them the truth about Zionist policy. Jews regretted they had been sending their money to Israel, which was corrupt. Even Americans told the President he was the first head of state since the UN was founded to be frank. Others moderated their speeches for fear of some Super Powers.' Delegates who walked out of the Assembly had had other comitments.

Just before leaving the US Amin stealed himself to hold a reception.

Winding up his tempestuous 2-day visit at the New York Hilton, Amin described how, 11 years before, undergoing parachute training in Israel (he still wore Israeli Air Force wings on his chest), he had seen young Israeli fighter pilots chained into US-built Phantom warplanes and sent to raid Arab lands. 'I saw it myself,' he beamed. 'They were locked in. Palestinians are being murdered everyday, bombed by the Phantoms.'

He rambled on: 'I love Ford very much. He is looking after me, he kindly gave me secret service protection. The British are my friends. I love them very much too, but I don't want to see them kill the Irish Catholics because as a former colonial of Britain I feel embarrassed.'

Remissly, Amin also professed love for the country which weeks before he had threatened to declare war on. 'The people of Tanzania are our brothers and sisters. We love them and we love living with them.'

Why, then, were so many people afraid of such a profusely loving person?

'It is my brilliance that frightens them,' Amin finished.

A number of diplomats were noticed to have undiplomatically slipped away after passing the introduction line at Big Daddy's party. The Americans and British did not turn up at all. Overflying the United Kingdom on his homeward journey Amin radioed a ground station and asked a sleepy operator to pass his felicitations on to Queen Elizabeth.

What Moynihan had achieved in a single tragic blow was to unite Africa behind a tyrant.

The pendulum swung slightly the other way.

So far the OAU had failed to make any headway in bringing an end to the Angola fighting. November 11, the date set for independence from Portugal was drawing nearer. Pleas to the three warring African Liberation Movements for a ceasefire had been drowned out; the OAU's preference, a new government of national unity incorporating all the rivals, had come to nothing. Chairman Amin's handling of the OAU's approach to the matter brought him fresh criticism— and renewed efforts to unseat him, but clung to the idea of sending an African peace keeping force to Angola which he himself could lead.

After November 11 eight African countries recognised the Marxist Popular Movement (MPLA) as the legitimate government of Angola. Two of them, Congo and Guinea, canvassed for Amin's resignation because he had not recognised the Popular Movement—and this was tantamount to formenting civil war waged by the National Front (FNLA) and Unita with western aid, and mercenaries, channelled through South Africa and Zaire.

As yet, Amin had also stubbornly resisted requests by other OAU governments to convene a crisis summit on Angola. But he kept a grip on the OAU chair.

Angola rubbed Amin against the abrasive Russians. As he put it, Kampala ambassador Alexei Zakharov came to him drunk on vodka and tried to dictate what Uganda should do about Angola. Russia supplied the Popular Movement with arms. Moscow's surrogates, the Cubans, sent thousands of troops. Zakharov demanded Amin recognise the MPLA.

'I am not a puppet,' Amin carped. 'I don't dance for criminals who try to act like the vice president of Uganda. He would break off diplomatic relations with the Soviet Union unless he received an explanation from the Soviet Communist Party about both its involvement in Angola and 'the behaviour of the Soviet ambassador in Uganda' within 48 hours. He would immediately kick out the several hundred Soviet technicians and military advisors unless Moscow sent a high-ranking emissary for talks, he would not deign to see any junior official.

Zakharov, a tubby, white-haired 65-year-old former Soviet foreign minister, had also complained to Amin that Kampala radio delighted in blasting out the anti-Soviet sentiments of Pro-FNLA Zaire.

'It is a pity the Soviet Union comes all the way to Angola from Moscow to impose imperialism. The Soviet attitude is equivalent to the OAU chairman going to Moscow to advise what policy to follow in Czechoslovakia.'

Moscow responded to Amin's 48-hour challenge by straight away recalling Zakharov and suspending its relations with Uganda. Amin, complaining the Russians had not kept up the flow of spare parts necessary for his 60 million US dollar Soviet-supplied armoury, shot off 40 cables to OAU members telling them to hurry up and form the African peace keeping force for Angola.

Russian experts were recalled from the provinces and ordered to remain within the Kampala city limits. But the drinks party at the Uganda-Soviet Friendship Club at Entebbe went ahead as scheduled. Big Daddy mixed with the reluctant revellers, telling them how Uganda soldiers and students had been discriminated against in the Soviet Union. Russia still had to fulfill a military aid agreement—delivery of 15 medium T55 tanks, a batch of 23 mm anti-aircraft guns and some Czech-made OT 64(B) armoured personnel carriers was still outstanding.

'If you really think you are a super power you will honour this agreement' Amin reasoned. 'I think you will but if you decide not to, I will never kneel to you.'

The Russians began leaving Uganda. Amin promised as a farewell gesture of 'friendship and forgiveness' to play his accordion to departing Russians at the airport.

The rupture, however, healed itself in a mere six days. It was Moscow's turn to accuse Amin of insulting behaviour. But an exchange of opinions had taken place and diplomatic relations would be fully restored.

Idi Amin had backed down. Athough Soviet armaments had killed 30,000 Africans in Angola, Amin said, he conceded South Africans were involved in the conflict too. He would choose the lesser of two evils. He had received the message he required from Soviet leader Leonid Brezhnev and was prepared to bear-hug and make up as long as the Russians didn't send Zakharov back to Kampala.

That was an easy demand. The Russians knew how badly Amin needed them to keep his 20,000 man army well-equipped. It was still worth their while to humour him—though with their new hold in Angola it would not perhaps be necessary to carry on the relationship with the same vulnerable intimacy as before.

CHAPTER XIII

'The Organisation shall have the following
purposes:
To promote the unity and solidarity of the
African states:
To coordinate and intensify their cooperation
and efforts to achieve a better life for the
peoples of Africa:
To defend their sovereignty, their territorial
integrity and independence:
To eradicate all forms of colonialism from
Africa:
To promote international cooperation having
due regard to the Charter of the United Nations
and the Universal Declaration of Human
Rights.'

Charter of the Organisation of African Unity.

Makerere students were meant to take part in
parades celebrating the fifth anniversary of the military
takeover. Jeep-loads of soldiers arrived at the campus to
check the undergraduates who had been practising and
were up to standard. A pistol-waving captain yelled at
the students, soldiers jostled them with rifles. Amin's

son Tahan watched keenly, an automatic pistol in the crook of his arm. Tahan had been sent home from the Soviet Union before completing his aviation technology training. His teachers had given him a less than commendable report. Now he had installed himself in staff accommodation at Makerere and was studying nothing in particular, sometimes engineering, sometimes languages, sometimes medicine. Mostly, he swaggered through the campus as the son of his father wearing a pistol, or swinging the automatic at his side.

The soldiers went from the university to check school preparations for the parades. A pupil slapped back at the captain. The student was shot.

Makerere scholars signed a petition demanding disciplinary action against the captain. He was promoted....

Third year law student Paul Serwanga took his girlfriend to the end of term Leavers' Ball. After the dance the couple and two fellow students stayed on chatting in Serwanga's room in the halls of residence until 3:00 a.m. All four then walked towards another block not far from the university's Wandegeya gate. They were hailed by three State Research Unit men who had earlier barged into the dance. The students ignored them. The car stopped. The men grabbed Serwanga. The first pistol shot hit him in the chest; he fell to the tarmac. Several more shots were fired into his body.

Hearing shots, other students ran to the Wandegeya gate. The three men seized one, and beat him. They drove off at speed to Wandegeya police station where they said they had just killed a robber whose body should be picked up from the road.

A small group of students and Makerere wardens identified Serwanga's body at the mortuary. Early the following morning about 100 students and university staff converged on Mulago—but the body had been removed. Senior police had found the student's identity papers and knew protests would follow.

They were right. By midday, virtually the whole Makererer student population had gathered on the main campus in Freedom Square. The mood was one of bitterness and anguish. The procession moved out of the main gate; passing through the streets more cityfolk joined in.

'Save us from Amin!

'Save us from murderers!'

'Save us from oppression!

'Save us from slavery!'

In central Kampala the demonstrators listened as student leaders addressed them. Uniformed police began breaking up the crowd, scuffles developed. Armed soldiers were brought in to reinforce the police. Key student leaders escaped and hid. The demonstrators gradually dispersed.

That night, and the following morning, students tore down portraits of President Idi Amin at Makerere. The portraits were burned.

'We do not recognise the Amin regime.'

For once Big Daddy was at a loss for words. And even if he hadn't been, there was no-one to hear them except university officials and the service chiefs who came to Makerere with him. Students stayed away from the main hall where Amin was to address them. They had barricaded themselves in their rooms with tables and chairs.

As a token gesture Amin said a commission of inquiry would be established to investigate Serwanga's death. There was another unreported token: a handful of students were taken to Naguru for disciplinary action beatings.

Kenyan student Esther Chesire was flying home from Entebbe for the vacation. Passing through airport customs to catch EAA flight EC 692 plainclothesmen singled her out, demanding her student identity papers.

Esther was taken to an office and searched.

She was never seen again.

At the Makerere graduation ceremony a few days later Idi Amin received an honorary law degree. Said the citation in part: 'Field Marshal Amin has restored law and order, contained armed robbery and made

Ugandans live their lives free of fear.'

Graduates were told by Professor Kiapi: 'The President has excelled himself as a public administrator, a God fearing ruler and reconciliator. He has puzzled the best classroom political scientists. He is an outstanding advocate of oppressed people. As the champion of Afro-Arab unity he has amply won the admiration of all academics at Makerere University."

The government said Serwanga had been caught breaking into a house on the night of the Leavers' Ball. He and his accomplices defied challenges to give themselves up. Police had no choice but to open fire.

The government said Esther Chesire was no longer in Uganda—she left Entebbe on the day she intended.

Why then was Nanziri Bukenya, warden at Esther's residence, Africa Hall and the only woman at Makerere with a higher in mathematics, dragged off by State Research agents to sign papers describing Esther as 'a loose girl who spent nights out without the authority of the university.'?

Nanziri Bukenya's body was found dumped in Namanve Forest. Esther Chesire was later reported to have been told she was a spy and taken to Makindye Prison. She was raped, her throat cut.

Nothing in Idi Amin's Uganda had changed.

Truck driver Kamau Gitau and turnboy Mununa Mulinge were collecting bananas from a farm 35 miles from Kampala. Two government cars, one of them carrying CID officers, arrived at the farm. The police demanded to see the driver's trade licence, which was valid and backed up by a photocopy of a Bank of Uganda draft cheque covering his latest transaction for bananas. The two men were told the papers were not satisfactory, and that banana dealing had been banned. The cars escorted the truck to Naguru. A senior police officer—without asking to see the papers—ordered 20 whip strokes and held them in custody.

'We were led into the cells. There we found a truck wheel rim. We were ordered to kneel down, put our heads through the ring and stay in that position until the lashing ended. Any movement, we were warned, would be demanding more punishment, like being "sent to the moon", which we later understood to mean we would be shot.

'I warned Mulinge to keep calm otherwise we were going to die. We swallowed the pain without moving our bodies at all. They did not strip us. They assured us that anyone getting into their cells had first to be initiated with the whip.'

The cell was crammed with 50 prisoners—including policemen and soldiers.

'We heard shots. During that night, six people were shot dead. The shooting could be heard by us in our cells because it was done within the station.

'The next night we heard two more shots. One of the prisoners who shared a cell with us was killed that night. He had told us that he had stolen a car.'

Mulinge was called out of the cell. 'I was led to a police vehicle within the station. It was about 11:00 p.m. The shots had been fired about an hour back. I was ordered to clean the vehicle of blood. It was all over and I had to do it. I knew it was not animal blood. As I finished cleaning I was lashed with a whip. I was chased back to the cell. We stayed there awaiting our fate. There was horror and panic in the cells . . . no-one knew what would happen to him.'

But Gitau and Mulinge were fortunate. Their employer paid a ransom of 10,000 shillings in Kenya currency for their release. Smuggling accusations were dropped as quickly as they had been thought up.

Kenyan businessman John Oyuga Danga paid more for his life. After two months in jail under the constant threat of death he bribed his way to freedom with 180,000 shillings.

Uganda soldiers, armed with the latest automatic weapons and mortars, crossed remote stretches of the border into Kenya, stealing livestock and killing tribesmen who resisted. At Kapchop Konyao Reserve 14 Kenyas were killed by the troops. Among the dead

205

were four children.

The troops plundered the trains from Kenya.

Ticket inspectors Patrick Mungau and Francis Owino were pulled from the train at Tororo, just inside Uganda. Mungau was stripped and whipped beside the track.

'The lashing was so severe I fell on my back. They then kicked me and stamped on me. They passed the whip to take turns to lash me.'

Passengers told Owino his colleague had been taken. The second inspector went looking for Mungau. 'I found him weeping, with whip cuts all over his body.'

Owino was not allowed to help his friend back to the train. And the soldiers who ordered him to reboard the train alone had second thoughts.

'They made me march around with my hands in the air and then forced me to kneel. Then they flogged me. They took me to the police station and told the officers there they had taught me a lesson.'

A small group of Ugandan soldiers came to Makenge village near Jinja. They stormed into the house of a Kenyan businessman and, holding him at gunpoint, sexually assaulted his wife. The enraged Kenyan grabbed for a panga. The volley of gunfire hurled him against the wall.

In the morning troop carriers arrived at the village. A bugle was sounded. A soldier shouted: 'We're hunting for Luos.'

It was a reference to Kenya's second largest tribal group, closely related ethnically to Ugandans, settled in the western region close to the Uganda border.

Fish trader Obonyo Nyandeta was beaten, bayonetted and left dying in the sand. James Oduori died in hospital from stab wounds. The soldiers moved from house to house. They raked the home of sub-chief Cornel Ogola with gunfire.

Ten villagers were herded onto trucks and driven away.

James Otieno ran to hide in the nearby Papco factory. 'When they came to my house they hit me several times with the butts of their rifles. I was left lying on the ground when the others were taken away.'

Villagers fled into the forest. Soldiers broke into the village grocery shop and loaded all the goods onto their trucks. A bar was ransacked. Other troops swarmed through the houses looking for valuables, and smashing breakables.

'Where is your husband?' The soldier demanded. 'Say or we kill you. You choose between life and death. Where is he? Tell us woman.'

Amin sent a resume of his argument to the OAU secretariat. The next day four trucks owned by the Kenya National Transport Company KENATCO were seized on their way through Uganda. They carried explosives for a Chevron Oil Company prospecting project in southern Sudan; the eight drivers and a mechanic were jailed at Luzira prison. From then on, Kenya took Amin seriously.

Kenyans staged countrywide mass rallies at which effigies of Amin were burned.

'Demanding our land is demanding your death,' crowds chanted.

'We are ready to destroy this paper tiger.' they called.

What kind of a leader is this? He cannot even feed his own troops. Can hungry troops fight us? He cannot even provide his soldiers with soap with which to wash their pants.

'Amin should get his own medicine: shoot him and throw him to the crocodiles.'

Kenya variously described Amin as a mad dreamer; a fascist warmonger and sadist, the black Hitler, a megalomaniac who should be taken to hospital for psychiatric treatment', 'a monstrous animal specimen that has massive flesh but lacks brain.' One village rally offered 800,000 shillings for Amin's head 'on a platter.'

'Make food, not war.'

'Get your blood-thirsty tentacles off.'

Amin fanned Kenya's anger by saying he would establish a jet fighter base on the border. Roared Kenyatta: 'We shed a lot of blood to free our country

and we shall shed it again before we allow anyone to take
even a quarter of an inch of our land.'

Late in the afternoon a bugle sounded again. Five
bodies, including that of a child, were heaved onto one
of the booty-laden trucks. The hum of the vehicle
engines faded into the distance: Villagers crept timidly
out of hiding, stunned and afraid.

TWO DAYS after Esther Chesire's disappearance
OAU chairman Amin delivered his bombshell. Parts of
Kenya and the Sudan historically belonged to
Uganda—and the Defence Council had agreed to follow
up means of getting them back. One chunk of territory,
he claimed, stretched from the existing border to within
20 miles of the Kenyan capital, Nairobi—a total
distance of some 200 miles. Amin wanted the British to
explain why their colonial administration had given
Kenya fertile Ugandan land when the colonial boundaries were demarcated. 'I will not go to war to reclaim this
land because I want peace. The British made many
mistakes in this matter. My job is to liberate all Ugandan
territory and put right all the mistakes of the British.'

Amin revised an old warning that he would not
hesitate to go to war if Uganda's trade route to the sea
through Kenya was ever threatened.

The rascally British preferred to settle in Kenya—and
that was why they had expanded that country. Big
Daddy thought of the people of western Kenya and
southern Sudan as his children. 'Look what the British
did to Palestine. They transferred it to all the Israelis and
made the Palestinians homeless. If the people they
transferred to Kenya are not happy with the administration in the area they should be allowed to come back. I
am a military leader and I must be taken very seriously
because I am not joking like most politicians do.'

Dockers at Mombasa began boycotting Ugandan
goods at the port. Locked in the blockade were
ambulances and troop carriers from Libya. Amin said
Kenya had confiscated the cargo, adding the military
vehicles were urgently needed 'to enable farmers to

transport their goods to collection centres.'

Trains and heavy goods vehicles stopped at the border...

Big Daddy backed down. He had not foreseen the intensity of Kenya's irritation. 'I have nothing but peaceful intentions. I do not want to interfere with the affairs of neighbouring countries. In fact, if Kenya, Zaire or Sudan are ever in trouble I am not joking when I say I will come to your assistance. I will be in Kenya in a second to protect Kenya and guard Mombasa from warships.'

Of his service in the British Army against Kenyatta's Mau Mau guerrillas (of which the rallying Kenyans made much) Amin claimed he had actually been a Mau Mau informant.

'I contributed to saving the lives of many Mau Mau fighters. I did this because I wanted Africa to be free.'

Amin ended his olive-branch offering to Kenyatta with belated 'best greetings to all Kenyans for a prosperous and Happy New Year.'

But Kenyans were not so easily soothed. And if Amin wanted to patch up the quarrel his contrition did not last long. Kenya's projected road link to Sudan was part of an Israeli masterplan to dominate East Africa, he said. Recklessly driven Kenyan trucks were killing Uganda children and therefore would not be allowed to drive Uganda roads after dark. A group of Uganda-bound Palestinians passing through Kenya never reached their destination. Israel wanted Kenya to shut off Uganda's oil supplies. Kenya forced down two Ugandan military helicopters which had strayed into its airspace and subsequently tortured and killed their crews. Kenyan forces raided Ugandan border villages.

Amin reeled off his complaints.

Just out of Athens two men rose from their seats, pulling out revolvers. 'We are revolutionaries and this aircraft is now our property. We are going to take you where we please.'

A young woman in a blue skirt and blouse held a

grenade as she walked the aisle snapping for silence. Pistols poked at the passengers. 'Put up your hands.'

A slim well-dressed man snatched up the cockpit microphone: 'We're Palestinians.'

The twin-jet Air France airbus, flight 139 from Tel Aviv to Paris via Athens, put down once for fuel-in Libya. With dawn approaching it began a gentle descent over Lake Victoria to Entebbe. The 258 passengers and crew were led to a decrepit, out-of-use terminal wing. Rats scurried off as they entered the building.

Ugandan soldiers mounted guard over the hostages. The hijackers laid explosives in and around the airbus. Amin arrived at Entebbe in his full dress uniform with medals and strode into the terminal, small son Mwanga (also in military uniform) at his heels, to welcome the hostages to Uganda. 'We want your stay to be as nice as possible.'

Through Uganda radio the hijackers made known their demand—the release in two days of 53 'freedom fighters' imprisoned in Israel, France, Switzerland, West Germany and Kenya. (The list included Melchite Catholic Archbishop Hilarion Capucci, convicted of running guns to Palestinian guerrillas, Kozo Okomoto, survivor of the Japanese Red Army group which massacred 27 people at Lod airport, Tel Aviv in 1972 and six members of the West German Baader Meinhof gang.) Kenya denied it held any Palestinian prisoners, though Amin's earlier mention of Palestinians missing in Kenya probably referred to a foiled attempt by Palestinian guerrillas to rocket an Israeli El Al airline taking off from Nairobi's Embakasi airport in January.

From the moment the Air France jet touched down at Entebbe Idi Amin Dada was in his element. He was in the limelight, enjoying himself. He sauntered among the hostages. 'Some of you know me and some don't. For those who don't know me, I am Field Marshal Dr Amin Dada,' he said cheerfully. 'I looked after you. I arranged for you to get off the plane and stay in Uganda.'

Amin—who had earlier embraced the Palestinians—

told the passengers he thought the hijackers' demands very reasonable. 'Tell your government to solve the Palestine problem. That is my advice to you.'

Uganda troops guarded the hostages while the four hijackers went off to bath and rest. A Ugandan aircraft had brought three Palestinians from Somalia to join the hijackers at Entebbe. Uganda soldiers gave automatic weapons and ammunition to the hijackers. French ambassador to Uganda Pierre Renard was not allowed to deal directly with the hijackers. Negotiations for the freeing of the captives would be conducted through Somali ambassador Hashi Abdullah Farah or Amin himself. On the second day 47 hostages were unexpectedly handed over to Renard and flown to Paris.

Colonel Baruch Bar-Lev had been head of Israel's military mission in Uganda when Amin seized power from Milton Obote. Bar-Lev had won Amin's trust. Aware of Obote's growing hostility to Israel Bar-Lev forewarned Amin of the plan to arrest him on his return from Cairo. Prior to the coup the experienced Israeli officer advised Amin to base more loyal Kakwa troops in the capital. Four Israeli-trained Ugandan paratroopers killed Obote officers planning Amin's arrest at the time of Singapore Commonwealth conference. Bar Lev had helped Amin achieve power in 1971 ...

From his villa outside Tel Aviv Colonel Bar-Lev telephoned Kampala.

'How are you, my friend?' Amin said.

'How are you feeling, sir?'

'I'm very pleased to hear your voice today.'

'I am speaking from my home. I heard what has happened. May I ask something of you?'

'I agree because you are my good friend.'

'I know, sir.' Bar Lev said. 'My friend, you have a great opportunity to go down in history as a great peacemaker. Many people abroad, in England, in America, in Europe are writing bad things about you, and now you have an opportunity to show them that you are a great peacemaker, if you free those people, you'll go down in history as a very great man and that will be

211

against those who speak against you.'

Amin conveyed the Palestinians' deadline to Bar-Lev. '... they will blow up the French plane and all the passengers at twelve noon tomorrow. So I advise you, my friend to report to Rabin, General Rabin, the prime minister, I know him, he's my friend, and to General Dayan, I know that he's my friend. Your government must do everything possible to free the hostages immediately, that is the Palestinian demand.'

'Mr President, you are the ruler in your country. I think you have the power to free these people.'

'I want you to know you are my friend for always.'

'Can you do something to stop them from killing?'

'I can stop them, if your government accepts their demand immediately.'

Four hours before the deadline Israel said it was prepared to talk. The hostages were ominously separated into Jewish and non-Jewish groups. About 100 captives in the latter were freed. The deadline was extended to noon, Sunday, July 4. Israel prepared the alternative to submission. Mossad, the Israeli intelligence service, slipped black operatives into Uganda. Released hostages arriving in Paris were intensively debriefed.

They said the terminal building had not been wired up with explosives. About 70 Ugandan troops were deployed at the airport. Israeli agents questioned El Al staff in Kenya for additional local information before securing Kenya's secret promise of cooperation. The Israeli construction firm which had built Entebbe airport a decade before provided the plans, but these were discarded because of later modifications. A replica of Entebbe for commando training was built from satellite data and aerial photographs supplied by the Pentagon.

Amin flew to Mauritius to relinquish chairmanship of the OAU, claiming there that several African leaders had actually asked him to serve a second term, but he declined so he could spend more time on Uganda's domestic affairs. His 'excellent' OAU record had been made possible because of his country's 'tremendous' economic development. Amin did not read the relief of many OAU delegates when he flew back to Entebbe on July 3.

Big Daddy paid another visit to his 'guests' in the terminal. 'The problems haven't been settled but there's some advance in the negotiations. I want you to tell Colonel Bar-Lev how well I treated you, and how I looked after you.'

The Israeli aircraft flew over the Red Sea, escorted at first by Phantom fighters in case of interception by Egyptian or Saudi Arabian air force planes. They veered inland over Ethiopia and Kenya. A Boeing 707 carrying 23 doctors and fitted out with two complete surgical cabins landed at Nairobi. The three C 130 Hercules transports, and a second Boeing, a headquarters and communications plane, slipped out of the Nairobi holding pattern making for Entebbe.

One of the transports dropped flares and explosives over the west end of the runway, distracting the Ugandan defenders. The other two drew to a halt and disgorged jeep-borne paratroopers, infantrymen and two armoured vehicles. Fifty minutes later the C130s were airborne again.

Three hostages had been killed in crossfire. Israeli ground commander Colonel Yoni Netanyahu had been fatally hit by a shot from the control tower. Three hostages and five Israeli soldiers had been wounded.

All seven terrorists lay dead, as did 20 Ugandan soldiers. Eleven Uganda Air Force MiGs had been blown up. They burned slowly at a corner of the airstrip. Ugandan soldiers were shooting into the dark long after the raiders had gone.

The Israelis stopped four hours in Nairobi.

At 1:00 a.m. in Kampala the Field Marshal was handed the phone.

'Sir, I want to thank you for your cooperation and I thank you very much,' Colonel Bar-Lev said.

'You know I did not succeed.'

'Thank you very much for your cooperation. What?

The cooperation didn't succeed. Why?'

'Have I done anything at all?'

'I just wanted to thank you, sir, for the cooperation.'

'Have I done anything?' Amin said, irritation in his voice.

'I did exactly what you wanted.'

'Wh. . . . Wh. . . . What happened?'

AT THE head of an armoured column Amin raced to Entebbe. First to suffer Amin's revenge were four radar operators who were dragged out onto the tarmac and shot.

Dora Block had been on her way to Paris to see a brother and visit the grave of another. Then she was to fly on to New York for the wedding of her son Daniel, political correspondent for the Tel Aviv newspaper Davar. Fluent in five languages, Mrs Bloch volunteered to help as an interpreter during the hostages' ordeal at Entebbe. Amin jovially asked her occupation.

'I am just an old mother,' replied the 73-year-old white-haired Mrs Bloch.

Eating lunch at the airport a piece of meat lodged in Mrs Bloch's throat. She was taken by ambulance to Mulago Hospital. Travelling with Mrs Bloch was one of her three sons Elan Hartuv, who asked to accompany her to hospital.

The request was refused. But the hijackers permitted him to telephone Mulago. 'All is well and you can expect the release of Mrs Bloch in a day or so,' a doctor told him.

When the Israelis raided, Dora Bloch was left behind. On Sunday afternoon Peter Chandley, the British commercial attache, visited her in hospital and agreed to bring her some food. Returning an hour later Chandley was barred from entering the hospital. Mrs Bloch was dragged out of bed and pulled, screaming, to two State Research Bureau cars waiting outside. Her fate was not immediately known. Britain recalled high commissioner Hennessy from leave to tackle Amin. Mrs Bloch held duel British-Israeli nationality. The Bloch family despatched a heartfelt appeal to Amin. 'On behalf of all her children and grandchildren we beg you to release Dora Bloch, and sent her back to us.' Daniel Bloch desperately asked world boxing champion Mohammed Ali to use his influence with Amin. Israel called for International Red Cross intercession.

Uganda's reply confirmed the family's worst fears. Mrs Bloch, it said, had been returned to Entebbe before the Israeli strike. 'When Israel invaded Entebbe airport she assumed by force responsibility for all hostages. The Government of the Republic of Uganda ceased to be responsible for them.'

'Members of the invading force took away all the hostages—dead, injured or otherwise. Reports (that) one diplomat saw Mrs Dora Bloch in hospital on Sunday are false. There is no concrete information about it.'

The British High Commission was told Chandley's expulsion papers were being drawn up. Jimmy Parma, chief photographer in the Ugandan Ministry of Information, photographed Mrs Bloch's body in Namanve Forest. An attempt had been made to burn it with petrol.

Parma, suspected of frequently tipping off foreign journalists, was confronted in the street near his office at the Voice of Uganda. He was tied up and bundled into the boot of a car. All his exposed film was destroyed. Like Mrs Bloch, the 45-year-old photographer was strangled and dumped in Namanve Forest. Parma's body was also disfigured—but with knife and gunshot wounds.

Amin answered the telephone again. It was the Israeli newspaper Maariv. 'I am counting the bodies of my dead soldiers,' Amin simpered. 'I am carrying the bodies in my hands. You mistreated me. I believe you reciprocated to my kindness with ingratitude. I am the victim of Israel though I defended the hostages . . .'

'All I have left to do is count the bodies. Your planes came and my soldiers did not want to fire at them as we would have shot them down. Had my soldiers wanted to fight they would have fought, but they were killed.'

The Uganda soldiers and Palestinian guerrillas were buried side-by-side after a short funeral ceremony at Kampala's Kololo airstrip. A eulogy from the Popular Front for the Liberation of Palestine said its fighters were being buried beside the Ugandans as a symbol of their common objectives. Big Daddy ordered two days of national mourning for the dead and vowed vengeance. 'Everyone responsible for this will pay heavily ...inside Israel or elsewhere. Don't think our Air Force is not strong. . . . We don't keep all our eggs in one place.'

A government decree made it a capital offence to joke about the Israeli raid. Two Kampala bar girls disappeared after they were overheard saying their boyfriends were 'as strong as Israeli pilots.'

Amin awarded a posthumous medal to the Ugandan soldier who killed the Israeli commander before being cut down by retaliatory fire. The soldier was named as Sergeant Gogo. Another medal, the Uganda Distinguished Service Order, went to Colonel Isaac Lumago, Amin's high commissioner to the tiny southern African country of Lesotho. Lumago had warned Kampala of the arrival in the Lesotho capital, Maseru, of a transport aircraft bearing the Star of David insignia of the Israeli Air Force and predicted an elaborate military rescue operation may have been afoot. As it was, the aircraft had no connection with the Entebbe strike and in any case Lumago's suspicions were ignored by Uganda army chiefs and Amin at the time was absent in Mauritius.

Israeli prime minister Yitzhak Rabin received an idiotic telegramme. Uganda would attack Israel unless compensation was paid within seven days for the destroyed MiG fighters, the damage to old Entebbe airport and 'expenses incurred on hospitality for the hostages on the French Airbus. 'I want you to understand I am not joking like the Arabs who are now killing each other in Lebanon instead of attacking their common enemy, Israel.'

Amin had already told French ambassador Renard

he would keep the airbus until compensation equivalent to its value (about $20 million) was paid. Eventually, however, he turned the aircraft over to Renard and Air France officials discovered all the baggage on board had been looted.

Libya replaced the destroyed MiGs and Amin returned Uganda's remaining 10 Israeli-made jets. 'I am sending you the planes because I am not a thief,' Amin said.

Big Daddy advanced the theory the Israeli commandoes intended to kidnap him in the rescue raid, explaining that six Israelis burst into the presidential suite at Entebbe's international terminal. Only a few people knew the layout of the upstairs suite which comprised of an office, lounge and bedroom. 'Obviously they wanted to capture me. They knew where to look, but I left the airport three hours earlier.'

Author William Stevenson says the idea to seize Amin came up during preparations for the raid but was rejected by the Israeli cabinet.

At last Amin admitted Dora Bloch may not have rejoined the hostages at Entebbe before the raid. She had been discharged from hospital and could subsequently have disappeared. Britain's protests on behalf of Mrs Bloch stemmed from jealousy, Amin ghoulishly remarked. 'They are jealous because I have not married a British woman. They wanted me to be their brother-in-law or their father-in-law.'

At the United Nations Israel escaped world censure for the Entebbe raid. But Idi Amin Dada once again won the concerted support of African and Arab countries. The Organisation of African Unity described the action as wanton aggression against Uganda. UN Secretary General Kurt Waldheim called the raid a serious violation of Uganda's national sovereignty and territorial integrity—and African countries drafted a resolution to that effect for approval by the Security Council. The raid was both an affront to an independent African nation and a challenge to African unity as a whole. Although the African resolution was withdrawn

217

at the last moment because it could not be sure of getting the necessary nine votes in the 15-member Security Council a second resolution sponsored by Britain and the US calling for universal condemnation of international terrorism was not adopted either. Seven Security Council members sidestepped: the point at issue was not the overall question of terrorism but specifically the Uganda episode.

The Security Council session ended without it agreeing on anything. 'Israel has not been condemned and thereby has been vindicated,' delighted Jerusalem's UN ambassador Chaim Hertzog. Hertzog's submissions to the four day debate were as carefully planned as the raid itself. 'I am in no way sitting in the dock as the accused party,' he said. '. . . I stand here as an accuser of this rotten, corrupt, brutal, cynical, bloodthirsty monster of international terrorism and all those who support it in one way or another, whether by commission or omission.'

Uganda's advance cooperation with the hijackers, Hertzog said, was unquestionable. The Air France Captain had stated that one of the hijackers, Wilfred Böse, a German national, knew Entebbe to be the aircraft's final destination.

When the plane landed at Entebbe one of the hijackers said: 'Everything is OK; the army is at the airport.'

The Ugandan airport manager had been told to cater for 260 expected passengers and crew. Hertzog also cited the behaviour of Amin and his troops throughout the hijack period, noted the hijackers had been unconcerned and relaxed at Entebbe. Cars driven by Ugandans—and many other facilities . . . were put at the hijackers disposal; Uganda radio broadcast a Palestinian announcement praising Amin for his stand against Zionism . . .

Israel's evidence of Ugandan complicity was lengthy. Among many more observations: 'Ugandan soldiers, under the direct orders of President Amin, supervised the separation of Jewish passengers from non-Jewish passengers. This was a development of a nature so sinister and so pregnant with memories of the past that no member of the Jewish people, whether in Israel or abroad, could fail to recall its horrible significance. There flashed, immediately, upon the inward eye of every member of our people, the memory of the terrifying selections carried out during the most horrifying holocaust that mankind has ever seen and which beset our people. We recalled the selections carried out by the Nazis in the concentration camps as members of the Jewish people were singled out for the gas chambers and extermination.'

Hertzog recalled Amin's oft-repeated admiration for Adolf Hitler—and notably the 'Hitler was right to burn 6 million Jews' telegram.

Nazi persecution of the Jews had been raised during the hijack itself. Böse had seen the concentration camp number tattoed on the arm of a Buchenwald survivor among the hostages, Yitzhak David. David said to Böse: 'This is what your fathers did to me. I have been telling my sons that your generation of Germans is different. How am I going to explain to them what you are doing to us now?' During the Israelis' raid Böse burst into the passenger lounge and aimed his machine gun at the Jewish hostages cowering on the floor. According to Mrs Bloch's son Elan Hartuv Böse braced the weapon to shoot, hesitated indecisively for a moment, turned and ran outside, opening fire into the muzzle-flashed darkness.

For Uganda at the Security Council, Foreign Minister Col Juma Oris Abdullah denied any Uganda complicity in the raid, in advance or otherwise, indicted Israel for for barbarism and banditry...and drew Kenya into the fray. 'I have done my best to avoid mentioning Kenya, as it is a sister state and neighbour state of Uganda. I had in mind not to mention much about Kenya...(However) I should like the Council to follow exactly what are the facts regarding Kenya...' Kenya had readily granted Israel all the assistance required of it. 'Uganda still regards the people of Kenya

219

as their brothers and sisters. We express the hope that the authorities in Kenya were somehow misled into collaborating in this heinous act. Accordingly Uganda does not intend to undertake any retaliatory measures against Kenya for this collaboration.'

Even as the Ugandan colonel spoke, Field Marshal Amin was moving troops to the border with Kenya, instructing them to be ready to strike at a moment's notice. Sensing the tension the US lent its staunch African friend Kenya two Philippines-based P3 Orion long range reconnaisance aircraft, which soon confirmed Amin's build-up along the 350-mile frontier. For show, the US frigate Beary arrived in Mombasa and six more ships of the American Indian Ocean fleet, headed by the carrier Ranger, set out on what was officially called a routine trip to the Kenyan port.

Amin's Kampala radio then peremptorily blabbed: 'We are being invaded by Kenyans. Field Marshal Amin is in control of the situation. Citizens should be prepared to give blood.' The smokescreen did not amuse the Kenyans. Nor did seizure by Amin of 30 Kenya trucks carrying fuel through to Zaire, Rwanda and Sudan. Worse still, Amin's embarrassment over Entebbe—his anger that Israelis got away through Nairobi—showed red.

The first count by the Kenyans of their nationals killed in Uganda in the days which followed the Israeli attack put the number of dead at 245. The hunting down of Kenyans was carried out under Amin's personal orders. In one incident at Mbombo, southwest of Kampala on the Masala road 30 Kenyans were dragged into the open and shot to death. Seventeen Kenyan fishermen were machine-gunned and thrown into the water at Lake Mobutu Sese Seko (formerly Lake Albert) and in Kampala itself troops scoured the suburbs looking for Kenyans. Seven were tied and shot at Namongo, others were snatched from their Kampala shops or businesses, the bodies of three Kenyans were found by relatives in a river near Mukoni, about seven miles from the capital, and 27—including a group of businessmen travelling in a Kenya registered car—were thrown into Makindye Prison. More killings took place in Entebbe and Jinja and, closer to the border, at Bugiri, Tororo and Mbale. Kenyans escaping across the border told the Kenyan authorities Ugandan civilians—mostly from Amin's Kakwa tribe—had joined the troops in looting and destroying their property. Ugandans associating with Kenyans—or with business connections in Kenya, West Germany and Britain—had not escaped the Amin's revenge. The bodies of two leading businessmen, one a partner in a West German international electrical and photographic business, the other the proprietor of a Uganda-registered firm with branches in Kenya, were found on a ranch at Nakasongola, outside Kampala. The pro-Kenya coach of Uganda's Express Football Club disappeared: his players had beaten Amin's Simba Regiment team. Kenyans who fled Kampala, having checked Mulago mortuary for the corpses of missing relatives or friends said the mortuary was 'overflowing with bodies which are piled on the floor and in every available room.'

Joseph Mpanga reported that two of his brothers working as porters at Entebbe airport were arrested and killed. Soldiers pumped 20 bullets into the body of one of them. Ouma Orege said the bodies of men killed by soldiers attacking the Kenyan-run Corner Bar in Kampala were left lying in the bar for 36 hours. A Catholic nun, Sister Hellen Mildret, told the Kenyans Amin's troops had killed 'most of the people who were on duty at Entebbe airport' and tortured Kenyans in the forest around Kampala. Four more prominent businessmen, an assistant district commissioner and a Saza chief were murdered—and their bodies burnt—after expressing ambivalence over the Israeli incursion, fugitives to Kenya reported.

Kenya had long been distressed by both the levity and lies with which Uganda treated its queries about the disappearance in Uganda of Esther Chesire, another unnamed Kenyan student beaten to death during the Serwanga incident and former Mau Mau guerrilla

221

Kungu Karumba.

After insisting Esther had left Uganda Amin conceded she had disappeared and convened an inquiry chaired by British Makerere academic Brian Langland. Prof Langland left Uganda before the inquiry's work was complete because the authorities refused to renew his work permit. Other Kenya approaches concerning missing nationals encountered a wall of silence.

As Uganda claimed Kenyans were invading and as more than 1,000 Kenyans streamed over the border from Uganda bringing more tales of Amin's vengeful atrocities Nairobi had had enough.

At first Kenya had simply broadcast a new serial on its national radio titled 'The Pranks of Sebastian' about a tyrannical, deranged chimpanzee which had taken over a game reserve.

Kenya's foreign minister Dr Munyua Waiyaki circulated a letter at the United Nations with an appendix detailing what it called the highlights of anti-Kenya utterances, provocations and incidents by Amin since the military take-over in 1971. The list included the presumed murders of 157 Kenyans in the period before the Entebbe attack. It maintained Kungu Karumba had been ordered 'to be taken to the Middle East'—another Amin euphemism for death.

On the latest killings in Uganda Dr Waiyaki's letter said: '. . . the Ugandan military authorities have engaged in systematic and indiscriminate massacre of Kenyans in Uganda. These citizens are lawfully residing in Uganda, contributing immensely in sustaining what little remains of the already shattered economy. The indiscriminate hunting down of Kenyans, torture and mass murder of civilians which has already claimed hundreds of innocent lives, indicates to the whole world the callous contempt that the Ugandan authorities have for international law, morality and human decency.'

A less controlled Kenya statement responding locally to further Amin charges that 30 Israeli and American aircraft were detected by radar approaching Uganda from Kenya in attack formation (most of the Ugandan radar equipment destroyed by the Israelis had not yet been replaced), said Kenyans sympathised with peace-loving Ugandans who found themselves living under 'the world's greatest dictator' in modern history. 'Since the military government came into being five years ago blood has been gushing from the throats of Ugandans whose only crime was having been within reach of the Ugandan armed forces when they went berserk.'

'The first exercise that the Ugandan government embarked on was the elimination and liquidation of the brainpower in Uganda that had hitherto placed that country rightfully in the path of 20th century civilisation.'

The Kenyans decried the 'dictatorial fascist ruler of Uganda who has been a constant threat to peace in East Africa'. 'He has been at war with almost all his neighbours. Remember in 1973 he unleashed a kind of bombing on Tanzania's lake region that has never been seen since the end of the second world war. Incessantly desirous of shedding blood sadist Amin has driven the government and people of Kenya to a point where tolerance and willingness to understand are no more a virtue.'

Israel had attempted to spare Nairobi the wrath—not only of Uganda but also most other pro-Arab African countries by saying it had forced itself upon Kenya. Kenya, in turn, said it allowed the Israelis to put down at Nairobi out of purely humanitarian considerations. Britain sided with Kenya and broke diplomatic relations with Amin's government—the first time it had ever cut ties with a member of the Commonwealth. Amin, just declared Uganda Life President, concluded with extraordinary logic that this proved Britain's collusion with 'the people who murdered Jesus Christ' and that 'the majority of Kenya government officials, including Kenyatta, are not Africans.'

Amin moved more troops to the Kenya border under the cover of a countrywide electricity blackout for what he called 'Operation Panga Kali': Operation Sharp Knife. He received a military delegation from Kenya's neighbour, Somalia.

Kenya saw a sinister portent in the Somali visit; Somalia claimed a large swatch of Kenya's eastern territory and had long fought a protracted guerrilla war for it. The presence of extensive Russian military installations in Somalia did not make Kenya feel any easier. Kenya put its 9,500 strong Army, Air Force and paramilitary General Service unit on a 24-hour red alert. Kenya's military would have been heavily outnumbered by Somali and Ugandan forces (23,000 and 21,000 respectively) and could never have outgunned its foes. Against Kenya's 13 armoured cars and 14 combat aircraft Uganda could show at least 30 heavy tanks, 15 scout cars, 100 armoured personnel carriers, 58 amphibious tanks and 46 military aircraft, Somalia, with 275 Soviet tanks and 52 warplanes, was one of Africa's best militarily equipped countries, even though its economy was one of the poorest.

As for Uganda, Kenya controlled the importation of all the oil required by Amin's fuel-guzzling armour and a conventional invasion was a non-starter from the beginning. But Kenya wasn't taking any chances.

It stopped upwards of 300 fuel trucks bound for Uganda from Mombasa and grabbed millions of dollars worth of Ugandan goods transiting Kenya, including 30 trucks destined for Amin's army.

The pinch hurt. Amin squealed.

Complaining to the Arab League, whose members supplied oil to Mombasa refinery in the first place, Amin said that even with strict rationing...a ban on private motoring was in force...Uganda had only five days' fuel left. 'We will take desperate action against Kenya. Uganda will have no alternative but to fight for its survival if this blockade continues.' As if to show he meant business Amin cut off electricity supplied from Jinja to Kenya under a 50-year bilateral hydro-electric agreement.

To Kenya the shut-down was but another irritation. And publicly the Kenyans said they were not blockading Uganda. Amin had simply not paid his bills. 'Pay up, or shut up!' snapped Dr Waiyaki. 'We are not obliged to subsidise the Ugandan economy. We have to pay for goods we import and there is no way we can give them to Uganda unless Amin's government sends payment with its orders.'

'We have not closed the border. There is nothing to stop Uganda trucks crossing the border to collect their goods but we cannot ask Kenyan drivers to enter Uganda knowing their lives will be in real danger. Uganda is either unable or unwilling to guarantee the lives and safety of our people. If his threat to attack is based on closure of the border—as the border is not closed—Amin is just looking for an excuse. If he attacks Kenya will be bound to use all her energies to defend herself. But the whole world should know we have no interest in fighting Uganda.'

Kenya had allowed Amin to fall 500 million shillings behind in oil payments and other dues in order to help alleviate the economic hardships of ordinary Ugandans. 'All Amin has shown in return has been provocation,' voiced Kenya vice president Daniel Arap Moi. 'The thanks of a donkey are kicks.'

Showing Amin they, too, could go arresting Kenya police seized ten Ugandans 'near vital installations' at Mombasa. The Ugandans, employees of the East African Railways and EA Cargo Handling Services, would be thoroughly investigated before being charged or tried. The Mombasa authorities said pointedly: 'If nothing substantial is found against them they will be released as Kenya believes in justice and human rights'.

Whichever way it was looked at, Kenya had Uganda where it wanted it.

Again Big Daddy backed down. He implored Kenyatta to be 'forgetful' of the two countries' differences. 'The people of Uganda and Kenya have blood relations and we in Uganda cannot possibly cross even an inch into Kenya and cause harm to our brothers and sisters. From now on our aims should not be diverted from the service of our people and the total liberation of Africa.'

Amin sent copies of the message to President Nyerere, Dr Waldheim and the OAU. 'We can solve our problems affecting our region peacefully within the framework of the Treaty for EA Cooperation, or the OAU or the nonaligned movement or the United Nations Organisation to which both our countries are members.' In a separate radio broadcast Amin blamed Britain for all the misunderstandings in the region and said that when everything had been properly ironed out he would honeymoon in both Britain and Kenya and pray at the Al-Aqsa mosque in Jerusalem—whether Arabs or Israelis liked it or not. Proof of his belief in East African blood ties was that he had two sons in Kenya Njuguna and Njoroge, by a Kikuyu girl named Wanjiru.

Kenya asserted that if this was true the boys were the offspring of Kikuyu schoolgirls Amin raped while fighting against Mau Mau insurgents in Central Province.

Kenya agreed to receive a 15-man Ugandan delegation in Nairobi, and then slapped a seven-point peace plan onto the table.

- Stop laying claims to any part of Kenyan territory.
- Stop the killing of innocent Kenyans legally residing in Uganda, and in accordance with international law and practice guarantee their safety and security against illegal arrest, torture and confiscation of property.
- Stop the threat of force against Kenya.
- Stop the hate and smear campaign which is aimed at giving us a bad name internationally. (An inference of pro-Israel sympathies).
- Uganda must pay for goods and services she has received or wishes to receive.
- Uganda must not hold hostages the neighbouring states of Rwanda, Burundi, Sudan and Zaire by confiscating goods destined for these countries. Kenya has not closed its border with Uganda nor interfered with her unimpeded access to the sea. She must in return and in accordance with international practice give the

226

same unimpeded transit of goods through Uganda to these neighbours.

• Stop all acts of belligerence against Kenya by removing all troops from near our border.

'When we talk of peace we do not mean only peace between two states: We mean peace between states and within each state. We believe peace and the prosperity of Kenya is intertwined with the peace and prosperity of all its neighbours,' Foreign Minister Waiyaki said.

The Ugandans readily put their signatures to the 'Memorandum of Understanding'... but hardly had the ink dried when five Kenyans were shot by soldiers at Gulu north of Kampala, a Kenyan *dukawallah* was beaten and his shop burned down in Kigumba region, and ten other Kenyans escaped from the same area by bribing whooping Amin soldiers. It took a further five weeks for Amin to pull his troops back from the border, apologising lamely that the withdrawal had been delayed by fuel shortages.

'Amin is talking of peace with Kenya but he does not mean it,' protested a Kenyan spokesman. 'The Ugandan leadership cannot be trusted. Amin is killing our people.' Another Kenyan official said transit goods were still going missing. 'The Ugandans are liars and thieves. Our drivers have come back showing visible injuries and signs of beatings by Amin's military men.' Still without satisfactory answers to their questions about the treatment of Kenyan students at Makerere Kenyan academics at home urged the suspension of university exchanges with Uganda until Makerere ceased to be 'a military playground'—and the 'lawless flogging of innocent Kenyans under Amin's jungle rule' ended. In so far as Idi Amin Dada is concerned we are dealing with an individual who is suffering from *dementia praecox*.'

At later 'normalisation' talks in Addis Ababa Amin claimed Kenya was holding 140 armoured personnel carriers he was anxiously waiting for. As it was, the shipment of military vehicles had been late in arriving at Mombasa. The bickering at Addis Ababa served to remind the Kenyans of the difficulties in dealing with

Amin.

Power Minister Col. Dusman Sabuni arrived in Mombasa to find out how much Uganda owed Kenya for unpaid freight. 'Abnormal?' he said. 'We are not abnormal. We are normal. If we were abnormal we would not have whites coming to settle in some parts of Africa. We have been brothers right from the beginning. This talk about normalisation is only a formality.' Sabuni said Kenyan businessmen wishing to start new ventures or resume old ones in Uganda would be assured of success and safety. There was no immediate noticeable rush of Kenyans eager to take him at his word.

FROM THE day he seized power, Amin had been threatened. But for more than five years, belying reports by former intimates and seniors that he was of low intelligence, he had survived all attempts on his life.

That he commanded loyalty there can be no doubt, whether through fear or respect.

How long it would last no one could predict. Amin had amazing resilience—a capacity for survival as cunning as the leopard with a brute strength equal to that of gorilla.

Clearly, he was clever, and devious, if lacking in formal intelligence. Equally clearly, he was a master at organising secret intelligence—and when that was lacking, at anticipating with uncanny intuition those moments when his life was possibly in danger. He had one such intuition not long after July 4.

AMIN's radio appeal for Ugandan citizens to donate blood had nothing whatsoever to do with a Kenyan invasion—or anyone else's invasion. Nor was his aberrant demeanour after July 4 solely created by the Entebbe rescue.

Two bombs exploded at the Command Post, killing an unspecified number of Amin's guards. A third was discovered in the building and disarmed. Amin was not at the Command Post when the explosions occurred.

228

After a passing out parade, at Nsambya Police barracks, hand grenades were thrown at Amin's jeep. Three soldiers died and 36 were injured in the attack—but Amin walked away unscathed. In a third attempt on his life, Army mutineers who attempted to storm the Command Post using bazookas and heavy machine guns were repulsed by loyal soldiers. Shooting spread briefly through Kampala but the following morning Uganda radio gave this explanation:

'President Amin has instructed his family in the use of heavy weapons. The new, most modern and sophisticated Soviet anti-tank and anti-aircraft weapons were operated in the Presidential Lodges and the command post by the president, his wives and some of his children under the age of seven.'

The shooting had disrupted an early evening football match at Nakivubo Stadium. The game was abandoned midway as both players and spectators hastily made for the exits and dispersed towards their homes. Beerhalls nearby had emptied fast.

Amin needed blood donors for his private war. Morale in his Army—even among the Kakwa—had hit a new low. Many units had not been paid for weeks and rations were in short supply. Hungry soldiers swept through villages taking away sheep, goats and chickens for slaughter. Murchison Falls, famous for its hippopotamus, had been turned into an open-air abbattoir for hippo killed at night; hundreds of buffalo were killed in Queen Elizabeth National Park by heavily-armed foraging parties from a newly-formed squad known as the Special Hunters Regiment. Troops mounted cattle-rustling forays across the Kenya border—and bands of deserters offered to exchange their weapons and equipment for bread, maize meal, tea and civilian clothing. Supplies of green bananas, *matoke*, were over-ripe by the time they reached outlying garrisons and much of the protein-rich hippo and game meat was also inedible. (No salt for salting the meat; animals had been killed with automatic weapons and sometimes anti-tank rockets.)

Two battalions—about 2,000 men—at Kampala and Gulu refused to obey their officers' orders. Afraid of their soldiers' discontent, a group of Amin's most trusted, and brutal, commanders confronted him. Public Safety Unit head Col Ali Towelli, Lt Col Juma of the Malire Mechanised Regiment, the commanders of the Paratroopers and Command Regiments and 20 other senior officers presented themselves at the Command Post and asked Amin to step down.

Amin gave the officers short shrift. Five of them were marched off to the Nile Hotel where, according to Amin, they were put under 'low grade house arrest as a precautionary measure against possible mutiny.'

But mutiny there was already. A list of soldiers' demands calling for comprehensive reforms within the Armed Forces and a countrywide reconstruction policy in consultation with civilians and international bodies was delivered to the Defence Council. Four Uganda journalists were arrested after being found with leaflets demanding Amin's resignation attributed to 'civilians of Uganda and military rank-and-file.'

Amin swung into effect the only counter-measure he knew. His Praetorian guard of Kakwas, Nubians and Arabs relentlessly sought out the ringleaders and middle-ranking soldiers known to bear a grudge against the leadership. The effect rippled through the forces, leaving an estimated 1200 soldiers and civil servants dead. The threat of war with Kenya was all too convenient a ploy Amin had found effective in the past—danger from without distracted attention from dangers within—It also enabled him to string troops out along the border and reduce the effectiveness of any possible mass revolt.

Libya sent Big Daddy a new set of bullet-proof vests and a British electronics company processed a Uganda order for a powerful, mobile broadcasting station which would be fitted into eight bullet-proof Land Rovers. The order said the electronic equipment would be used to find underground radios operated in Uganda by opponents of Idi Amin and to intercept other relevant information on the air as and when necessary.

Aware that the equipment could give critical strategic advantage to the beleaguered Uganda regime by broadcasting normal programmes and bulletins in the event of popular uprising British Liberal Party leader David Steel pressed for a Board of Trade investigation and ultimate suspension of the contract. To which the suppliers replied: 'We are in business not politics and we have the highest respect for Amin. We will meet our commercial committment.'

The radio equipment was to come under the responsibility of the State Research Bureau.

By dint of Amin's experience of opposition, the newest was snuffed out. The key to his personal survival was that the assassination attempts were always betrayed by friends of the plotters. 'It has taken us a long time to realise Amin has a hard corps around him loyal to him and him alone,' said one a surviving dissenter. Amin himself accused the American CIA of 'engineering an attempt on his life.' The plan went everywhere, through the churches, through other organisations and everything, but I came to discover this. Anyone cooperating with the American Intelligence Agency will 'face trial by military tribunal and execution by firing squad.' Amin inexplicably released seven men he said were implicated in the Nsambya grenade attack, including an Army sergeant, a government commissioner of veterinary services, a south western district administrator, an official of the Ministry of Culture and a Kenyan identified by name as Macharia Kamau.

Amin chose to announce the alleged assassins' release during an hour-long speech at Entebbe Cricket Club. 'I know they did not plan to assassinate me of their own accord but because they had been bought by certain non-Africans,' Amin said.

'Ugandans must stop hating the Army,' he continued. 'It was the Army which saved them from the Israeli invasion. Ugandans must love the Uganda Army and stop writing anonymous documents asking me to resign—or else such people will be taught a lesson by the

231

Army they will never forget.'

STUDENTS were moving from Lumumba Hall to Freedom Square when the first soldiers arrived at the campus. The square slowly filled. The protest demonstration was to have climaxed with speeches by black, white and scarlet-robed student leaders. In all 900 students had gathered when the cordon of troops closed in on Freedom Square.

More than 100 students were brought down by quick volleys fired straight at them. Pandemonium. Panic. The soldiers advanced, bayonets drawn.

CHAPTER XIV

'The emancipation of Africa is being gravely harmed by one man—President Idi Amin of Uganda. He is the worst visitation by one individual that Africa has had in living memory. It is an unhappy circumstance that pits one black man against another, but the truth has to be faced bluntly: Idi Amin is an unmitigated disaster for the entire continent.'

Wole Soyinka.

'War is the only answer,' declared Idi Amin Dada, life president of Uganda. 'The fire has been lit in the liberation struggle and will continue and intensify. The freedom fighters in Southern Africa must redouble their efforts to regain their lands on the battlefield.'

Few Africans disagreed with that. For most the sooner whites were dislodged from Rhodesia, Namibia and South Africa by force of arms the better. In the eyes of independent Africa the sub-continent stood for all that was left of the bad old days—colonial oppression, injustice, racism.

'Kill them all—all the Europeans in Rhodesia, whether they hide in homes, trees, rivers or jungles,' Amin said. 'War is war. Zimbabweans must take over the land of those Europeans, and have 100 per cent control of their motherland.'

That was almost palatable too—even if it was a somewhat extreme solution.

Amin turned down an invitation to Johannesburg from South African boxing promoter Jaap de Villiers. 'I will never go to that part of Africa until it has been totally liberated and the people who are killing our African brothers and sisters have run away into the sea.

'Freedom fighters must fight a suicide war against the minority regimes in their countries and must be prepared to die right from the beginning. Africans must show the criminal reactionaries their courage and determination to be free.'

A draft resolution circulated by Uganda at the United Nations bid the Security Council expel South Africa, then take punitive action-embracing the use of force—if that country did not revoke apartheid. 'It is the sacred duty of the United Nations Security Council to live up to its obligations and dignity and deliver a just and long overdue judgement by removing the seeds of this evil that threaten the very existence and usefulness of our organisation.'

Amin harked back to the combined African invasion force for southern Africa. 'The time has come for freedom fighters to abandon guerrilla tactics against fascist regimes because this strategy has not yielded good results.' Uganda would contribute seven regiments to the combined force. 'South Africa is too strong for guerrilla tactics. It has fighter planes which go at 2000 miles an hour and it is impossible for guerrilla fighters to cope with such things.

'Once we have liberated the people they must elect a president instead of letting power hungry individuals cause bloodshed.

'I am fed up with all this talking. Palestinians and Africans are living under trees and in trenches because of imperialism. African states must cross the River Zambezi (into Rhodesia) like Egypt courageously crossed the Suez Canal.'

Big Daddy staged another mock attack at Bulingugwe Island in Lake Victoria. This time it was a less showy affair than the capture of Cape Town. 'The Capture of Johannesburg' was spearheaded by the Suicide Regiment supported by police and prison officers. 'South African' forces were caught off-guard enjoying an afternoon siesta lulled by a cool breeze and warm sunshine.

Amin said 'I am very impressed by the accuracy of our shooting because there have been no casualties during the exercise.'

It was Rhodesia that went on the offensive, however. After Rhodesian forces crossed into Mozambique to attack guerrilla bases there Amin decided to send Air Force Commander Lt Col Sule to assess how Uganda could assist Mozambicans against unwarranted aggression by the illegal racist regime of Prime Minister Ian Smith. Amin's munificence cut little ice with Mozambique President Samora Machel. But Amin named a Ugandan air base after himself and kept bombers and MiG fighters on alert all the same.

'Africa is more than ready in terms of material resources and manpower to fight these international bandits who are continuing to occupy the African territory illegally. All peace-loving countries should give more military assistance to the freedom fighters'.

Amin turned north. Egypt had hoped he would not attend the Afro-Arab summit conference in March 1977. But there he was, larger than life in a neatly-tailored khaki safari suit and Cowboy hat, bouncing down the steps of his executive jet at Cairo. President Sadat had greeted other African visitors and left the airport. The photographers had gone too. Amin donned his blue Air Force uniform and medals for the meeting.

'There are no prisons in Uganda,' he said, tapping the rostrum emphatically. 'We all live in peace and security. Uganda is clean and its people have prosperity.'

The conference listened glumly. No prisons, only slaughter houses.

'How many enemies does Black Africa have now?

Black Africa has only two: Rhodesia and South Africa.'

Some of the delegates reflected bitterly, however, that Amin had miscounted. He was Africa's third enemy.

THE announcer read the 10 a.m. news bulletin on Thursday, February 17. 'A government spokesman has announced with regret the death of the Minister of Land and Water Resources Lt Col Orenayo Oryema, the Minister of Internal Affairs Mr Charles Oboth-Ofumbi and the Archbishop of Uganda, Rwanda, Burundi and Boga-Zaire the Most Reverend Janani Luwum, after being involved in a motor accident yesterday in Kampala. The three men were being driven away from the Kampala International Conference Centre by Major Moses for interrogation of their involvement in a plan to cause chaos in the country. The spokesman said the accident occured when the three men were trying to overcome Major Moses in order to escape. Major Moses was taken to hospital where he is still unconscious.'

A later bulletin expanded the story. The Range Rover in which three were being taken for questioning hit a second car only a few hundred yards from the Conference Centre, slid across the street and overturned. Its roof caved in. When the Archbishop and the two ministers were pulled from the wreckage they were already dead. Post mortem examinations showed Luwum died from a ruptured liver and lung, Oboth Ofumbi cranial bleeding due to internal brain damage and Oryema from internal bleeding and extensive brain damage caused by a fractured skull. Oryema's chest was completely crushed.

The radio quoted Amin: 'The accident was a punishment of God because God does not want the others to suffer.'

The day before the three men had been publicly accused of involvement in a plot to overthrow him. It was a bizarre spectacle on the lawn of the Nile Hotel. A pile of Chinese weapons and ammunition was on display. About 3,000 troops had assembled. The Archbishop and ministers had been summoned to the rally. Three trembling prisoners were pushed in front of the crowd. An attempt to kill Amin was to have taken place on January 25, the sixth anniversary of his own coup, they confessed. Archbishop Luwum held the golden cross hanging against his purple robe and shook his head as his name was read out in a letter—a letter which was purported to have come from Milton Obote.

'What shall we do with these people?' called Amin's vice president General Mustafa Adrisi. 'What shall we do with them?'

'Kill them' shouted the troops. 'Kill them now!'

Shortly afterwards Luwum, Oboth Ofumbi and Oryema were under arrest.

Nearly a fortnight earlier the Archbishop's home near Namirembe had been searched for weapons. In a written report of the incident, sent to Amin as part of a formal protest, Luwum said he had been woken by the barking of his dog at about 1:30 a.m. on Saturday, February 5. 'The fence had been broken down and I knew some people had come into the compound. I walked downstairs very quietly without switching any lights on and as usual I stopped at the door.' Luwum drew aside the door curtain and saw Ben Ongom, whom he knew, standing outside. Ongom, his face bruised and cut, cried for help.

'I opened the door and immediately these armed men who had been hiding sprang on me, cocking their rifles and shouting: "Archbishop, Archbishop, show us the arms." I replied: "What arms?" They replied: "There are arms in this house". I said: "No".'

The men pushed into the house and their leader, a Nubian speaking in Arabic, jabbed his rifle into the archbishop's stomach. Luwum was frisked.

'(The leader) pushed me with the rifle shouting: "Walk, run, show us the arms, take us to your bedroom." So we went up to our bedroom where Mary my wife was asleep. We woke her up and they began crawling underneath the bed. They opened the ward-

237

robe, climbing right up into the upper deck of the cupboard. They searched the bedroom thoroughly looking in suitcases, boxes etc. but finding nothing. They proceeded to search the children's bedrooms repeating the same exercise of searching thoroughly everywhere.'

Ongom, now handcuffed, told the Archbishop he had been found with ammunition. 'You see, sometime back we brought some ammunition and divided it up with Mr Olobo who works in the Ministry of Labour in Kampala. I kept some and Mr Olobo kept some. Now mine has been found and certainly because of involving myself in politics I am going to die in any case for it,' Ongom said.

Ongom, it transpired, had led the search party to Olobo's home and then to the house of a fellow Acholi, Dr Lalobo, the medical superintendent at Mengo Hospital. Nothing had been found but both were arrested.

'I suggested to the security men that Dr Lalobo might have transferred the ammunition to the Archbishop's house. This is why we have come to you,' Ongom told Luwum desperately. 'Please help us. If the arms are not here, tell us the location in any Acholi or Langi homes at Namirembe so they may be searched.'

'...We pray for the President. We pray for the security forces—whatever they do,' replied the Archbishop. 'We preach the gospel and pray for others. That is our work, not keeping arms.'

The search went on.

'They demanded we open the study,' Luwum wrote. 'They searched there. We opened the chapel. They searched there, even looking underneath the Holy Table. They searched the food stores putting their hands into sacks of sim-sim, millet, groundnuts trying to feel for hidden objects. We went to the guest wing. They searched through the toilets, bathrooms, etc. They searched the cars parked in the compound.

'My neighbours, Bishop Kauma and the Provincial Secretary had rung Old Kampala Police Station when

238

they saw there were men with arms in our compound thinking they were robbers. When the police came these men sent them away before they entered the compound. At about 3:00 a.m. these men left. They requested we open the gate for them to go out but my wife suggested they should go the way they came. I said we were Christians . . . we had clean hearts. We would open the gates for them. They left and entered their cars which they had parked down the road. The number plates were covered.'.

Archbishop Luwum possessed a telephone number— Kampala 2241—which he had been told would reach Amin at any time of day or night. He finally got through at 9:00 a.m.—but was asked by the operator to call back an hour later because the President was busy with visitors. The operator fobbed him off a second time. Amin had gone out with his visitors and would not be contactable by phone. Could the archbishop leave a message?

Luwum telephoned vice president Adrisi at home. He was out, too. 'Later on I managed to get Col Maliyamungu. I told him of the incident including the doctor's arrest and other arrests. He let me speak to the Vice President. I spoke in Swahili. He comforted me and assured me that he would call the people concerned and follow the matter up.'

The Archbishop heard nothing more from Adrisi. That evening Amin's security men visited the Bishop of Bukedi, the Rt Rev Yona Okoth. Not feeling well, Bishop Okoth had gone to bed after evening prayers. 'At about 10:00 p.m. my aunt reported two cars full of people near my home. They seemed agitated and were carrying guns. I got up and welcomed them.'

This time Ben Ongom was in chains. The security men asked to search the Bishop's house.

'Do you think I am having arms? Is that my work? Are you mentally disturbed? I do not know what you are talking about,' said Bishop Okoth.

'How many men do you have here?'

'A watchman and my driver.'

'How many arms do you have?'

'I have a rifle and a shot-gun which I use for shooting animals and birds. I possess the necessary legal documents.'

Bishop Okoth's house was ransacked. 'At once they scattered over the house, searching everywhere but finding nothing. They went into the sitting room, the food store, the bedrooms. At one point they found a large package. My new water pump had arrived and was still unpacked. They tore it open but found nothing. They searched and searched—every corner of the house. Then they heard noise. One of the men shouted: 'There are many people here.' I said: 'Take a lamp, go and see.' They came back and reported they had found only cows.

'We are sorry we have to do this, but we have been given a directive from our boss,' the leader said. 'We are sorry but we shall have to take you.'

'I am not afraid. If it is death for me it is the gateway to the Lord. If life, I will continue preaching the gospel,' said Okoth.

The Bishop was driven to Tororo in eastern Uganda. To his second house. 'We reached Tororo at 6:30 in the morning. Ben Ongom was left in the car. The others came into my house and began to search everywhere. They read through all my correspondence. When they found a game mentioning the word weapon they were elated until I explained it was only a game.'

At last, the men completed their search—but warned the Bishop not to talk of the incident.

'They shook my hand and said I was a free man. They returned my shot-gun and rifle. They cautioned me again not to spread the news. 'Go on working normally' they said. I replied: 'These are not normal times, if you suspect me, a man dealing in spiritual matters, what of others?' As they left people were already beginning to go on their way to Church and they wondered what was happening at the Bishop's house.'

The following Tuesday the House of Bishops of the Church of Uganda, Rwanda, Burundi and Boga-Zaire met at Namirembe under the chairmanship of Archbishop Luwum and drafted a letter to Field Marshal Amin. 'We...humbly beg to submit our most deeply felt concern for the Church and the welfare of the people whom we serve under your care.

'In presenting this statement we are in no way questioning the right of the Government in administering justice, to search and arrest offenders. We believe that Government has established structures and procedures for carrying out this kind of exercise. These structures and procedures give the police, the intelligence and security forces a framework within which to work. When these procedures are followed in carrying out their day to day duties this gives the ordinary citizen a sense of security. It creates mutual friendship and trust between such officers and the general public irrespective of uniform. But when the police and security officers deviate... in carrying out their day to day duties citizens become insecure, afraid and disturbed. They begin to distrust these officers.

'Your Excellency, you have said publicly on many occasions that Religious leaders have a special place in this country and that you treat them with respect for what they stand for and represent...

'The gun whose muzzle has been pressed against the Archbishop's stomach, the gun which has been used to search the Bishop of Bukedi's houses is a gun which is being pointed at every Christian in the Church, unless Your Excellency can give us something new to change this situation.

'The security of the ordinary Christian has been in jeopardy for quite a long time. It may be that what has happened to the Archbishop and the Bishop of Bukedi is a climax of what is consistently happening to our Christians. We have buried many who have died as a result of being shot and there are many more whose bodies have not been found, yet their disappearance is connected with the activities of some members of the Security Forces. Your Excellency, if it is required we can give concrete evidence of what is happening because widows and orphans are members of our Church.'

241

Other concerns of the churchmen were that Ugandan Muslims in powerful positions were coercing Christians into adopting the Islamic faith; that the killing of educated Ugandans had forced many to flee and subsequent fear had made the country's progress and stability impossible; suspicion and hidden hatred had destroyed the last vestige of mutual trust between civilians and soldiers.

'The gun which was meant to protect Uganda as a nation, the Uganda as a citizen and his property, is increasingly being used against the Ugandan to take away his life and his property. For instance many cars, almost daily are being taken away at gun point and their owners killed. And most of the culprits are never brought to justice. If required we can enumerate many cases. Too much power has been given to members of State Research who arrest and kill at will innocent civilians. Therefore, that which was meant to provide the Ugandan citizen with security is becoming the means of his insecurity.'

Luwum and the 18 Anglican clergy who signed the letter pointed to the growing gap between Church and state. 'We had been assured by you of your ready availability to religious leaders whenever they had serious matters to discuss with you. You had even gone to the extent of giving His Grace, the Archbishop, the surest means of contacting you in this country wherever you may be. But a situation has developed now where you have become more and more inaccessible and even when he tried to write he has not received any reply.

'While you, Your Excellency, have stated on the national radio that your government is not under any foreign influence and that your decisions are guided by your Defence Council and Cabinet the general trend of things in Uganda has created a feeling that the affairs of our nation are being directed by outsiders who do not have the welfare of this country and the value of the lives and properties of Ugandans at their heart. A situation like this breeds unnecessary misunderstanding. Indeed, we were shocked to hear over the radio on Christmas

242

Day Your Excellency saying that some Bishops had preached bloodshed. We waited anxiously to be called by Your Excellency to clarify such a situation, but all in vain.'

Archbishop Luwum had signed his own death warrant. The letter was typed and copied, ready for distribution on Thursday February 10. On Sunday, a British newspaper reported that Amin had uncovered a plot against him and unleashed a savage purge against Christian Acholi and Langi tribesmen during which Luwum had been questioned.

According to the report the assassination of Amin was to have been carried out on January 25, Amin's coup celebrations and hundreds of suspects had been seized and massacred. On Sunday evening Amin telephoned Luwum—not to consult him, but to scold him. He demanded to see the Archbishop at State House, Entebbe in the morning.

Radio Uganda reported the meeting at length.

Amin told Luwum 11 crates containing automatic weapons, ammunition and grenades sent to Uganda for Obote-backed plotters had been found by a group of schoolchildren near the Archbishop's house after the security search.

The frame-up was easy.

'Four people who were arrested with some of the arms and ammunition confessed that they were destined and confined only to the Langis and Acholis with the aim of destroying the property and killing all the people of the other tribes,' said the radio. 'Dr Amin told the Archbishop that among the many people in Uganda included in Obote's plans was the Archbishop himself as confessed by those who were arrested. He said that after learning of the Archbishop's involvement in the plan an order was given to security forces to go and carry out a thorough search of his residence at Namirembe.'

Security men had been directed to the Archbishop's house by Ben Owong, Abdalla Ayulu, former chairman of the Public Service Commission, both Langis, and two other conspirators, both Acholis. Another arms cache had been found at a Gulu lodge and the manager and owner of the lodge were shot dead while resisting arrest.

The British newspaper had reported that an unknown number of bodies had been loaded into Army trucks at Gulu and tipped into the Nile at Karuma Falls. Prison service trucks collected the bodies of another 116 Gulu civilians.

A further arms cache, Amin claimed, had been captured near the house of Bishop Okoth at Tororo. Bishop Okoth was responsible for receiving armaments and transporting them to Archbishop Luwum. 'He is at the border where the arms from Dar es Salaam through Nairobi can easily be channeled.

'The aim behind the whole affair was that Obote wanted the Langi and Acholi to have full control of the whole country through churches, parastatal bodies and other key bodies.'

Amin warned Luwum that as soon as investigations were over, a public rally would be held so that Ugandans could judge the evidence themselves. 'Even if Obote would not have succeeded he wanted to see all big people in the country, particularly those in key positions, killed. Documents have also disclosed all the major engineers of the plan are to be found in Kenya, Zambia, Tanzania and other countries abroad. According to those arrested Obote's plan got the full support of the Israelis and President Julius Nyerere of Tanzania.'

The weapons, Amin added, were originally intended for Southern Africa liberation movements but were diverted for use against Uganda. 'God did not want bloodshed and saved us. You must forget all these selfish subversive activities and preach the word of God. Pray for peace in the country. We will keep cool and calm, but should never be mistaken to be sleeping.'

Archbishop Luwum fought back. The allegations had left him speechless at first.

'It is quite clear Ben Ongom...was acting under duress and torture that if he did not find the arms he was going to die that night.'

Amin's men had provided no proof that weapons had

been found near his house—or that children had found
them on the night of the search or the following day. 'If
school children came to our house with the Security men
and found the arms I was not present on that day, but
still, none of our family including the servant told us of
any further searching team with children anywhere near
our place . . . For the sake of myself and the Church that
lead I would like more concrete evidence about these
serious and far reaching allegations.

'Many of our people in Uganda have either fled the
country or been liquidated on baleless allegations such
as this.'

The house of Bishops fought back. It was futile now.
On the day of Luwum's death it drafted its response at a
meeting at the Kampala conference centre. 'Our Church
does not believe nor does it teach its members the use of
destructive weapons. We believe in the life-giving love of
Christ, we proclaim that love to all without fear. We
speak publicly and in private against all evil, all
corruption, all misuse of power, all maltreatment of
human beings. We rejoice in the truth, because truth
builds up a nation, but we are determined to refuse all
falsehood, all false accusations which damage the lives
of our people and spoil the image of our country.'

Archbishop Luwum and the two ministers, almost
certainly were shot a very short time after their arrest.
Not so certain is where the shootings took place.

One supposition is that after the Nile Hotel Rally
broke up. Colonel Maliyamungu stepped in front of the
microphone and told the soldiers and government
representatives to make their way to the nearby
conference centre where Life President Amin would
address them.

Archbishop Luwum was led to room 270, Amin's
permanent suite on the second floor of the Nile Hotel.
Oryema and Oboth Ofumbi had already been taken to
the suite, and were seated. Luwum took the sofa
opposite Amin.

The two men were face to face.

'You have prayed for peace in Uganda,' Amin raged.

'It shows something was going to take place. You knew there was going to be bloodshed in Uganda.'

'I have always prayed for peace in Uganda.'

'Admit you knew about this plot then the matter will end here.'

'I have nothing to do with the arms and I say once again I am not involved.'

'We were led to your house. You preached: God should save the people of Uganda from bloodshed.'

Archbishop Luwum began praying, his words just audible. Amin drew his pistol and fired into Luwum's face. The first shot hit the Archbishop in the mouth as he was lowering his head and turning sideways. The second tore into his shoulder and a third missed as Luwum spun backwards with the impact. Amin's guards rushed into the suite, training their rifles on Oreyema and Oboth Ofumbi. Amin jumped up, walked to the telephone and dialled.

'I have lost my temper. I have shot the Archbishop. Do something.' It was a little after 5:00 p.m. Amin crossed to the Conference Centre where some of the soldiers at the earlier meeting had gathered and for half an hour spoke of the 'evil influence' of the Ugandan Church.

Oreyema, Oboth-Ofumbi and Luwum, bleeding profusely but still alive, were shoved into a car by State Research officers and driven to Lubiri, the barracks of Malire Regiment while the 'road accident' was being staged using two already damaged Government cars.

In the early hours of Thursday morning the bodies of Archbishop Luwum and the two ministers arrived at Mulago mortuary in the back of an Army truck. Soldiers guarded the mortuary. The first civilians to see the bodies were a duty doctor and nurse at Mulago. Bishop Festo Kivingere of Kigezi said the two Mulago staff had confirmed the 'accident' victims had been shot. 'One of our Bishops spoke to the nurse who said she had seen the Archbishop's body with two bullet holes in his chest and blood in his mouth. An hour or so after that we heard from the doctor who had managed to see the bodies while the guards were being changed.'

Fearing for his own life after the murder of Luwum and his two cabinet colleagues, Health Minister Henry Kyemba fled Uganda and corroborated that the three had been shot 'at very close range.'

The Health Ministry promised church leaders Luwum's body would be handed over for a traditional burial service at Namirembe Cathedral on Sunday. However, Amin detailed the Army to bury all three victims on Saturday. Luwum was interred at his home village near Kitgum in East Acholi district, Oryema on his farm in West Acholi and Oboth Ofumbi at his village 20 miles from Tororo. Each hasty ceremony was attended only by the soldiers and small huddles of mourners.

At Oryema's burial, armed soldiers warned the mourners not to show outward signs of grief.

In Kampala troops, sealed off Namirembe Hill.

The murders shocked even those who had become blase about Amin. In Nairobi the All Africa Conference of Churches declared: 'Member churches and churches throughout the world are urged to press their governments to censure and isolate the Uganda government for its flagrant violation of human rights . . . and campaign of terror unleashed against Christians. We cannot afford to remain silent while the regime in Kampala persists in sabotaging Africa's legitimate struggle against the tyranny of minority white rule on our continent. Archbishop Luwum is one more victim of the wave of killing in Uganda against which the AACC has consistently protested.'

The cancellation of the Archbishop's Namireme funeral was proof—'if any proof were needed'—of the Uganda government's 'cover-up'.

'Even the racist and minority regimes in Rhodesia or South Africa are not as callous in their treatment of the dead or of their bereaved loved ones. How much longer will the people of Uganda have to endure the tyranny of the Amin regime. Will Africa do nothing? Will the rest of the world do nothing?'

The National Christian Council of Kenya, Nairobi said: 'We wish to remind the government of Uganda that the cry of the blood of martyrs has reached the ears of God.'

Radio Tanzania, Dar es Salaam: 'Thousands of innocent Ugandans have been found floating in the River Nile in what the dictator and butcher Amin calls accidents....If Black African states condemn white minority rule they must also condemn atrocities committed in black ruled states.'

The World Council of Churches, Geneva, radio Tanzania added 'This is one more in the series of brutal events which have characterised a six-year reign of terror in which thousands have been summarily killed.'

The Church Board for World Ministries went on: 'Outrages against human beings in Africa whether perpetrated by whites or blacks cannot be accepted by the Christian conscience.'

The International Commission of Jurists, Geneva condemned: 'The pretence that they were killed in a motor accident will deceive no-one. This latest act of arbitrary violence gives added urgency to the case for an impartial investigation of the United Nations Commission of Human Rights of the consistent pattern of gross violation in Uganda.

US Ambassador the UN Andrew Young, New York thought: '...in a case like the assassination of the archbishop under the guise of an automobile accident in Uganda—as well as the reported 18th police prisoner jumping out of a window in South Africa—that kind of conduct by a government—the world knows better than that.'

Hundreds more messages flashed around the world.

From Dar es Salaam Milton Obote flatly denied he had been behind a coup attempt involving Luwum, Oboth Ofumbi and Oryema. The letter read by the aged and frail Abdalla Anyuru implicating them at the Nile Hotel rally was 'a concocted document'.

Kyemba said it was written on Amin's own official

notepaper. Said an Obote aide in Tanzania: 'Our information is that Anyuru was arrested on January 31 and thoroughly tortured. We sent no arms to Uganda. We had thousands of them (Chinese arms) when we were in power.'

From Nairobi the All Africa Conference of Churches wrote off to the then-secretary General of the Arab League, Egyptian vice president Mahmoud Riad. It appealed to Islamic states holding sway with Amin to help end all forms of persecution in Uganda. The consequences of the Archbishop Luwum's murder, and the massacre of Christians by Ugandan Muslims from the beginning of Amin's rule, endangered the relations between Muslims and Christians throughout Africa and jeopardised Afro-Arab collaboration.

'Muslims and Christians share a common veneration for sanctity of human life. Both religious traditions belong to Africa. It is therefore impossible to reconcile current events in Uganda with authentic Islamic or Christian teaching; just as it is not possible to see how such tragic happenings will contribute to the peace and solidarity between our two regions which are so essential to the success of the struggles for liberation that our peoples are today waging.'

It looked as though the international outcry was having some effect. Amin cabled the OAU and Arab League to say Uganda was calm despite exaggerated reports of recent events and a campaign of lies by the All Africa Conference of Churches. 'Any government is welcome to send a delegation to Uganda to see for themselves what has taken place.'

Britain and the United States called on the UN Human Rights Commission to take up Amin's offer at once—and UN Secretary General Waldheim sought clarification of it through Uganda UN ambassador Kinene. In Washington President Jimmy Carter deduced that the Uganda murders had disgusted the entire civilised world.

Within two weeks Amin had changed his mind about the international investigation. Speaking at the Afro-

Arab summit in Cairo on March 8 he said foreign observers would be barred from entering Uganda. 'There is no cause for alarm in Uganda. What happens is a car accident, like thousands of people are killed in New York. Somebody dies in a car. This is a police case, not a United Nations case.

'Uganda is a friend of all religions.

'There are no atrocities in Uganda. People guilty of crimes are tried according to the law. Sixteen people are in prison in connection with a plot to cause chaos. The masses asked for these people to be executed immediately but I did not want this.

'Do people talk about the British killing Catholics in Northern Ireland, the butchering of Palestinians by Israel, the assassination of President Kennedy, the massacres by the Americans of Red Indians, Blacks, Vietnamese and the Japanese at Hiroshima? They talk only about Amin because Amin is strong.'

But no matter how much he believed himself, time was running out for Idi Amin Dada.

HE was a Christian, and lived on the Jinja Road. A Public Safety Unit Land Rover drew up outside the house; four uniformed men, one of them a sergeant.

'You have stolen a pair of bedsheets from your master, Captain Sebi. Bring then now,' said the sergeant.

He had been told to throw away the old, torn sheets but he had kept them with a thought of mending them for himself.

'*Wewe Kondo! Lala Chini!*' the sergeant shouted (You are a robber! Lie down!)

The men kicked him to the ground. Two of them sat on his legs and chest. The sergeant put a knife to his neck.

'Bismillahi,' said the sergeant. (Bismillahi Rahmani Rahiim: In the name of God the Most Merciful the most forgiving...)

'We say Bismillahi only when killing an animal for food,' remonstrated one of the Nubian soldiers.

'King Faisal presented our president with a sword to spread Islam,' replied the sergeant. 'Whenever we kill the enemy of Islam with the sword or knife we must say it!'

The sergeant slashed with the knife until the jerking body lay still. Cutting at the neck he wrenched the head until it was severed.

'They loaded the body into the vehicle, leaving the head on the ground,' said an eyewitness. 'One man placed the head upright and then brought a cup of tea from a tray in the house. He placed the cup near the mouth as if the man was drinking from it. They went to find the man's wife and told her: "See your husband taking tea." They took the head, put it into the vehicle and drove off.'

More than 200 corpses were discovered at Mabira Forest between Kampala and Jinja. Most of the dead were Acholis and Langis.

A soldier had died in a skirmish with coffee smugglers on the banks of Lake Victoria. Army reinforcements ferried a group of suspected smugglers to Kigulu Island, tied them down, covered them with sacks, doused them with petrol and set them alight. The wife of a Langi soldier saw her husband arrested by military police. 'They came back and started rounding up children and their mothers very roughly and pushing them into a lorry.'

Bodies floated in Luzira shipyard.

Three senior academics at Makerere University—one of them Oboth Ofumbi's brother—disappeared. Senior civil servant, John Male, under-secretary in the Ministry of Culture Mark Sebaliba and the director of the Uganda National Theatre Dan Kintu were shot after the production of Male's play 'The Office Is Empty', seen to imply Uganda did not have a popular leader. Kintu replaced Byron Kawadwa as National Theatre director. Kawadwa's body had been found in the wreckage of a burned-out car in Kampala.

Tororo farmer John Kasule was injected with a massive overdose of lethal drugs by three soldiers who

251

had ransacked a nearby clinic.

Geoffrey Mugabi, one-time youth winger in Obote's Uganda People's Congress party, was arrested at Kisenyi Kampala in mid-February and jailed at Makindye. 'When we got to Makindye they asked us: What are your preparations with Obote to overthrow the government? We said we did not know anything and we did not know where Obote was.

'On February 18 at 9:00 a.m. the Commanding Officer of the military police and other officers came and registered all the prisoners by name, tribe and occupation. At 2:00 p.m. many military lorries came carrying soldiers who had been arrested. They were put into rooms C and D we knew as the elimination chambers. At 3:30 Military Police came to cells in block B and called out names. All those whose names were called were taken to rooms C and D.

'During the night of the killings we did not hear any gun shots. Only some thudding noise came from the adjoining rooms. You could hear a short cry and then silence. I think they were being strangled and then their heads were smashed.' Mugabi was one of the prisoners forced to load some of the battered corpses onto an Army lorry.

He was released after lying to the Commanding Officer that he had been arrested for 'refusing to allow some soldiers to take my girl away.'

Robert Kamau among eight Kenyans arrested for 'spying' on April 9, was thrown into Kololo Hill prison. At 5 o'clock one evening a group of about 100 people were brought to the prison.

'Through the cracks and keyholes in our cell we watched in horror as each was tied up and battered to death with a hammer. The murders were committed by a large group of soldiers who were not in uniform. Each victim was hit 18 to 20 times. The bodies were unrecognisable . . . they were pulp. It took a long time. The killings went on until about 10 p.m. and everything was quiet again. We don't know what happened to all those bodies.' The following day another 80 people were brought in. 'Some of the soldiers were youngsters. This time there were two women among those murdered. They were hit on the head with hammers . . . again and again.'

Kamau said the Kenyans planned their escape after being forewarned of their execution. 'We had nothing to lose . . . the last-ditch plan was to try and somehow overpower one of the soldiers and get his gun. But first we tried to cut the wire grid on our cell window. We used everything we had. It was a tedious job. It took a whole afternoon to cut the inside wire. A belt buckle was the most useful tool we had. To remove the outer wire was even more difficult, especially because the job was being done at night when the guards could easily detect the noise.'

JOHN Sekabira had been in detention for more than a year. For the latter part of his detention he was held at Murchison Bay prison where, he said, vacant land just beyond the prison fence was used for mass burials. Of one burial detail he said: 'We were taken to a military land rover . . . in it were 12 people all badly beaten and obviously dying. Some had their hands chopped off, others were wearing military uniforms of the Uganda Air Force. The driver started the engine and drove for a few yards. We were told to start digging graves for the bodies. The whole area was full of skulls and human bones, many of them newly buried. After digging two big graves we were told to start putting the bodies in. Nine of the people were dead but three were still alive. One asked the military officers what the people had done. They told me that they were thieves. For our work we were all given a packet of cigarettes. Not even two days had passed before the military police came again. This time they were in a big lorry almost full of bodies. This time I did not go to the burial but those who did told me the dead were all well-dressed people.'

On March 1 a purge of both officers and inmates at Murchison Bay and nearby Luzira Prison began. 'At 3:00 p.m. on that day State Research men arrived with heavy machine guns and a list of those they wanted. They ordered everybody to sit down and told them anybody trying to run away would be shot. The first man on the list was Mr Okurut, senior superintendent of prisons and the officer in charge of Murchison Bay, followed by another senior superintendent Mr Kataba-zi. Principal Officer Ondong was shot dead when he tried to run.'

Later, Sekabira and about twenty other prisoners were taken by motorboat to a Lake Victoria island off Port Bell, south west of Kampala where a beach party was being arranged, complete with a band for police, prisons and army officers. 'Colonel Maliyamungu came with State Research Officers and said there were still some bad elements and those elements would not leave the island alive. Major Faruk, officer in charge of State Research Bureau produced a list of 150 names of prisons army and police officers.

The listed personnel present were shot, and then buried by the prisoners, Sekabira said. Amin arrived on the island, inspected the graves . . . and led singing and dancing. Sekabira was released after serving a 21 month sentence on unspecified charges.

The head of Uganda's Muslim faith Chief Kadhi Sheikh Yusuf Matovu had presided over the wedding ceremony of Vice President Mustafa Adrisi's daughter Toma at Arua in West Nile. Near Karuma, about 40 miles north of Kampala, ambushers sprayed the car with gunfire. Its driver killed at the wheel, the car careened out of control. The Chief Kadhi was taken to Mulago with multiple injuries, including a ruptured bladder. The back of Muslim Supreme Council secretary Hadji Kaliisa was broken in the crash. A highly placed Uganda official was to say later: 'A certain army lieutenant colonel, himself a religious fanatic, wanted him killed so that he could take over the Kadhi mantle.'

On March 7, a detachment of Nubian troops arrived at Kabamba barracks in western Uganda, seeking out Christian officers. Three Protestant majors—Onyaiti, Zozo and Kliza—were shot. In the south-Western

Masaka coffee producing area, Christian owned farms and businesses were taken over—and about 300 Christian civilians arrested. Truckloads of Christian property and building-materials were driven north of West Nile, southern Sudan and eastern Zaire. Uganda Air Force planes bombed forest land near Mutukulu and the Tanzania border after what was officially described as a running battle between Amin's Masaka-based Mechanised Brigade and suspected coffee smugglers. Sixteen suspects—all Baganda Christians—were reported by the Army to have been killed in the action.

On March 17, Amin called Uganda's Anglican bishops to an 'emergency meeting' in Kampala. 'I am not anti-Christ in any way,' he said. 'I will never allow the Church to die.' Ten bishops attended the meeting—the other eight signatories of the House of Bishops protest letter had fled into hiding or exile. A white man among them, Rt. Rev. Brian Herd, Bishop of Karamoja, had been deported.

The Bishop of Madi and West Nile Silvanus Wani was announced as Archbishop Luwum's successor.

The Anglican Church postponed its centenary celebrations set for June 30. Before Luwum's death the church had annoyed Amin by stopping him interfering with arrangements for the centenary—particularly with a gift of Mercedes cars and money from West German churches intended for the celebrations. Amin wanted the cars for the government's run-down fleet; he wanted details of the sizeable cash donation. The Government subsequently claimed that tin badges advertising the centenary were being sold by the church to raise money for anti-Amin guerrillas. In one recorded incident troops forced a group of Christians to eat the tin badges they were wearing.

'We have no time or money to waste feeding unwanted people in jail. The best way is to get rid of them,' said a Military Police commander.

'I saw my uncle taken from his house,' a Kampala student told social workers of Kenya's Joint Refugees

Services in Nairobi. 'I saw corpses floating in a drain and one in a car just outside our college.'

'In my diocese I did not come across anybody who didn't cry because he lost someone to Amin,' said Bishop Benoni Ogwal, from northern Uganda.

AMIN's personal blood lust had never been in doubt.

For some time Sarah Amin, a dancer and singer in the Suicide Regiment Jazz Band when Big Daddy met her, suspected her husband had had her boyfriend, bandleader Jesse Gitta, murdered. After Amin's wedding to Sarah Gitta had written a satirical song about it.

Moses Aloga worked as a house servant at Amin's Command Post. During a visit to the Command Post Sarah asked Aloga if he knew what was kept in one of two fridges in a room there called the Botanical Room.

'I said I did not know, but thought it was for drinks for the President's important visitors. She was not content with my answer and asked again about the fridge, which she said he had not seen open since she became Amin's wife. She told me she would give me a large sum of money if I would open the fridge for her. I told her that I and another servant, Abud Khalim, were responsible for the key of the fridge and if I opened it for her my life would be in danger.

'But Sarah promised me she would not tell anybody. It would be a secret between us and she promised me a job at her own house (Amin's Cape Town Villas) with a bigger salary. After these big promises I opened the padlock which joined the fridges by a chain. She opened one which contained beer and other drinks. Then she opened the left hand one.

'In it were two heads . . . One was the head of Jesse Gitta. . . . She looked at it . . . for a few moments, then tried to take it out. Her body was trembling. . . . She was crying and sobbing . . . She fell down in a faint.

'The other head was of a woman called Ruth Kobusinje, a beautiful girl who had been coming to Amin and who he suspected was running with other men. One day, when I was cleaning the fridges with Abud we saw Ruth's head there and recognised her as the girl we used to see with Amin.

'I tried to lift Sarah up but couldn't, so I picked up the fridge key and ran out into the main room, forgetting to lock the fridge. It was then about 1:30 in the afternoon. I was afraid of telling the other servants what had happened to Mrs Amin and didn't know what to do.'

Amin walked into the Command Post accompanied by Juma Oris, Lt Col Mondo and Major Faruk.

'In his usual mood Amin asked us if we had had a good day. Then he asked where Mrs Amin was, as he had seen her car and driver outside. I said she was inside but I did not know where. He looked in some of the rooms then looked into the Botanical Room where he found Sarah crying. I heard Amin asking her what was wrong. Then he must have noticed the open fridge because he started to beat her and she was screaming. He came into the main room dragging Sarah behind him, with a pistol in the other hand. He was very very angry.'

Juma Oris tried to calm Amin, but Amin waved the pistol at him.

'Leave me alone,' Amin shouted, hauling at Sarah. 'I will kill you for this. I will kill you for this.'

Aloga ran out of the back door. 'The next day I heard Radio Uganda saying that Mrs Sarah Amin was leaving for Tripoli in Libya where she was going for an operation. I think she went to have her face and body healed after Amin's beating but I cannot be sure.'

Nurse Monica Nansamba worked at Kampala's Nbuya military hospital. She accompanied an Army doctor Captain Mawazi, to Makindye Prison. After treating a number of prisoners the doctor and nurse were approached by an Army colonel and three soldiers.

'He ordered them to go with Captain Mawazi to another place I didn't know. After a few moments I heard gun shots, then Doctor Mawazi came back with his white coat spattered with blood. He said we were going back to Mbuya hospital in a military truck taking with us six bodies the president wanted us to work on very urgently.

'When we reached Mbuya hospital the bodies were taken by the soldiers to the mortuary and the truck went back to Makindye. It was then lunchtime and Captain Mawazi told me to go for my lunch in the officers mess, and that I should come back early because the urgent work for the president had to be done that day. After lunch we went to the operating theatre and Captain Mawazi told the ward maids to bring the bodies from the mortuary. They were covered in blankets.

'One of the dead girls I was shocked to recognize as a school friend of mine, Jane Nansinkombi Kabugo, daughter of Mr Peter Kabugo, a high official in the Information Ministry. She had been the personal secretary of the chairman of the Uganda Development Corporation. Captain Mawazi was also shocked because Peter Kanugo had been a classmate of his at Makerere University. But I was under orders and the job had to be done. It wasn't the first time we had cut heads from dead bodies, which I believed were taken to the Command Post.

'At 3:00 p.m., after the work had been done, I had to shave the heads and applied some liquid spray to preserve them. Captain Mawazi told me he was going to the army headquarters officers mess. When he was gone I locked five of the heads away in the fridge, smuggled out Jane's head in a basket and locked it in the boot of my car. I gave the keys of the fridge to the guard to be handed to Captain Mawazi.'

Nurse Nasamba drove to the home of her school friend's parents. Mrs Kabugo telephoned her husband to return home at once. 'When he arrived I took the basket out of the car and showed them the head . . . In a state of shock Peter Kabugo took the head and said he was going to the president to hand him the head officially as he apparently wanted it.'

Kabugo's wife tried to stop him driving away. The nurse learned military police had gone to her Kampala flat looking for her and drove on to her sister's home. She telephoned Mrs Kabugo who anxiously said her husband had not returned.

'My sister went to a major dealer to sell my car so that I had money to leave Uganda. Next day at my sister's a phone call came from a friend to say that the bodies of Peter Kabugo and Captain Mawazi had been found on the Kampala-Masaka road in Peter Kabugo's car without their heads.'

Nurse Nasamba escaped to Kenya.

'My brother was killed because he would not allow the soldiers to steal bananas.'

The men of the small village near Masaka had formed a vigilante group to protect the banana groves. Nakasero State Research Bureau captain Adam Bisgin—a bus conductor before Amin's take-over—called it an anti-Government group. Six villagers died in the attack.

Former minister of Agriculture Justus Byagagaire was found shot dead in a Zaire registered car near the Uganda Zaire border. Unruly soldiers shot senior State Research Bureau officer Ramathan Biryabikwa dead by mistake. Not long before, Biryabikwa had stabbed a tour operator to death in the elevator of Kampala's International Hotel.

Biryabikwa's speciality, with fellow officer Captain Hassan Gale, was to force prisoners to fight gladiator-style duels with axes and pangas in the basement at Nakasero.

'The winner is immediately presented with another opponent, until in the end all die.'

At Lake Victoria fishermen found the body of Entebbe district commissioner Uma Abal. Hours earlier the official had been arrested by military police. 'When the military police were told about the body a group of them came back and tied a rock to the DC's corpse and it sank to the bottom of the lake. They did this in full view of the fishermen.'

By the end of March an estimated 10,000 Ugandan refugees had fled to Kenya. From January between 2,000 and 5,000 people were reckoned to have died in

Uganda.

'Amin eliminates his problems rather than solving them. To him you are either his friend or his enemy. When you are his enemy you have to die.'

In London the Archbishop of Canterbury Dr Donald Cochran said he was praying for the overthrow of field marshal Amin.

'The Archbishop of Canterbury should visit Uganda and find out the real truth about the country,' said Amin. 'As the highest leader of the Anglican Church in the world he should not listen to rumours spread by Jews and Uganda church men, he should not be misguided by Ugandan exiles who are only looking for money. Dr Coggan should not mix politics and religion. I have direct access to God and the world should judge his prayers by which of us will meet God first.

'As a revolutionary leader I am strengthened by the news that the Archbishop of Canterbury is praying for my downfall.

'Imperialist confusing agents and the CIA are using the Church as a weapon for subversive activities and assassinations. Church leaders must not involve the Church in politics because if they do the people will lose confidence in them. They should only preach the word of God and not politics, and pray for peace and not bloodshed.

'Uganda will not allow imperialists to interfere with the Church. Uganda is rich and there is no reason why religious denominations should beg from poor Europeans and Americans to whom Uganda is in a position to give financial aid. We are ready to give farms and ranches to the Church of Uganda, the Muslims, the Roman Catholic Church so they can make their own funds to build and maintain churches, mosques and schools.'

Two attempts were made to kill Amin in April.

Amin visited his home area, Koboko in West Nile, for a cousin's funeral. He drove himself to the funeral in his

Range Rover, but chose to return to Kampala in another government car.

Snipers fired at the Range Rover as it sped towards the capital, killing two occupants and wounding another. One of the survivors flagged down a north-bound car and finally intercepted Amin leaving the funeral—an aircraft was sent to collect the man with a sixth sense.

In the second attempt, about 20 Air Force personnel of the small Bakige tribe attacked a reception at Entebbe. The plotters opened fire on the old airport building—but Amin had already left the function. Three security guards were killed in the fusillade.

Amin was beginning to realise his infallibility could not last forever. Rather than his sixth sense failing, he knew he had made too many enemies ever to feel safe again.

He increased the strength of his bodyguard and formed a new unit designated as the Clearance Squad. This unit was filled exclusively by Sudanese whose purpose was to precede the president wherever he went.

The protection was absolute. On the road between Tororo and Mbale a Uganda Electricity Board van jutted slightly off the verge. The technician was up a ladder repairing the power line. The Sudanese pulled their Land Rover to a halt and called the technician down—but as he began descending he was thrown off the pylon by a burst of automatic fire.

CHAPTER XV

*'I'm going to London and no-one can stop me.
Whether they like it or not I am taking a
delegation of 250 and some members of the
British reserve forces as my bodyguards. I want
to see how strong the British are and I want
them to see the powerful man from the
continent of Africa.'*

Idi Amin Dada.

London's turn had come for the biennial Commonwealth Conference—and the storm was blowing hard.
Britain didn't want him. 'Amin is a murderer on a grand
scale and should not be permitted into this country,'
cried Member of Parliament Greville Janner. Zambia
didn't want him—and told African countries to walk out
if Amin turned up.

'Whatever happens, other African leaders must not
be seen to condone his presence, whatever garbage
spews from his lips.' New Zealand was unsure whether
club rules permitted a member to be barred. Even if he
was a homicidal maniac. And Canada wanted human
rights violations high on the agenda, either with or
without Amin present. British host Prime Minister
James Callaghan worried the summit would become a

circus, with Amin as the clown prince of tragedy.

The Commonwealth Secretariat thumbed through its protocol references. The situation was made significantly more complicated by the fact that the summit coincided with Queen Elizabeth's Silver Jubilee celebrations, on Amin's past form was a temptation he would be unlikely to resist.

As Britain had broken diplomatic relations with Uganda there was technically no procedure by which Amin could have been invited to the Buckingham Palace festivities. Commonwealth procedure, however, obliged Secretary General Sonny Ramphal to inform every member country of the dates of the heads of government meeting and contained no specific precautions against the attendance of an unwanted leader other than that the host country would not pay his hotel bills.

Much to Amin's delight the Commonwealth was in a spin. Ramphal's concern was that the issue could lead to a polarisation of Commonwealth members on racial lines, with white countries appearing to gang up against a black president. Ramphal cautioned Commonwealth countries against taking a 'holier than thou' attitude to Uganda. Britain sniped back, saying a consensus of Commonwealth views on Amin's attendance would have been more helpful and despatched a veteran Commonwealth specialist, Lord Thomson, on a tour of African, Asian and Caribbean countries to get one. Putting out soundings of its own, the Secretariat showed itself willing to go along with a total ban on Amin as long as other members supported it.

Two years before Amin had stayed away from the Commonwealth meeting in Jamaica on his own accord. Britain's newly-appointed Foreign Secretary Dr David Owen thought Amin's exclusion from the London conference would necessitate Uganda's expulsion from the Commonwealth. 'This is something to be discussed within the Commonwealth. No member state has ever been expelled from the Commonwealth. South Africa decided to leave. It (Uganda's expulsion) would be a major step.'

Just then the respected International Commission of Jurists in Geneva released its updated report on mass killings in Uganda during Amin's seven-year reign of terror. It said 80,000-90,000 people died in the two years following Amin's take-over and the figure had climbed steadily ever since.

Amin's rule had seen a total breakdown of law and order in Uganda and persistent gross violations of human rights.

Ironically, the Commonwealth's own human rights Declaration had been drawn up at the Singapore summit of 1971 during which Amin had deposed Milton Obote.

Uganda Health minister Henry Kyemba fled to Britain while attending a medical conference in Switzerland. 'I am ashamed to admit that on several occasions he (Amin) told me quite proudly he had eaten the organs or flesh of his human victims,' said Kyemba.

'I have no doubt he was serious when he told me that he had eaten human meat on a number of occasions. He remarked emphatically that it was salty. When I was Minister of Health doctors often told me that bodies delivered to hospital mortuaries had been tampered with in curious ways.

'I know there has been a great deal of international speculation about Amin's sanity. I have certainly seen him in situations when he gives every indication of being insane. If he is provoked he can react like a wild animal and go into a kind of fit. During these periods he is completely out of control and no-one around him is safe.'

Kyemba and the ICJ report had an inevitable effect on opinion. 'If the Commonwealth cannot stomach the exclusion of this evil man its unity is not worth preserving,' editorialised Britain's mass circulation *Daily Mirror*.

'Imagine if you can, a White Amin, one tenth as tyrannical? Would the African and Asian members of the Commonwealth have agreed to attend any conference from which he was not formally and categorically

264

excluded. It is enough to ask the question to know the answer,' voiced the conservative *Daily Mail.*

'The Commonwealth, if it is to be anything, must strive to be a forum where racial equality is an ideal to be revered above all others. Yet it operates double standards that amount to colour discrimination. For as long as the bestial Amin regime endures Uganda should be suspended from the Commonwealth.'

'It is said (by the British Government) that if a country is excluded from a Commonwealth Conference now, others—on more dubious grounds—might be excluded in future.... This is an excuse for dodging the issue,' said the *Financial Times.*

Added the Archbishop of Canterbury: 'I hope the members of the Commonwealth will say: No we will not have this man present.... Britain cannot make the decision alone. It can only make one thirty-sixth of a decision in the Commonwealth.... I just want to see an end to this appalling regime in Uganda as soon as possible.'

In case Amin set foot in Britain Ilan Hartuv took out a writ claiming damages for the death of his mother, Entebbe victim Dora Bloch.

The London High Court writ named Amin and Major Sarick Minawa of the State Research Bureau as responsible for Mrs Bloch's murder and acknowledged that while British courts had no jurisdiction in Uganda it would be effective if served on Amin in Britain, where Mrs Bloch's will making Hartuv executor was lodged.

In all the years of his rule by military power—whether by acknowledging him as a legitimate rule of a legitimate government or quietly shunning him—nations which should have known better had only served to entrench Amin's hold as the most evil dictator since Hitler. He was a master of exploiting equivocation. But one man who had resolutely opposed him from the start, President Nyerere, was already beginning to strengthen a resolve he had made in 1971.

At last the Commonwealth reached unanimity. The word went out: Amin was just not welcome in Britain.

Still clinging to the hope Amin would not risk leaving Kampala for fear of being overthrown—and to keep the decision as low-key as possible—Whitehall did not immediately announce a formal ban. But it did begin quietly drawing up contingencies should Amin attempt to gatecrash the summit.

A week before the conference was due to open Amin said he had received 'a confidential letter' from Callaghan indicating 'Uganda is not going to be represented at the conference.' In a telegram to Ramphal, Amin accused Britain of setting a dangerous precedent for the future of the Commonwealth Organisation, continuing: 'Uganda has been barred because it could find out the true mistakes made by Britain during her colonial rule. I wish to make it clear that gone are the days when Britain had the power and authority of an imperial master over the Commonwealth.'

But Amin was not taking the rebuff lying down. He announced his own contribution to Queen Elizabeth's Silver Jubilee celebrations. British nationals in Uganda would carry him shoulder high in a sedan chair all the way from Entebbe to Kampala, a distance of 22 miles. (The announcement was of course reminiscent of a similar spectacle—'The White Man's burden'—at the OAU Kampala summit in 1975).

'The Field Marshal's celebrations of the Queen's Jubilee must resemble in all respects the way black African slaves were made to carry the Whites during the colonial era,' said Uganda radio.

Then, in every news item, the radio reported that Amin had left Kampala for London—despite Commonwealth consternation. At first Amin had planned to travel as far as Paris with Zaire's President Mobutu who was going for talks with the French Government. He was to go by car from Paris to a channel port and hire a boat to take him to England. Uganda's representative in London Idi Osman advised Britain: 'The President will arrive in London during the current week, openly, and not by any back door.'

The bluff—for bluff it was—threw Europe and its press into confusion. Kampala said Amin's aircraft would land at Brussels. Belgian troops and police cordoned off the airport. No, the aircraft was diverting to Ireland. An unscheduled Aer Lingus plane on a test flight was refused permission to land at Dublin. It circled until it persuaded the control tower, it wasn't Big Daddy. A Ugandan jet was scheduled to touch down at Britain's Stansted airport at 5:00 a.m. on Sunday. The plane would be allowed to land—but Amin would not get any further than the airport lounge—where Home Office officials would tell him he could not stay in Britain for security reasons. The plane would be refuelled and that would be that.

Amin never left Kampala—he simply kept out of sight at Kololo. Vice President Adrisi fed his fictional travel plans to the radio station. Uganda's chair in London remained empty.

Well before the formal London sessions opened Zambia's Kenneth Kaunda was on the attack. 'Look, brother, we condemn terror wherever it is. I have been condemning Amin since he took power. I condemned him when he was the chairman of the Organisation of African Unity, and I will continue to condemn him until the people of Uganda get rid of him.'

'Those of us who condemn racism and facism which lead to the destruction of human life and property in southern Africa as a whole must have the same moral strength to condemn the atrocities of that man. He is an evil man, a criminal against mankind as were Hitler and Mussolini.'

Jamaica's Michael Manley said: 'Amin's oppression is a source of embarrassment to developing countries and a cause of shame to all mankind...Uganda atrocities have been confirmed. The evidence is there for all to see.'

In session, the Commonwealth's revulsion to Amin was clear—but differences arose over what to do about him. Nigeria, for one, was still troubled by procedural principles. 'We should not pass a resolution about a fellow member or his country when he or it is not present at the conference. Whatever anyone may think, the principle is that the leader of Uganda should have come to Lancaster house to say his say.

'For all of us in the Commonwealth it is not right for any one country to try and exclude any other member.... After all, ours is an association of free and independent countries. We want to see it flourish....'

The Commonwealth objected to Amin—not Uganda. Australian Prime Minister Malcolm Fraser said Uganda's expulsion from the Commonwealth 'wouldn't seem to be conducive to helping the people of Uganda.'

'In our discussion of human rights we cannot ignore what is happening in Uganda. There have been violations which the Commonwealth cannot ignore. This is a subject on which the Commonwealth should speak out with clarity and strength.'

In their summing up of proceedings—proceedings overshadowed by Southern Africa and the overthrow in his absence of President James Mancham, leader of 60,000 Indian Ocean Seychelles islanders—Commonwealth heads delivered an unprecedented attack on a fellow member.

But the final communique was a compromise of the wishes of African states for a strong censure of Amin and others that feared the issue would harm black African solidarity and distract attention from southern Africa. It neither mentioned Amin by name nor spoke of specific measures against him, least of all his expulsion from the Commonwealth grouping.

'Cognisant of the accumulated evidence of sustained disregard for the sanctity of life and of massive violations of basic human rights in Uganda it was the overwhelming view of Commonwealth leaders that these excesses were so grave as to warrant the world's concern and to evoke condemnation by heads of Government in strong unequivocal terms.'

The wording adroitly provided any Commonwealth leader with the chance, if the need arose, to say he was not one of the heads of government referred to.

The communique went on: 'Mindful that the people of Uganda were within the fraternity of the Commonwealth fellowship heads of government looked to the day when Ugandans would once more fully enjoy their basic human rights which were now being so cruelly denied.'

If it seemed to some Amin had got off lightly, Big Daddy himself was anything but pleased. He advised his detractor Kaunda to cry into 'a 25-year-old pair of the Queen's nickers', decided to sell Uganda High Commission buildings in Trafalgar Square and Hampstead to Saudi Arabia and slapped new restrictions on the activities of 300 or so Britons still living in Uganda. The restrictions prevented British nationals travelling outside Uganda without government permission and threatened them with jail sentences if they gathered or moved around in groups of more than three. Amin also ordered the French Embassy in Kampala to close down its British Interests section.

There was always to be an individual victim.

The Commonwealth Summit had moved into its second day when jovial, stocky and bushy moustached Scanlon was picked up in Kampala. The charge: spying. The penalty: death by firing squad (if found guilty of treason by a Military Tribunal).

Scanlon, 50 years old and the father of three, had spent nearly 14 years in Uganda; he was well known in the white community and to Amin. He had been one of the Britons who carried Amin into the OAU reception in 1975; he worked for the Uganda Transport Corporation and then as a manager for a car dealership in Kampala, Cooper Motors.

Two years before his arrest—at a time Amin wanted to expel all British nationals from Uganda—Scanlon took out Ugandan citizenship.

Amin's radio broadcast typically muddled accounts of Scanlon's supposed crime.

A powerful battleship-grey radio transmitter had been found at his house. Scanlon had turned to spying for the British Government after being fired from

Cooper Motors because of his negative attitude to Africans. Cooper Motors had not in fact dismissed Scanlon. Smuggling was also mentioned by the radio.

Amin dangled Scanlon on the end of a string. Since he was a Ugandan citizen Britain would get nowhere if it tried to intervene. 'All representations must stop immediately. Anyone who has committed a mistake will have to face the laws of this country. The person if found guilty will be shot and there will be no case about it.'

In London Osman fended off inquiries. Scanlon would be given a fair trial the outcome to which would be made public. (He simultaneously attacked the I.C.J report and Kyemba's revelations saying: 'Do you think 11 million people would sit back if President Amin was really a despot and eccentric?') Another Kampala news bulletin said Scanlon was being held in a remote part of the country because of the seriousness of the charges against him. 'There will be no question of handing over his body to anybody. Likewise no announcement will be made about the time or place of execution, which will not be made known to anyone.

Scanlon was never tried. His wife Gloria received no official word of him: her requests to see him were studiously ignored, as were her personal appeals to Amin. Rumours were plentiful...That Scanlon had been shot and his body burned ... That he was gravely ill at Makindye military prison. For Scanlon's family the weeks dragged by. A Briton who had become a close advisor to Amin, Bob Astles, assured Mrs Scanlon her husband was alive and well. Astles, a long standing friend of Scanlon and the man who had arranged the White Man's Burden episode, told the family to await 'developments'. This inferred that Scanlon was being held in reserve for one of Amin's public gimmicks; after encouraging all manner of dramatic rumours a robust-looking Scanlon would be released at a suitably opportune moment. It was hinted by Astles that such a moment could be the opening of the United Nations General Assembly.

Scanlon was never released.

Radio Uganda claimed Scanlon escaped from custody pending his trial. A nationwide manhunt was in process. 'It is apparent that Scanlon was stolen from prison by British Imperialist Intelligence for whom he was spying. As such the Uganda Government no longer holds itself responsible for him. It is British imperialists who have stolen him who are now responsible.'

Bob Scanlon was dead.

The following sequence of events unfolded. On the foundation of their friendship Scanlon had agred to take charge of a number of business deals for Astles. Scanlon soon found himself caught in a web of murky intrigues. According to Christopher Twesigye, a Uganda Foreign Service official, Scanlon once travelled to Britain on Astles' behalf to supervise the purchase of transformers and electrical equipment which was later converted into torture apparatus at the State Research Bureau's Nakasero headquarters—with engineer Scanlon's assistance. 'Scanlon,' said Twesigye, 'was up to his neck in what was going on.'

Astles also assigned Scanlon to buy spare parts for the Uganda Transport Corporation's fleet of British-made buses. At the time British Leyland had refused to supply parts to Uganda. Astles believed Scanlon, using his contacts in the motor trade, could circumvent the embargo.

The transaction was to involve a large sum in foreign currency—and because of its nature under-the-counter payoffs were only to be expected. By this time Astles had been given the rank of major in the Uganda Army and appointed head of the government's Anti-Corruption unit. In this capacity—and as Amin's right-hand man—Astles was not unjustifiably labelled a killer. The blame for countless deaths—whether of borderland smugglers, civil servants, businessmen or Amin opponents generally—was laid squarely at his feet. Major Bob Astles collected enemies. . . .

Astles had already salted away a small fortune and prepared a bolt hole for the day Big Daddy's time ran out. Now he suggested that during Scanlon's circuitous negotiations for the bus parts no-one would be any the wiser if they both siphoned off some of the money for themselves. Astles instructed Scanlon to deposit his share into a secret bank account in Europe. Whether Scanlon accepted the proposition is not clear. What is clear, however, is that no new payment was received by Astles' bankers during the period of Scanlon's search for a seller. Scanlon's spending showed a shortfall and Astles immediately suspected his friend of taking all the loot. He confronted Scanlon, who denied it. Astles wanted to know where Scanlon had deposited the missing money. Scanlon wasn't saying anything . . . but there were ways of making him talk.

On Astles' advice Amin called in the State Research Bureau. Spying was Astles idea. Corruption would have drawn things too close to home. And smuggling made it not unreasonable for the head of the Anti-Corruption Unit to have special interest in the prisoner's interrogation.

Scanlon was taken to Makindye prison. In the hospital wing he did indeed receive medical treatment— but for ulcers, an old complaint. He was transferred to the smaller less conspicuous Kololo Hill prison, converted from a colonially-styled house overlooking Kampala that had once served as the residence of the British High Commissioner. Three months after his arrest Scanlon was led from the storeroom which had been his cell. He and four other men were gagged and pushed along the corridor. Scanlon was beaten to death with a sledgehammer.

If there was any information to give, and if Astles got it, Bob Scanlon knew too much . . .

SCANLON's replacement in Kampala at CMC—the Nairobi based car and aviation conglomerate whose chief executive was Bruce McKenzie—was gruff, burly Bob Brown, a long time company executive.

Despite all of Amin's whimsical moods, his tirades against the white man, CMC maintained an extremely amicable relationship with Big Daddy.

They were the only company functioning in Uganda

allowed to expatriate their dividends to Kenya.

Bob Brown became fairly close to Amin—for business reasons in his capacity as CMC's Uganda chief.

One night, with his wife, in their home in a Kampala suburb they were disturbed by noises in their garden. Brown had Amin's private telephone number. 'If you ever need my help,' Amin had told him, 'just call me on this line.'

Brown did so now. 'Lock your windows, bolt your doors,' said Amin. 'Don't move. I'll be there in five minutes.'

The time was about 3 a.m. Sure enough, almost on the dot Amin, and a guard of heavily armed soldiers pulled up outside the house. They offloaded and fanned out into the garden. The Browns heard machine gun, machine-pistol and rifle fire.

Amin knocked on their door. 'They're all dead,' he said. 'Now we can relax over a drink.' The Browns and Amin sat sipping spirits for about 90 minutes before the President left.

Within 36 hours the Browns were back in Nairobi. 'We had no reason to continue living in Kampala,' says Bob Brown. 'How could we know we could always depend on Amin for help? Next time it might have been us.'

But Brown's departure did not alter the relationship between CMC and the Amin regime. Not long after, McKenzie himself—a former Kenya Cabinet Minister (his secret portfolio was Minister for Security)—began to commute regularly between the Kenya capital and Amin's capital.

In the few months before his death in a mysterious plane explosion over the Ngong Hills on the approach to Wilson Airport with a Vickers arms salesman, the moustachioed South African born ex-farmer turned politician turned business magnate had visited Kampala 48 times.

Mystery still shrouds his death although several explanations have been put forward. Perhaps the most convincing: Amin and McKenzie exchanged words in an angry session during the last visit.

McKenzie walked out. When he and his party reached Entebbe Airport there was a message from Big Daddy which said, in effect, that the President was sorry. He wanted to make amends. Could they delay their flight while he sent a gift for them.

The delay extended beyond Amin's promised deadline. Almost as McKenzie was giving up, again in anger, the gift arrived. It was a lion's head trophy.

Forensic scientists have confirmed that in the scattered wreckage strewn over the Ngong Hills there were pieces of hair and the hide of a lion. The theory is that Amin had an explosive device fitted inside the head which was detonated by a time switch.

But before this, just after Scanlon's disappearance Astles very nearly had to use his fugitive's fund. The plot was codenamed 'Operation Mafutamingi' after the swahili dub—meaning "much fat"—Amin had given to his expulsion of the Uganda Asians. The plotters, calling themselves the Uganda Liberation Movement, worked in complete secrecy. Their weapons had been gradually stolen from Amin's Army; the key to their success was the support of Amin's Air Force, for the coup attempt entailed the bombing of State House, Entebbe, with a simultaneous mortar, machine gun and small arms attack. The flight to State House, half a mile from Entebbe airstrip, would have taken only a few seconds. Take-off was planned for 6:00 a.m. on June 19.

A narrow 90 minutes beforehand the telephone roused Amin. The secret had been broken—and just how, nobody knew. A column of trusted Amin troops coverged on Entebbe Air Force base immobilising the aircraft. Amin mustered a convoy of security cars and set out towards Kampala.

There was no time to round up the conspirators. Nor was there time for them to plan anew. Realising their scheme has collapsed a small group of the conspirators tried desperately to salvage it. They sped ahead of Amin's convoy and chose ambush positions along the Entebbe-Kampala road near the village of Baitababire, only two and a half miles from Entebbe. It was unlikely Amin would be travelling in his only official Mercedes and it was impossible to pick out any single target. The ambushers' only hope was to throw so much at the convoy that Amin would be hit.

The cars accelerated through a barrage of shooting and grenade explosion at Baitababire. The presidential Mercedes swerved off the road and crashed; hundreds of shots punched into the escort cars, Amin's protectors fanned out into the roadside undergrowth returning sprays of fire. Amin's hulking form was seen dashing for cover from a halted car, its windows shattered.

The attackers rose and ran before Amin's body-guards rallied the search. Reinforcements sealed off the Village. The houses were smashed open. Clothing, pots and pans and furniture were hurled outside. The Baitababire elders were bunched onto the trucks and driven away—some never to return. The Uganda Air Force was grounded—and to make doubly certain Army sappers blew up five MiG fighters standing at Entebbe. Roadblocks were established on all the main approaches to Kampala. Three permanent blocks on the trunk road from Kampala to the Kenya border were supplemented by another nine new ones. Outside Kampala loyal marines and soldiers of the Mechanised Reconnaisance Battalion fought scattered battles with rebel soldiers and airmen for eight hours. The skirmishing fizzled out when the rebels, prepared only for a quick strike, ran out of ammunition. Several hundred combatants died. About 1000 servicemen, mainly Baganda and Basoga, from Entebbe and Bombo barracks north of Kampala had been behind the overthrow attempt.

Amin's men never punished suspects alone.

'The situation here is very tense. Bodies of men, women and children are being thrown into the lake. Those of the Baganda, Busoga, Nyankole, Bakiga and Bagishu tribes are being taken to Entebbe barracks. The soldiers are going around homes between Entebbe and Kampala and arresting the people of these tribes.'

What had happened to Amin? One of a group of 13 officers involved in the plot who made it to Kenya said Amin seemed to have been wounded in the Baitababire ambush. Hit by the blast of a grenade, Amin's car hurtled off the road and in the ensuing firefight two of his immediate bodyguards fell dead. As he made for cover firing his pistol Amin had fallen clutching his other arm into his side.

For five days Amin was neither to be seen or heard. Unusual as this was, the speculation was feverish. It was conceivable Amin had succumbed to wounds. A cook at the Command post told an inquisitive telephone caller Big Daddy had arrived there injured, but left again after a few minutes. He could be traced at none of his other official houses in Kampala. He must have been undergoing medical treatment in hiding. It was conceivable he had been flown to a friendly country— probably Libya—for hospital care.

Vice President Adrisi conveniently stationed himself beside the telephone at the Command post. Amin, he said, had disappeared.

Even for Uganda the situation was odd. 'We have not found him yet,' Adrisi told a reporter calling from Kenya's *Daily Nation*. 'We don't know where he is. If you find him, please contact Uganda immediately.'

Troops and police were sweeping the country, looking, Adrisi said Uganda radio was unusually silent. An item announcing Amin would attend a celebration in the north west was suddenly dropped from the bulletins and no further mention of him was made in the following days.

The international speculation grew—and so did the headlines . . .

The hoax worked perfectly. Attention was on the mystery, and not on the latest bloody purges. His purpose achieved Amin resurfaced, claiming he had just been on a belated honeymoon with Sarah at a remote island hideaway in Lake Victoria. 'I've been trying to keep out of the news,' Amin said jauntily.

Big Daddy couldn't resist putting the record straight.

He denounced worldwide consensus that an assassination attempt had taken place as imperialist and Zionist propaganda. But he admitted there had been a number of arrests in connection with consignments of arms smuggled into Uganda from Kenya and Tanzania. Christian churches in the neighbouring countries had been involved in trafficking the weapons into Uganda. Amin appeared on Uganda television meeting a group of Black American visitors. He wore a long sleeve shirt and remained seated during the televised chat with the Americans—and was less animated than usual, although the tenor of his talk hadn't changed.

'I am not liked because I am not a puppet leader.' The Commonwealth Conference had failed to solve the Rhodesia dispute because of British weakness and Moshe Dayan would not be a good Israeli foreign minister—he was too hot tempered.

If Amin had been injured the wound could only have been a superficial one. He turned up at the OAU's annual summit in the Gabonese capital Libreville a few days later showing no outward signs of discomfort.

'He's the uncrowned King of Africa,' yelled a young admirer as Amin's limousine drew up at the Libreville conference hall. Amin jumped out, his medals jangling on his chest, his revolver to his hip. Inside the hall one or two stony-faced heads of state kept their disapproving composure as a deafening ovation greeted the Ugandan. Delegates roared with laughter as Amin disclosed his defence council had awarded him the CBE, the Highest Order of the Conqueror of the British Empire. He had earned the honour, Amin grinned broadly, for making the British run away from East Africa.

A *volte-face*. For ten minutes Big Daddy entertained his listeners with a colourful account of the Baitababire attack. 'I captured some of the people who tried to assassinate me. I've got them. They were Western inspired. The whole Western Press knew what was going to happen to me. They were sending people to Uganda to kill me, to Angola to kill President Neto, to Benin to kill President Kerekou and to Guinea to kill President

Sekou Toure.'

The murder of President Marien Ngouabi of Congo-Brazzaville in March, Amin said, had been part of the same Western conspiracy; (even though Ngouabi had been one of Amin's more vociferous OAU critics.)

'They wanted to kill me and some of the strongest anti-imperialist leaders of Africa,' declared Amin. 'But I ate them before they ate me.'

IT WAS the Carter administration's first foreign policy crisis. 'Godammit,' complained a White House official. 'We couldn't have asked for a less dignified start.'

Idi Amin had ordered all Americans living in Uganda to assemble at Entebbe airport on Monday morning. During the week-end Ugandan security forces would prevent Americans leaving the country. This news had been picked up from a routine Kampala radio bulletin monitored in Nairobi; the signals reached the State Department's Operations Centre as dawn came up over Washington. As national security advisor Zbigniew Brzezinski took word of the ominous development to Carter's routine morning briefing secretary Cyrus Vance and top State Department officials already had their coats off and their shirtsleeves up.

The 200 Americans living in Uganda were mainly missionaries stationed in remote country areas. The rest, a handful of pilots, aviation engineers and their families, kept Uganda Airlines and Amin's personal jet, a Northrop Gulfstream II, in the air and had not registered with the US Embassy in Nairobi, as Americans going to Uganda were advised to do. Nor had they reported to the West German embassy in Kampala which had been handling US affairs in Uganda since the United States closed its embassy in 1973. The pilots and engineers were excused from attending the Monday meeting—if they were too busy to do so, said Amin.

By mid-morning on Friday Uganda's acting charge d'affaires in Washington, Paul Chepkwurui had been summoned to the State Department and told the US would not tolerate its nationals being used as political hostages. Chepkwurui insisted Amin only wanted to reassure the Americans that nothing would happen to them. Cables buzzed from Washington through Bonn to Kampala.

Amin's next move was disquieting for Washington. It confirmed what Washington already thought: Amin was engaged in another blatant exercise in international blackmail prompted by Carter's proclaimed disgust at the deaths of Archbishop Luwum, the two cabinet ministers and Uganda's human rights record as a whole. Inimitably, Amin ordered his regional administrative officers to prepare a list of all Americans and their property 'including chickens, goats, pigs and other animals.' He accused the US of supporting the coup plot in which he had implicated Archbishop Luwum and the cabinet ministers and charged that even now a 2,500-strong American, British and Israeli mercenary force was marching through Kenya towards the Uganda border. The rambling message indicated Amin's belief that Carter was in the pocket of Israel and suggested that instead of delving into Uganda's domestic affairs the US should look at its own international crimes.

Amin promised to send Carter copies of the post mortem reports on Luwum, Oboth Ofumbi and Oryema. 'It appears that all you have said about Uganda is false and all those feeding you with information have not set foot in Uganda. They base their reports on hearsay.'

Amin noted that among American crimes was the murder of world leaders by the CIA. 'The US should examine this before pointing an accusing finger.' Amin warned Washington against using the 5,000 marines he knew were ready to stage an Entebbe-style rescue of the missionaries because Uganda had the strength to crush any invaders. He ended in vintage Amin tone: 'I ask you to pass my greetings to all Americans, both White and Black. I hope to visit you in the White House in the near future.'

Thus, the Americans were left to fathom out Amin's

intentions. Carter, who asked for hourly reports on the situation, favoured a low-key approach on advice that Amin would act rashly on the slightest provocation. The nuclear aircraft carrier USS Enterprise was cruising in the Indian Ocean... a thought to send the ship to Mombasa bounced between officials of Carter's Uganda Special Working Group. In any case, the Enterprise did not have the capability (it could muster 200 marines) to mount the sort of rescue operation that would be required and flag-waving might not impress Amin. The carrier was instructed to keep a watching brief, and Washington asked African and Arab leaders on good terms with Amin to urge restraint instead.

Amin told Crown Prince Fahd of Saudi Arabia that the Americans had no cause for alarm and cheekily expressed wonderment that 'some leaders have become telephone operators and messengers for America.' Once more, Amin was delighted with the stir he started. He postponed the Monday meeting until Wednesday so that, he said, he could lay on a thank-you-for-your-excellent-work-in-Uganda party for the Americans. He would invite an additional crowd of 3,000 and everyone would be serenaded by his favourite folk-dancers, Heartbeat of Africa.

At the last moment Amin cancelled the meeting altogether, lifted the travel ban and redeployed the armed guards who had been tailing American citizens since the episode began. It had all been a misunderstanding which had arisen partly from Carter's lack of knowledge of Africa, Big Daddy explained. 'I want good relations with the United States. I want them to reopen the embassy here as well as have more Americans working in Uganda.'

Despite his conciliatory talk Amin kept Washington and the missionaries on their toes for a little longer. The mercenary force was still on his doorstep, the US had established a military air base in an African country only an hour's flight from Kampala and he would ask the Russians to put more weight on the region's military power scales.

Amin was thoroughly content. The tussle with Carter totally eclipsed the wanton slaughter of the victims of Amin's latest witch-hunt—the purge in which more than 1000 Christian Langi and Acholi soldiers had died at Mubende and Mbarara barracks alone. And in which Milton Obote's home village of Apache had been razed to the ground.

Only one American suffered physical harm in Amin's manouevre. Visiting New York Law graduate Brian Schwartz was arrested at gunpoint while sipping a beer in a Kampala bar. He was roughed up under interrogation and twice taken out to lonely places by machine-gun wielding guards bent on scaring him. But Schwartz scrawled his name and passport number on a scrap of paper which he managed to throw to a Canadian passing along an alleyway outside his cell. The scrap reached the West German embassy and Schwartz was released and expelled to Kenya the next day.

'Uganda doesn't interest us,' declared the current Organisation of African Unity chairman Omar Bongo, president of Gabon.

'Uganda really is an internal problem and the most important problem is South Africa..."

'The Americans created a stir but we found out the next day everything was all right...'

'You shouldn't make the mistake of confusing the South African problem with the Ugandan problems...'

'Uganda is an independent and sovereign state and in that country there is only one race. For us Africans, South Africa is not an independent country. It is majority rule that counts. But in South Africa the White minority rules. The day when everyone has the same vote (as Prime Minister John Vorster) the problem will cease to exist. Vorster and Idi Amin are not the same....'

'There is no race question in Uganda, it is a question of justice...'

'Each government has its own ways of dealing with certain problems. Idi Amin has his own way of dealing

with problems to maintain his government. If he has to
do certain things, he has to do certain things....'

'...Africa is a continent of independent countries
and Uganda is only one drop of the water. Uganda is not
like the rest of the continent and you can't compare the
situation at all in the independent countries with the
situation Vorster has created in South Africa.'

No-one contested, however, that Idi Amin Dada
could not have done more for South African Whites.
Amin had become the African bogeyman, standing
threateningly over the slightest reforms. Extremists
could not have wished for a better ally, for better
publicity.

'Look what happens when a black man gets control...'

Amin gave the whole of independent Africa a bad
name.

'Maybe the world will see our problems in South
Africa a little more clearly...'

Black opinion in South Africa despaired: Yes, Amin
provided an abundance of ammunition for the enemies
of African aspirations. A black newspaper, one of the
few avenues of African expression in South Africa,
urged Amin's expulsion from the OAU and an
international trade and diplomatic boycott.

'How long can Africa and the international community go on tolerating the dastardly acts of this tyrant...?'

'We must now take effective steps to denounce
him... and restore the dignity of the Ugandan people...'

'There must be no room for the implementation of
double standards. Brutality is brutality, whether it is
initiated by a black or a white man...'

'We condemn Amin as a blood-thirsty animal who
has lost the right to be regarded as a human being.'

'The president would like to remind all Ugandans
that since the coming into power of the Military
Government and especially since the declaration of
"Economic War" and the expulsion of non-citizen

Asians Uganda has been the subject of hostile campaigns launched from many quarters, both here and far, intended to discredit the military government and cause chaos and bloodshed in the country.

'This campaign over the years has taken various forms—such as the 1972 Mutukula invasion and the 1976 Israeli invasion culminating the abortive plot to overthrow the Government in February, 1977.

'Following the capture of arms and ammunition smuggled into the country some of those responsible for this heinous and dangerous act were arrested. It was through their own confession of their part in the plot that they implicated some Ugandan high officials, including the former Archbishop of Uganda, Rwanda Burundi and Boga-Zaire and two cabinet ministers and some of the security forces.

'No human being in his right senses will stand up to deny that the way this plot was conceived and was to be executed was intended to turn Uganda into a bloodbath in which thousands of innocent Ugandans would have lost their lives and property.

'According to this plan Ugandans belonging to tribes other than the Langi and Acholi were to be ruthlessly exterminated to pave the way for the return of Obote and his henchmen who are in exile with the assistance of some murderers and Mafia-type criminals living in Uganda who were promised high posts in the event of the success of the plot.

'Moreover, the plot was based not only on tribalism but on religion. It is therefore not surprising that the Defence Council found no good reason at all to advise the president into pardoning the condemned prisoners.

'Anybody, be he a minister, a high ranking officer, a civilian, highly or lowly placed, can engage in subversive activity against this country simply because he has been bought by the imperialists by being promised big posts in Uganda or anywhere else. He is not only deceiving himself or herself and is actually committing suicide.

'Anybody in Uganda who aspire to high position in the government can get it only through hard work.'

283

Twelve men were convicted in a secret trial by the Military Tribunal sitting at Kampala City Hall: Ben Ongom, Abdalla Anyuru, Daniel Nsereko, assistant commissioner of police and under-secretary in Oboth Ofumbi's Internal Affairs Ministry, John Kabandize, a superintendant of prisons, Peter Atua, principal officer at Murchison Bay prison, Edward Mutabazi, superintendent at Kampala prison headquarters, Lieutenant Ben Ogwang, intelligence officer at Malire, Regiment, Y Y Okot, chief inspector of schools, John Leji Olobo, industrial relations officer at the Ministry of Labour, Elias Okidimenya, general manager, Lake Victoria Bottling Company, Julius Adupa, a teacher at Lira Polytechnic Institute, and Garison Anono, principal at Bobi Foundation School, Sulu.

Two men, Boy Lango, a ticket inspector with the Northern Province Bus Company, and John Obinu, a hotel waiter, were sentenced to 15 years imprisonment. Two others were freed because, said the tribunal, they attempted to report the plot to Oboth Ofumbi and were intimidated into joining it.

The executions were to be held in public. The smuggled Chinese weapons and ammunition were to be used 'so the plotters 'get a real taste of them,' Amin ordered.

Amin chose the Clock tower in Central Kampala— erected to commemorate Queen Elizabeth's visit to the city 23 years before.

All morning Army jeeps patrolled the vicinity. Oil drums were placed in position and filled with sand or water. Three Air Force MiGs screamed low over the capital to advertise the occasion. The twelve men's bearded faces, shown by their prison photographs, stared vacantly from the front page of the *Voice of Uganda* newspaper too.

Checkpoints were set up; citizens' identity papers were scrutinised. From noon crowds began gathering in the tree-lined Clock Tower Square. Soldiers in combat-readiness arrived. Troops brought the relatives of the convicted men under guard. The onlookers talked in subdued whispers, aware of the security men moving slowly back and forth among them.

For several minutes a rusty Makindye prison van nosed its way through the crowd. At 4:40 it stopped beside the Tower. The prisoners chanted as they were tied to the oil drums.

'Don't blindfold me,' said Dan Nsereko. 'I want to see.'

Nsereko tossed himself forward. He hung wounded—but alive—after the first volley. A pistol cracked. A doctor pronounced all dead. The bodies were roughly lifted into wooden coffins and loaded into the prison van.

When the early African darkness fell Clock Tower Square was deserted.

Two days before the executions the telephone rang in the Nairobi office of the American news agency, the Associated Press. 'The President is in a coma,' said Major Bob Astles. 'We believe he'll pull out of it. I'm going over to the hospital right now to see what's happening.' According to Astles Amin had not recovered consciousness after an operation at Mulago.

Uganda Radio did not elaborate. It had announced that Amin underwent surgery performed by a Russian doctor named as Dr Feodor Senkov. It did not say what Amin had been suffering from. 'Uganda recognises the great role the Soviet Union is playing in the medical field in Uganda.' But a nurse in Mulago's Ward 6B said the surgeon had removed a swelling from the back of Amin's neck.

'When we checked out at 5:00 p.m. on Wednesday we left the President here. When we returned this morning he was not here,' she said.

An explanation fed to callers had it that Amin had been transferred to an island in Lake Victoria for security reasons. 'It looks serious,' said a well-rehearsed member of Astles' staff. 'We cannot get Major Astles because he is at His Excellency's bedside.'

Amin's coma had all the hallmarks of another hoax.

'President Amin is not in a coma and reports that he is are pure fantasy,' Ambassador Pierre Renard told a French radio station. 'Uganda Television showed Amin in Mulago hospital and announced he would undergo a minor operation of no urgent nature. We were then shown the President at Mulago surrounded by members of his family, the Soviet Ambassador and Soviet doctors who were to operate on him. This story of a coma is from a novel.'

Other Kampala diplomats affirmed that Amin had walked away from the operating table.

'We had the impression it was more a public relations exercise on behalf of the Russians rather than anything medically necessary. He would certainly not have gone into a coma as a result of that operation. He did not even have a general anaesthetic.'

Besides, none of the Lake Victoria islands had more than basic medical dispensaries.

Hoax or no, Amin was incommunicado. Conscious or not, he ignored appeals for clemency on behalf of the condemned men by Gabon's President Bongo, Liberia's President Tolbert and Muslim groups, some of whom wanted him at least to postpone the executions until the end of the holy Islamic month of Ramadan.

In a coma Amin could hardly be held responsible for the executions going ahead as scheduled.

The disappearing trick, like his June honeymoon, would make news. It would take emphasis off the executions.

Amin wanted the executions to be a lesson to all other would-be opponents. Amin, his muscle and his mystique were a match for the best of them. Ten days after the Clock Tower showpiece Amin returned from Ngunze Island and was declared 'medically fit' by his Soviet doctors, Uganda Radio announced.

CHAPTER XVI

'This year will be the year for love, peace and reconciliation'
                    Idi Amin Dada, January 25, 1978

If the year did open in a less tempestuous manner than the other seven, it was not of Amin's doing—but more of the weather on another continent. Unusually severe frost in Parana state the year before had wiped out 80 per cent of Brazil's coffee crop and the subsequent world shortage pushed up the price of East African Coffee from £400 a ton to £3,000. The money had begun to flow back to Uganda.

The economic partnership between Kenya, Uganda and Tanzania known as the East African Community (encompassing common market tariffs and shared services) had been dissolved in 1977. One reason: Tanzania's Nyerere refused to attend any meeting of the East African Authority—the overall body headed by the three member presidents responsible for ironing out mutual problems—if Amin was to be there.

By the end of 1977 once-prosperous Uganda ranked among the world's 25 poorest countries. Until then it had only been saved from total bankruptcy by a steady flow of Arab aid and the arrival of Arab and Pakistani experts to replace skilled Ugandans who had fled abroad. (More Ugandan doctors worked in Britain than in Uganda.) Amin's economic chaos also produced conditions in which up to 90 per cent of the population lived away from the towns, supporting themselves in small traditional communities.

At first, there were high hopes for the coffee money. The government published a three year 'action programme' which emphasised the reorganisation of communications and the rebuilding of Uganda's industrial infrastructure. Factories began re-opening. Daimler Benz offered to set up a repair depot, ship in spare parts to put 40 cars and 15 lorries back on the road daily, and assemble 400 new vehicles a year ...

The rosy outlook did not last long. Too much damage had already been done. Finance Minister Brig Moses Ali admitted the military administration did not have the money to finance most of the projects in the action programme. From 1972 right through coffee, cotton, tea, tobacco and sugar production had fallen because of poor administration and continuous shortages of labour, fuel and chemicals. Despite the record coffee price a massive deficit was forecast for the fiscal year beginning in 1978. What's more, much of the coffee income found its way to Amin's soldiers. That, if any, was a good enough reason for apparent calm.

In the army barracks shops shelves groaned under the weight of colourful shirts, shoes, sports jackets, watches, pens, tinned food, clothing for women and children, cigars, cigarettes, cameras, glassware, radios, cassette recorders, battery torches, cigarette lighters, wines and spirits, all of it tax free. The luxuries were airfreighted by Uganda government Boeings flying twice weekly from Britain's Stansted airport—flight known as the Stansted whisky run. Amin himself let it be known he was in the market for another executive jet. And he had his eye on a Hawker Siddeley 12T, worth a cool £1.5 million.

In the past there never had been a shortage of suppliers willing to take Amin's money. No credit, strictly hard cash. This had long been the basis of

Uganda's unofficial relationship with Britain. No formal embargoes existed between the two countries and British officials could not interfere with the comings and goings of Ugandans.

They came to keep Amin's coteries happy. If the preordered goods weren't ready, the aircrews headed off to the cash-and-carry store at Bishops Stortford, not far from Stansted, their pockets bulging with £10 notes. They scooped up bread, washing powder, dog food, bottles of aftershave lotion, liquor.

They came for shopping sprees in the West End of London, buying up fashionable clothes, jewellery, rare cheeses. . . .

They came to check on the activities of Ugandan exiles in Britain. Once, Lieutenant Colonel Charles Alele, a familiar Amin luxuries buyer, and his No. 2, Lieutenant Issa Aligo, were caught by British immigration officials carrying the passport of Elizabeth Okite, a Ugandan businesswoman in London. The immediate suspicion was that the officers' mission was to kidnap former Amin foreign minister Elizabeth Bagaya. It turned out, said the Uganda Interests section at the Saudi Arabian embassy, that the real Elizabeth Okite, a Langi who had been in import-export trade in Britain for three years, lost her Ugandan passport and applied for a new one. It was preposterous to suggest the two officers came to kidnap Miss Okite.

Alele and Aligo were hastily recalled to Uganda and severely ticked off by Amin for drawing attention to themselves, and to the whisky run. Quite why Alele had Elizabeth Okite's passport was never fully or convincingly clarified.

On another occasion two of Amin's security men were detained briefly at Stansted and then deported from Britain. They had apparently been assigned to ensure Uganda Airlines chief representative at Stansted Enok Bainomugisha returned home to Kampala after his dismissal from the job. Doubtful of his safety in Uganda Bainomugisha tipped off Stansted police, and remained in Britain.

In Kenya the Joint Refugee Services organisation agreed agents of Uganda State Research Bureau mingled with exiles, passing themselves off as refugees. In Nairobi a Ugandan, Mohamed Jugai, was convicted of possessing .38 special calibre ammunition. Kenya police maintained that Jugai worked for the State Research Bureau. His documented employers, the transport firm Transocean Uganda Limited, had been a known front for security activities.

A State Research Bureau lieutenant defected. Lt Magidu Abudy Waye had been responsible for the training of girl spies for Amin. The girls were chosen for their looks, physical fitness and intelligence. The girls had been trained in the use of firearms, micro-photography, radio techniques and unarmed combat. Many had been prostitutes and still used prostitution as a cover. Others found jobs as secretaries or worked in Uganda embassies in world capitals, reporting information on refugees to the embassies' passport officers.

'They were taught a little psychology, the art of approaching suspects, how to extract information and how to write reports. Because a lot of their work is angled to sex and the art of luring men a woman assistant police commissioner teaches the girls how to use contraception and how to set about getting an abortion.'

Ugandans came to Britain for pilot training. Charles Balidawa defected during a course at Perth in Scotland.

Balidawa had been a captain in Uganda Airlines. Amin decided civilian pilots should join the Air Force— Balidawa was given 20 minutes marching drill, a uniform and the rank of Lieutenant. Under Amin's supervision he took part in farcical exercise at Entebbe airport. 'With a handful of armed troops aboard my plane I was instructed to taxi at high speed along the runway, then brake dramatically. The soldiers would leap out, weapons aimed in previously specified directions and they would take up positions as though they were invading some place.

'... this was repeated time and time again before

Amin grew tired of all the play acting and the whole business was dropped and never mentioned again. He would wave his arms, or leap up and down and stamp with rage or he would laugh and bellow with satisfaction. We weren't supposed to know what it was all about, but Amin asked me several times if our planes had the fuel capacity to take troops and weapons to Mombasa nd back.'

Carrying 16 British guests, including a group of Essex farmers (Uganda had just ordered 3,000 Essex cattle and 100 breeding bulls), Balidawa force landed his Twin Otter aircraft across the border in southern Sudan. Within hours of being acclaimed as a national hero by Amin, the pilot was arrested by the State Research Bureau and accused of having links with anti-Amin guerrillas. At State Research Headquarters he was stripped of his watch and clothes. 'I was led to a room to wait for a senior officer and on the way, they took me past an open door where there was a man I had known well, a fellow pilot, who disappeared a few days before. He was barely recognisable, he had been so beaten and tortured. One of his eyes had been gouged out.'

Balidawa was released—but his mind was made up. To the Ugandans at Perth Balidawa appeared a staunch admirer of Amin—until his family was safely out of Uganda.

Former Royal Air Force wing commander Jim Cobb slipped quietly out of Uganda too. Cobb had been hired as a civil pilot—but then he was charged with the training of Amin's first batch of 12 teenage girl pilots. Once qualified the girls would join the Uganda Airlines Air Force combat squadrons. The girls had had only the most basic schooling. Inaugurating their training with Bob Astles at his side, Amin told the girls: 'The world will soon see what the women of Uganda are capable of. From now on you will always be in the nation's eye.'

'I trained the girls every day, with only Sundays off,' Cobb recalled. 'They stayed in their own barracks as Astles didn't want them to mix with the male members of the air force . . .' At Astles' bidding Cobb's 14 year-old daughter taught the girls elementary mathematics, the use of navigational slide rules and map reading. One day Astles insisted one of the girls went ahead with her first solo flight.

'I didn't think she knew enough,' Cobb said. 'But Astles simply shrugged and said: 'Well, if any of them crash we'll give her a heroine's funeral.

'Feddi did well and made a good landing. But instead of stopping she opened the throttle, took off again and made another circuit. On her next landing she bounced along, then again took off. The next landing wasn't bad—but again she opened the throttle and shot towards a wood beside the runway. She missed the trees . . . looped the plane around and careened towards the trees on the other side. She just missed those, turned towards the middle of the runway and managed somehow to stall the engine. We all . . . ran to the plane. Feddi got out and collapsed with nervous fatigue. All the girls fussed over her, and there were lots of tears.'

Finally, the girls were sent to Scone airfield, Perth, where a private company had taken on the students for £150,000. 'The poor girls never wanted to fly in the first place. They were ordered to,' said Cobb.

Jim Cobb left Uganda after Amin suggested he should lead Uganda Air Force jets into battle, and Astles sinisterly wondered why, having been specially given Ugandan citizenship by Amin, he had not renounced his British nationality. Astles had arranged the ceremony at which Cobb and other Britons bowed before Amin as they were sworn into the Ugandan Armed Forces Reserve.

Cobb described Astles as the Mephistopheles of Uganda.

'When he points a finger somebody is arrested or disappears. . . . He was the only man in constant contact with Amin. He always carried a walkie-talkie and their private call sign was the Ugandan word for "bird".' At that time Astles travelled in a black Mercedes driven by a hefty Ugandan bodyguard named Abbas, Cobb said.

'Bob joked that Abbas was the man "who collects

them and takes them away" ...'

Silver-haired Astles had left Britain as a serviceman in 1942. After ten years in the Middle East, he moved to Uganda and became a roads department foreman under the British administration. He took out Uganda citizenship soon after independence and joined Uganda's fledgling television service, where—always an opportunist—he set himself up as an unsolicited publicity man for Milton Obote. The relationship never matured. In fact, Obote detained Astles for a time and revoked his citizenship.

Astles got to know Amin at boxing contests when Amin was Uganda's heavyweight titleholder. Soon after the military take-over Amin jailed Astles for eight weeks. On his release Astles' Ugandan citizenship was restored.

Astles never looked back. First, Amin appointed him his security advisor. Then special advisor on British and European affairs. Then head of the anti-corruption unit, with the honorary rank of major. He married Mary Senkuituka who became Amin's culture minister.

To some of his acquaintances Astles was a straight-forward man and not noticeably intelligent. 'He is a typical roads foreman—the sort of man who can make it anywhere else but in a place like Uganda at present.' Others were surprised how easily and completely he seemed to have won the confidence of the whimsical Amin. Sheer ruthlessness?

Earlier recollections of Astles in Uganda have him as mostly diffident, sometimes abrupt. He was a knowl-edgeable astronomer. He was popular with children—at outdoor Sunday parties at his Kampala bungalow youngsters, sitting at their own low table, called him 'Uncle Bob'. A sideline: Astles caught baby crested cranes and other African birds for export to foreign zoons.

But there was a mysterious, enigmatic side to Uncle Bob, the roads foreman.

A conversation with visitors turned to Tibet. 'To everyone's astonishment Bob grew terribly heated and vehemently denounced the Dali Lama, to the point of producing photographs which he claimed to have taken ... of holy lamas robbing graves.'

Astles owned a Lake Victoria Island. 'At the top of the cliff was dense undergrowth ... there was no sign of human habitation until Bob gave a series of peculiar penetrating whistles. Then teenage boys, about a dozen or 15 of them sprang into view.... Later he explained that his island was used for a regular exercise. He collected groups of boys every Friday evening from a town on the shore, took them by boat to the island and picked them up again on Sunday evening. During their time on the island they had to prove themselves self-sufficient. He was teaching them commando tactics, he said.'

On another occasion Astles surprised those who knew him as an outspoken supporter of the Kabaka of Buganda and the Kingdom's political party, Kabaka Yekka. 'They should hang them. Hang every one of the Kabaka Yekka! Obote is the man for the people,' Astles shouted from the steps of the National Assembly.

In Amin's Uganda in 1978 'Major Bob', head of the anti-corruption unit, was a hated Mr Fix-it. In his own words:

'My correct role is that of anti-corruption. But there isn't much corruption now and I fill in with other things as I am asked. As I am employed by the office of the President these general duties can be quite varied.

'As I said, there is very little corruption at the moment. I think what happened was those who were corrupt were the ones who became exiles...'

Ugandan exiles had no time for Astles insinuations. They were planning a more emphatic reply, one which if it worked, would put Astles out of a job.

At Stansted Amin's jets were splashed with red paint by demonstrators. Foreign secretary David Owen declared himself utterly opposed to British trade with Uganda and promised to seek means of stopping it. And in the United States—where thirst for coffee had provided Uganda with a third of its export revenue—the first rumblings of a total Uganda trade embargo sounded. The advocates of the embargo said American trade helped keep Amin in power—and Amin was the personification of everything the US administration's human rights campaign stood against. The United States had been Uganda's largest single source of foreign exchange. A smaller point at issue was the Ugandan police pilots were also being trained privately in the United States.

Amin was back under pressure. Britain and America, in collusion with Ugandan exiles, were planning to invade, he told an Army parade. 'Military spies' had been captured in Uganda with armaments. 'They plan to kill all members of the armed forces and then form a new army. They also plan to kill all progressive civilians in all government and other sectors and institutions such as schools regardless of their religion or tribe.

'They want to turn the whole of Nile Province into a graveyard. All is in writing.' he said. 'Ugandans must fight the invaders with all weapons at their disposal— even spears, bows and arrows.'

Extravagant claims were nothing new.

The loyalty of the Defence Council was disintegrating fast; disagreements had emerged within Amin's ruling echelon. Amin was fighting another challenge to his supremacy—not only from outside, also from the men at the top, and in particular vice president Mustafa Adrisi. Differences had seethed between the two men for months, and Adrisi was gaining the support of more and more military men.

On the Jinja Road eleven miles from Kampala Adrisi's official car slammed into a slow moving lorry. Shooting followed the impact of the crash—between State Research men and Adrisi's own loyal escort. One explanation given later was that the escort must have mistaken the State Research group for ambushers. Officially, Adrisi received multiple injuries in the incident. He was flown to Cairo for treatment.

Two weeks after the 'accident' Amin stripped Adrisi of responsibility for the Ministry of Internal Affairs and promoted State Research Bureau chief Major Faruk to Lieutenant Colonel. He had already been busy reshuffling other ministerial posts and Army commands. He relieved Juma Oris of the foreign affairs portfolio and put the Foreign Ministry under his own control because, he said, it needed 'a lot of diplomacy and a cool head.'

Colonel Nasur, commander of the revolutionary Suicide Mechanised Regiment and hitherto notoriously loyal to Amin, was dismissed ostensibly because 'nobody is above the law and any soldier who transgresses army regulations will be punished.' Also to go: Army Chief of Staff General Isaac Lumago. His new job was to look after the Army's spare parts requirements. Then Amin fired Finance Minister Brig Moses Ali, whom he claimed had been allocating cars to girlfriends and relatives.

Ali's dismissal was also said to have followed a cabinet row in which Amin hurled an ashtray at him and the two drew pistols on each other.

The weeding-out was not confined to the top. Amin's favoured Maliyamungu, now a Brigadier, announced that a number of lower ranked soldiers had been arrested on suspicion of subversion, and he warned that he would not hesitate to call out tanks to flatten the homes of people harbouring 'subversive elements.' This was a warning to Adrisi's not inconsiderable following in the Army.

The year of peace, love and reconciliation was set to end in all-out war.

CHAPTER XVII

'Amin is the first African to quarrel and fight with us. He is the first African to try and undermine our development efforts and commitment to the African liberation struggle. He is the first to push us into hostile relations with a neighbour.

We will continue to prepare and consolidate our defence and continue to hit Amin hard.'

President Julius Nyerere of Tanzania

October 30th 1978.

Shielded by tank columns and a bombardment from the air, three thousand Ugandan soldiers streamed across the frontier into remote north-western Tanzania. The Suicide Strike Force spearheaded the onslaught. Tanzania's scattered border defences were caught unprepared. The Ugandans rolled on towards the Kagera River, killing, looting, and pillaging as they went.

The Kagera sugar mill, a squat structure in the sparse rolling landscape, was cleared of all its sugar and reduced to mangled metal and burned out debris. On the

river at Kyaka, a once busy trading centre, mortar
bombs tore gaping holes in the stonework of a hillside
church. Shells demolished the police post. The Ugandan
artillery turned on the National Bank of Commerce, the
post office and the state sawmill. The marauders then
ransacked the smouldering buildings. Some 15,000 head
of cattle were being herded away from the Tanzanian
Government ranch at Misenyi, midway between Kyaka
and the border.

Hundreds of unarmed Tanzanian villagers died in the
Ugandans' savage advance. The corpses bloated in the
sun, the stench of death carried on the humid breeze.
Some of the dead had been tortured and beheaded.
Soldiers swept into the hamlets shooting indiscriminate-
ly, and throwing teargas cannisters into the huts. They
stole personal belongings—wristwatches, transistor sets
and clothing—and set fire to the modest shelters.

John Joseph was at home at Byamgemba when the
soldiers came. 'They told us to lie down and they started
hitting us. I lost consciousness. When I came to my
father was dead and my two wives and children had been
taken away.'

Scores of villagers were taken hostage and made to
carry food and looted property to a Ugandan camp
across the border. Many were beaten fiercely by their
captors—and many were critically wounded.

Within days the Ugandans occupied a 700 square
mile triangle of Tanzania, the Kagera Salient. 40,000 of
the area's Tanzanian inhabitants fled to makeshift
refugee camps over the rain-swollen river. A mining
engineer blew out a section of the only Kagera bridge at
Kyaka to deter Tanzanian retaliation. None of the
Uganda army engineers was capable of handling the
task.

'The Uganda Armed Forces have made a record in
world history,' said Idi Amin Dada. The Annexed
territory, which he claimed had always traditionally
belonged to Uganda, had been over-run 'in the
supersonic speed of 25 minutes.' 'All Tanzanians in the
area must know that they are under direct rule by the

Conqueror of the British Empire."

Earlier in October Ugandan aircraft had twice made bombing forays over Tanzania's lake-side town of Bukoba. The first raid caused little damage—a bomb crater in the grounds of Bukoba's provincial hospital was put to use as a rubbish pit. In the second three Tanzanians were killed. The raids were part of a three week 'phoney war' relayed on Ugandan radio in which Amin said Tanzania had invaded southern Uganda in the first place. According to the radio, Tanzanian troops, fighting alongside Cuban soldiers, had marched 10 miles into Uganda, wiping out the small border garrison at Mutukula on their way. A later broadcast, accompanied by martial music, maintained that the Tanzanians and their Cuban allies staged further attacks using tanks and heavy weapons, and were intent on moving towards Kampala both by land and by the water of Lake Victoria.

'The public are being advised not to panic as the Uganda Armed Forces will contain the situation,' said the Kampala announcer. 'The Ugandan forces are determined to teach the Cubans a lesson they have never been taught before in Africa. All fighter bombers of the Uganda Air Force are ready for action and all officers and men on leave from the Uganda Army are ordered to report to their regiments immediately.' If the invading force did not withdraw, he said, Uganda would have no compunction about mounting full-scale bombing raids deep into Tanzania. President Amin and the Defense Council had selected Tanzania's main towns— Dodoma, Musoma, Tabora and even Dar es Salaam— as principal targets during a visit to Uganda's beseiged south. The radio, apparently oblivious that the Tanzanian capital was well out of the flying range of Ugandan Air Force jets, added: 'Places where the current invasion has been personally planned by President Nyerere have already been surveyed by the Uganda Air Force.'

At first, Tanzania played down these verbal volleys. Missionaries in northern Tanzania reported no build-up of Tanzanian forces along the border and Dar es Salaam dismissed Amin's invasion alarm as a baseless lie. 'We have no wish to enter arguments with this man,' said the Tanzanian authorities. So many times before had Tanzania heard demented war cries from the north.

Major Bob Astles declared that Tanzania's mythical October incursions had been repelled. 'The only Tanzanians left in Uganda are dead ones,' he bragged. For defence of the Ugandan motherland Amin deserved a place of honour in the annals of modern warfare.

Tanzania rightly concluded that Amin's war-mongering was another ploy to cover up internal crisis. Dissatisfaction had simmered in Amin's army since Vice President Mustafa Adrisi's car accident. Adrisi's followers were more convinced than ever that the accident was a put-up job intended to eliminate their general. At last, malcontents in the Simba (Lion) regiment at Mbarara in the south west, an Adrisi stronghold, in the Chui (Leopard) regiment at Gulu and in the Malire regiment at Bombo broke into open revolt. The mutineers were not all Adrisi supporters, but it was their action which spurred on soldiers still angered by Amin's continued favouritism for individual Sudanese Nubians and Kakwas.

The as-yet disjointed uprisings included a new attempt on Amin's life. But as a band of mutineers converged on the presidential lodge in Kampala Amin escaped by helicopter.

Amin avenged the challenge to his powers. Loyal troops overpowered the Malire rebels in clashes which left as many as 150 men dead, and headed to the seat of the revolt in the south-west. There they met stonger opposition and the first loyalist wave was fought back, suffering heavy casualties. The soldiers of the Simba regiment had the reputation of being a crack unit—and their defiance was not easily snuffed out. Only by the weight of numbers against them were the Simba rebels routed. Those who escaped made for the Tanzanian border, where their only hope—if they were to hit back—was to link up with Tanzanian-supplied anti-

300

Amin guerrillas.

For Amin, though all the ingredients of a sham invasion were readily available.

Amin's forces steamrollered after the rebels. At least 600 people caught in their pursuit were executed. Some were shot . . . most were grouped together and blown up in cells at the border prison of Mutukula. For the moment, the rebels were in disarray, but occasional encounters provided just what Amin needed to fill out his decoy. Invaders, said the radio, had pushed beyond Nbarara to Masaka and along the road to Kampala. But: 'The enemy supply line with Tanzania has been broken. The Malire Mechanised Battalion under the command of Lt. Col. Juma Ali has cut off the invaders from receiving supplies or reinforcements. The Tanzanians are not aware they have been cut off. The Tanzanian invaders are advised to surrender if they want to be safe and they will be treated as brothers. Uganda wants peace and has not yet gone into action.'

Amin already had his own plan in mind. His critical decision was influenced not only by the latest uprisings, although he was sure the rebels had found succour in Tanzania. Capture of the Kagera Salient would pre-empt the return of rebels and exiles—and with trade sanctions against Uganda beginning to bite, it would provide his soldiers with a chance of easy plunder. Fewer luxuries were reaching the soldiery.

There could be no taste as sweet as victory.

After the second October air attack at Bukoba, Tanzania's President Nyerere called cabinet ministers and military commanders to an emergency meeting in Dar es Salaam. A squadron of Tanzanian MIG fighters was moved to Mwanza on the southern tip of Lake Victoria. But just as Tanzania started sending more troops to the border region Amin struck out for the Kagera.

Tanzania stood momentarily stunned by the barbarity of Amin's blitzgrieg. Nyerere's eight-year hatred of

Amin was fanned white-hot. He vowed to drive the Ugandans off Tanzanian soil and teach Amin that Tanzania would no longer tolerate his deadly whims. 'We are going to fight this snake until it is out of our house,' Nyerere declared angrily.

Nyere's army, the People's Defence Force, geared itself up for a massive counter-attack. In Dar es Salaam trucks, buses and Land Rovers were commandeered to carry men and supplies to the war zone—a distance of 850 miles over poor, bush roads. Tankers set out for the Kagera, leaving petrol stations to run dry. In the capital thousands of citizens gathered to cheer each departing convoy.

The counter-attack started badly. The Tanzanian anti-aircraft guns brought down six fighter aircraft in the first week—three Ugandan and three of their own. Ground forces—about 10,000 had reached the front—were unable to cross the flooded Kagera River.

'We have only one task, it is to hit Amin,' said Nyerere. 'We have the ability to hit him. We have the reason to hit him and we have the determination to do so. We want the world to understand this clearly, that we have no other task. We are asking our friends who are offering to mediate to stop these efforts.'

Dar es Salaam announced immediate measures to raise money for the war effort. Cigarette and beer prices went up, further curbs were put on the allocation of fuel and finances were channelled from non-strategic ministries to the Treasury's war fund. The announcement warned Tanzanians to brace themselves for a long period of war, and appealed for donations from individuals and organisations alike.

Days after claiming the Kagera River as Uganda's new southern boundary, Amin suggested an astonishing solution to the dispute. The matter, he said, should be settled in the boxing ring. 'I am keeping fit so that I can challenge President Nyerere in the boxing ring and fight it out there rather than the soldiers lose their lives on the field of battle,' he said. Muhammed Ali would be an ideal referee for the bout and he, Amin, the robust former Uganda heavyweight champion, would give the diminutive, white-haired Nyerere a sporting chance by fighting with one arm tied behind his back and his legs shackled with weights.

The ridiculous proposal was Amin's way of answering Nyerere's outright rejection of any form of mediation. As far as Nyerere was concerned Amin had gone too far. Tanzania would not listen to calls for a ceasefire—and was particularly annoyed by one from Amin's mainstay, Libya. Emissaries from the Sudanese chairman of the Organisation of African Unity, President Nimeiri, were also met by an unrelenting Nyerere. 'There has been a naked, blatant and bragging aggression against Tanzania. I want to hear the OAU's voice. I want to know what the OAU will do about this. I expect African countries to tell Amin to immediately withdraw before people can talk of restraint. I expect no dithering.'

Tanzania's government-owned media reinforced the president's stand. 'To accept mediation is to turn the other cheek to a butcher. There is no going back on our resolve to drive Amin out of our boundaries.'

Nyerere's demands for wholesale African condemnation of Amin were largely unheeded. The OAU dithered. Amin did not renounce his claim to the Kagera Salient. 'If he has not renounced this claim, what do I say to the people of Tanzania?' Nyerere asked a Nigerian emissary. 'Is Africa asking Tanzania to pay for those massacres and wanton destruction of property? Africa would be setting a dangerous precedent if it allowed matters to end there.'

Tanzania, it was clear, was willing to go it alone. 'This is not a situation where the aggressor gets away with it,' Nyerere said.

Nyerere had no guarantee Tanzania would be kept unmolested in future. And it was time to punish Idi Amin once and for all.

Amin already assumed personal control of Ugandan troops occupying the Kagera Salient, having twice replaced his front line commanders for inefficiency. On

November 8 Amin said he was willing to withdraw from the Tanzanian territory provided Nyerere guaranteed to stop hostilities against Uganda.

A war of words began as a shooting war raged.

'It was not Uganda's intention to invade Tanzania,' Amin said, 'we took it merely as a precautionary measure to prevent exiles from infiltrating into Uganda.'

Ugandan troops would pull back as soon as promises were received through the OAU...and as soon as another demand, that Nyerere recognised Amin as Uganda's real ruler, was fulfilled. Amin also told Tanzania not to think he was unaware than an invasion force was amassing in Rwanda and that 50,000 British troops were on their way to bolster the Tanzanian army. 'Ugandans need not worry about this because I have already conquered the British,' he said.

A week later—without having received the guarantees he required—Amin said he had ordered his troops to evacuate the Kagera Salient. The order, proclaimed the Uganda radio, showed Amin's good intentions towards Tanzania and his respect for African neighbourliness.

'Complete lies,' retorted Dar es Salaam, 'the struggle continues. Amin is not withdrawing his troops. These declarations are aimed at camouflaging Amin's aggression.'

'This aggression constituted a declaration of war against Tanzania and was effected at great cost in Tanzania human life and property. Member states of the OAU should not forget these crucial facts.'

'Amin's soldiers have killed many of our people. His ill-disciplined troops raped women, razed whole villages, ran off with cattle. Our wisdon and sense of duty to Africa and the rest of mankind behoves us to deal with Amin in a manner he understands most— destroying him and his aggressor troops along with their weaponry.'

Tanzania wanted Amin overthrown. Tanzania would do all it could to achieve that end. 'Tanzania is now determined to end the sad story of Idi Amin's eight years of rule. The seizure of Tanzanian territory must be the last of Amin's mad actions.'

Sarah Amin gave birth to a baby boy. Amin said he had named the infant Kyaka. Medina bore a child too. Amin called him Kagera River. No-one saw the children. If they existed at all, Amin had found an early use for them—to revive the flagging popularity of his fatal Tanzanian adventure.

Amin addressed Tanzania: 'War has ended. Nyerere's forces have run away. I am surprised he says fighting is going on. The only living things I found there were three dogs and three cats.'

'Tanzanians therefore should not listen to Nyerere. Nyerere is a liar and a coward who collects his family around him to clap for him as if he were a madman.'

Replied Tanzania: 'We shall keep prodding that huge serpent to stop it from sleeping and until it sticks its head out. Then we shall crush it and drive it out with its head dangling.'

'The confrontation is still on. Our stance is unchanged.'

December 9, 1978.

The only event celebrating Tanzania's 17th anniversary of independence was a meeting of the ruling Chama Cha Mapinduzi party at Dar es Salaam's Diamond Jubilee Hall addressed by President Julius Nyerere:

'We have a big problem at hand. We do not think it is right under the circumstances to mark this occasion with all the usual festivities. I am not even sure it is proper for us to be on holiday today when our fellow countrymen are at war defending the country and spending nights in trenches.

'I do not like this man. Since Amin usurped power, he has murdered more people than Smith in Rhodesia. He had murdered more people than Vorster in South Africa. But there is this tendency in Africa—that it does not matter if an African kills other Africans. Had Amin been white, free Africa would have passed many resolutions condemning him. Being black is now

305

becoming a certificate to kill fellow Africans.'

Nyerere said Tanzanian forces had succeeded in defeating Amin's invaders. 'The position now is that Amin's troops have been kicked out of the territory although there are still a few pockets of resistance in the Kagera forest areas. Our troops are holding all strategically important positions. But this does not mean it is the end of our problem as the enemy is now amassing his troops along the border.

'Countries which have not condemned aggression have forfeited their right to talk to Tanzania about mediation. Even if Amin renounces his claim to any part of Tanzania we will still have to keep up our defences. Amin is a killer. Amin is a buffoon who cannot be trusted.'

Amin sent greeting to Nyerere. 'Dear Brother, we want peace to prevail between Uganda and Tanzania and Kenya so that our region may be stable for development. There is no reason for Uganda to be at loggerheads with Tanzania, or why misunderstandings between us should not be resolved.'

'I hope when the opportunity presents itself, I will be able to join with the people of Tanzania in the celebration of their independence anniversaries.'

For Amin it was the end of the beginning . . . and the beginning of the end.

The bodies of 120 Ugandan soldiers were discovered in a Tanzanian forest near the village of Minziro, north of the Kagera. The Tanzanian commanders deduced the corpses had been dumped to look as if they were battle fatalities, although they were actually executed mutineers.

Tanzania, using heavy artillery and tanks, had invaded Uganda, Amin said. Tanzania's intention was to topple the military government and reinstall Milton Obote as president.

'Tanzania,' said Tanzania, 'harbours no claim on an inch of Ugandan territory, has not done so in the past and does not intend to do so in the future. Despite our abhorrence of Amin we have never worked to topple his regime or undermine his country.'

Uganda said Tanzanian forces had kidnapped 1000 Ugandan civilians from its frontier district. 'We are studying the situation with grave concern and we warn the Tanzanians that if they do not return the innocent 1000 civilians and farmers they will suffer the consequences.'

Tanzania said 193 suspected Ugandan spies had been arrested after crossing the border, disguised as Tanzanians. 'There will never be peace in East Africa until Amin goes.'

Amin said he had been personally directing troops against the Tanzanian invaders, explaining another of his disappearances, this time for three days. He had repulsed occupying Tanzanian troops. 'If Tanzania continues with its aggression Nyerere will be sending his troops to feed the crocodiles.'

On December 21 Tanzania claimed that a second Ugandan invasion attempt using tanks had been driven back. 'The enemy suffered heavy losses and retreated in disorder. They are now regrouping at the border.'

Uganda acknowledged that a force of 80 Ugandan exiles had staged a water-borne attack at a town on the northern shore of Lake Victoria. But, Uganda said, for the capture of all the attackers only one Army lieutenant was killed.

Tanzania accused Uganda of violating its airspace over the Kagera region. Spy planes overflew the region. 'The reconnaisance mission, another act of aggression, is believed to be part of Idi Amin's plans aimed at his much orchestrated second-phase invasion of Tanzania.'

Uganda wanted Tanzania to cease providing refuge for Milton Obote and fellow Ugandan exiles.

Tanzania wanted compensation for the destruction caused in the Kagera Salient.

Uganda said its intelligence network have unearthed a plan in which Tanzania had offered $800 million to a French-based mercenary outfit known as "International Security Force" to attack Uganda.

In Tanzania—and in one of his rare public

statements—Milton Obote urged Ugandans to launch a nationwide uprising to dislodge Amin's regime. 'I call upon the Ugandan army and air force to rise up to their national duty by combining their efforts with the masses to overthrow Amin. I implore compatriots inside Uganda to organise themselves into bodies for the express purpose of prosecuting this struggle. Terror more than anything else has sustained Amin and his regime for the past eight years. There have been many attempts by Ugandans to rid themselves of this scourge. Now is the time for Ugandans to close ranks and co-ordinate efforts to overthrow this regime of terror.

'The main force for change must be organised from within. There should be no wishful thinking that there are foreign troops who will liberate the people of Uganda. Ugandans outside may be able to help, but no-one should be led to believe that the Ugandans outside, on their own, can change the situation.'

'We have been attacked again,' Amin declared. 'The situation on the border is very tense.' The attack had begun with a heavy artillery barrage. 'Captured Tanzanian enemy forces have revealed all their troops movements and possible invasion of Uganda any time now. Ugandan forces may be forced to break through if the enemy continues its aggression. Every member of the armed forces on leave must listen to the radio for possible recall.

'Three regiments of soldiers from African countries, Europe and Tanzania are approaching the Uganda border. I have obtained a secret and highly destructive weapon from one friendly country and I will not hesitate to use it.'

'Idi Amin's troops again tried to invade Tanzanian soil at Mutukula, Kakunyu and Minziro,' said Tanzania. 'During the fighting which started on January 20 a number of Amin's soldiers and weapons were captured. Fighting continues.'

'Tanzanian forces have reinvaded Uganda,' said Uganda radio on January 21. 'Six battalions have penetrated seven miles into Uganda to capture Murema,

308

Kigarama and Kasese villages in East Ankole district. The invaders are heavily armed with tanks and machine guns and are burning houses.'

Behind every feint, a real blow by Amin's opponents.

January 25, 1979.

The eighth anniversary of Idi Amin's military takeover was also a low-key affair. Parades there were— but small, brief ones at provincial army posts. In Kampala celebrations were modest. Gone were the fanfares, razamatazz and backslapping of previous years. Absent for the first time—on specific orders from Amin—was the scurry of foreign press and television men. Amin's anniversary touched only lightly on the crisis at hand:

'As I speak Tanzanians are inside our border. We only had one mechanical company who were repairing equipment there, including dead tanks and probably four armoured personnel carriers. They have now photographed the tanks and the APCs and the body of one soldier killed to fake their victory claims.

'I am grandfather Dada of all Ugandans. I am the most well-known leader in the world today. Tanzania should not deceive itself that it can capture Uganda. Tanzanian soldiers in Uganda are sitting on fire.

'I have combat experience myself. I study you first from the feet up, knees, stomach and even your nails. I study them all and then before going into fight, I know that when I fight you it will take me so many minutes or hours to capture you. That is why I say these people who have encroached on Ugandan soil are on a volcano. They have been sent here to meet their deaths.'

'They say they have destroyed three Uganda Air Force planes. I have just seen my pilots drinking coffee and there appeared nothing wrong with them.'

Amin's words gave little indication of events either in the border area or elsewhere in the country. That Amin's resources were sorely stretched was beyond doubt, however. He sent an unusually humble message to

United Nations Secretary General Kurt Waldheim. 'I appeal to you to inform the Security Council of the situation. My people have requested me to ask Your Excellency and the Security Council to prevail on Tanzania to withdraw from Uganda peacefully.'

Amin went in search of arms. Saudi Arabia sent him away empty-handed and suggested instead that tension would be better reduced if it paid $50 million compensation to Tanzania on behalf of Uganda. Amin's other principal ally, Libya, was in a more delicate position. Several Libyan soldiers attached to the Uganda army had apparently been taken prisoner by the Tanzanians and were now being held in Zanzibar. Having always expressed Libya's readiness to help Amin in case of trouble—and having done so often in the past—Gaddafi was in a quandary.

It was widely rumoured he offered substantial aid to Tanzania in return for the release of the Libyans, as well as a satisfactory accommodation between the two battling African neighbours. One figure mentioned was $100 million.

Nor was it beyond the realms of possibility that Gaddafi would offer armaments to Tanzania. This last convolution in the almost make-believe mix was noted by Uganda radio, which discussed it recklessly and at length.

A Tanzanian delegation did go to Libya—to ask Gaddafi to halt the flow of Libyan arms and manpower to Amin. Tanzania and Libya were barely on speaking terms, if Libyan Foreign minister Ali Toriaki's earlier visit to Tanzania was any measure.

Tanzania officials were incredulous to hear a British radio report that Libya had managed to arrange a meeting between Amin and Nyerere, and that Amin had agreed to a ceasefire while the Libyan peace plan was being implemented. The Tanzanians politely showed Toriaki the door.

In Tripoli Gaddafi did the same to the Tanzanians. During the first week-end of February explosive charges tore down three steel towers carrying a 132-

kilowatt power line from the Owen Falls dam to Kampala. Water pumping stations wers shut down by the power cut. Other explosions set fire to a fuel depot in Kampala's Bukoto district. While troops scoured the capital arresting hundreds of suspects in house-to-house searches, roadblocks were set up around the city. Amin at once blamed Obote sympathisers from Tanzania for the bombings. A killer squad had been sent by Obote to assassinate him and top Government personalities. 'The people of Uganda are fully aware of the imperialists and Zionists who are trying to disrupt peace in our country. It is nonsense for Tanzania and the imperialist media to attribute these incidents to internal problems.'

On Monday, a hitherto unknown group, the Save Uganda Movement, claimed the attacks had been its doing. The group distributed a clandestinely-produced leaflet echoing Obote's call to the Ugandan populace to rise up against Amin. Significantly, SUM described itself as a new group drawing its support from within Uganda itself. As such, SUM threatened Amin from close quarters, and represented the growing momentum of internal opposition to Amin. A week later saboteurs destroyed a section of Uganda's main rail link to Kenya at Busembatia in the east of the country. An anonymous spokesman for the saboteurs said they were not part of SUM. 'But we are in collaboration with SUM. It is part of the same struggle.'

In Arusha, Tanzania, a SUM guerilla identified by his operational name, Faki Kulle, declared that the group had 1,500 guerillas operating inside Uganda. High-ranking members of Amin's armed forces were helping the opposition movement, which described itself as apolitical without specific allegiance to Obote or other 'personality cults'. That its campaign had begun after Obote's call to arms was coincidental. 'Our aim is to overthrow Amin and restore democracy to Uganda.'

By now, Idi Amin asserted, Tanzanian forces and Ugandan exile invaders had pressed more than 30 miles into Uganda towards the south western provincial centre of Masaka. Amin said he had personally taken charge of an aerial reconnaisance mission to establish the whereabouts of the invaders. Over the shores of Lake Victoria he said he had observed 'some of the Tanzanian troops are already eating hot curry.' Back on the ground, he called together Lake fishermen. 'I advise you to continue fishing and fighting,' he told them. Then Amin needed the battlefront for his next theatrical scene.

Kampala radio claimed Amin narrowly escaped capture at the front. 'At one time the President and two of his ministers were cut off and one soldier in their party was killed. They called for air support from the Ugandan forces and made their way out, taking the body of the dead soldier with them.'

The radio made another melodramatic appeal for Ugandans to donate blood at transfusion centres throughout the country. When the response proved to be half-hearted soldiers rounded up donors.

Ugandan resistance was weakening, the morale of Amin's troops was sinking fast. According to Tanzania many of the Ugandans melted into the bush, abandoning their equipment. Amin's version was different, but typical. 'The fighting is as hard as a match between Muhammed Ali and Ken Norton. We have run short of ammunition but we are wrestling and boxing our enemies.'

The foundations of Amin's power were crumbling beneath him. The Suicide Battalion rebelled and took control of Masaka. Amin conceded that a mixed force of 20,000 Tanzanians, 'mercenaries' and Ugandan exiles had occupied the town and were moving out to Mbarara in the west and Kampala itself. A last minute attempt to end the fighting by an OAU mediation committee was spurned by Tanzania.

'Despite the gravity of the situation, Uganda will never give up,' said Amin's radio. 'The President will remain in Kampala with his family to control the situation.'

'The Life President urges all those Ugandans who believe in God to pray day and night.'

Gaddafi answered.

More than 3,000 Libyan soldiers were airlifted to Uganda. But the Libyan help was too little—and too late. Anti-Amin units had reached Mpigi, 25 miles from Amin's capital. Amin launched a counter-offensive, but its gains were temporary. On March 24, Ugandan exile leaders gathered in Moshi, Tanzania, to decide how to hasten Amin's fall—and what to do afterwards. The meeting elected an 11-man executive council under the chairmanship of a former Makerere University vice-chancellor, Professor Yusufu Lule. The council, under a new banner—the Uganda National Liberation Front—was to be assisted by three committees covering political, military and finance and administrative affairs and would begin by taking over the administration of the 'liberated areas' of Uganda.

Notably, Milton Obote did not receive executive responsibilities in the UNLF.

And Idi Amin was still talking. He had had to pull 25 Palestinian commando volunteers out of battle because they were too tough. 'The commandos killed more than 300 enemy troops and destroyed much of their equipment in only three hours of fighting,' he said.

He appealed for papal intervention. 'Nyerere is a Catholic. We hope that he would heed an appeal by the Pope. We appeal to Pope John Paul II to use his good offices to ensure Nyerere orders his forces to withdraw.'

Amin's radio was still talking too. One morning it broke into a music programme to tell Ugandans that enemy forces had cut the road between Entebbe and Kampala, trapping Amin at Entebbe. 'Although he is cut off from the rest of the armed forces he is not worried. He will try his best with the blessing of God to unite Entebbe and Kampala with the rest of the country. Even if he is cut off from all his family he will use any type of gun to the maximum to see that he makes a breakthrough.'

The bulletin said Amin had seen 12 tanks approaching his Entebbe State House. 'The President will show how only 20 men can fight against 20,000. He will have

313

breakfast with the enemy today.'

Sure enough, Amin appeared in Kampala the next day. If there was any truth in the story the tanks had probably been his own. It was to be Amin's last ruse. The final countdown had begun.

Artillery pounded the outskirts of the Ugandan capital.

A Supersonic Libyan Tupolev 22 jet bomber dropped five bombs on northern Tanzania. On Sea Nane Island, an animal sanctuary, six gazelles were killed, said a Tanzanian war communique.

Tanzania MIG fighters streaked over Kampala and Jinja. Bomb damage was slight. The MIGs strafed Entebbe airport, tearing up parts of the runways.

Amin appeared in Jinja. 'This will be my line of defence. I am prepared to die here,' he told bewildered citizens.

Entebbe fell to the invaders. 'I am still going strong,' cried Amin desperately. 'The enemy must know although they are now bombing Kampala and Entebbe and have dropped more than 200 bombs so far, that they have been cut off to the rear, left and right and we are just watching what is going on.'

In Nairobi visiting Ugandan Foreign Minister Matiya Lubega lamented; 'I don't think I can go home now.'

Many of Amin's Libyan defenders boarded aircraft bound for home.

Amin spoke over Uganda radio. 'There is no need for panic. The invaders are 40 miles from the capital and are being contained.'

Loyal Nubian troops of the Bondo Battalion reached Kampala from Amin's home region in the north-west. They were Amin's last card.

On April 11 Kampala fell. And with it, Idi Amin fell from power.

Amin's terror rule was over.

CHAPTER XVIII

*'We are committed to establish the rule of law
in the country, and restore the dignity of our
people. Ugandans can resolve never again to
allow a dictator to rule them.'*

Yusufu Lule

It was the first time in post colonial history that one
African country had invaded another and overthrown
its ruler. Loudspeaker vans drove through Kampala
crackling out their message: 'The fascist dictator is
finished.'

The Tanzanian column, headed by three T54 tanks,
wove its way into the heart of the city. The column got
lost: at one intersection the leading tank turned and
backed up several times before choosing the route. The
commander had picked up a Ugandan guide who gave
his name as Godfrey—and Godfrey didn't know the
capital as well as he professed.

Soldiers of Tanzania's 208th Brigade spread out from
the main force. To the sound of bugle calls and
brandishing a spear, Lt. Col. Ben Msekwa led charges
against the remnants of Amin's troops. Resistance was
light. Msekwa sipped tea with the North Korean
ambassador while Tanzanian gunners established

artillery positions in Kololo suburb. After daybreak
sniper fire and return volleys ripped through the stunned
quiet. Five Amin soldiers in a commandeered Mercedes
sped towards the Tanzanian column, their automatic
rifles blazing from the windows. The car disintegrated in
a barrage of gunshots from the forward ranks of 800
Tanzanian infantrymen.

Kampala accustomed itself to a new day. To a new
era. Citizens came out, unbelieving. It was over at last.
They garlanded the tanks with flowers, hugged the
soldiers and adorned them with green leaves and sprigs
of shrubbery.

They cried: 'We are free.'

Scrawled placards came out:

'A return to sanity.'

'Murderer, tyrant and cannibal dies permanently.'

'Long Live Nyerere.'

'Why should they arrest me?' said Amin's Minister of
Public Service and Cabinet Affairs, Raphael Nshekana-
bo. 'If the right people had been put in the right places
after independence the mistakes which have occurred
would not have occurred.'

In their haste to leave the city Amin soldiers stole cars
at gunpoint. Civilians removed the wheels from their
cars and hid them.

'We want your car.'

'The wheel is being repaired.'

'Fetch it.'

This citizen, a Muslim, recognised the soldiers as
Muslims and fetched his Koran from indoors. The
soldiers left him unharmed—but others were not so
fortunate.

Euphoria turned to anger. Crowds stormed the
buildings which symbolised Amin's rule. Government
office buildings were ransacked, the homes of Amin's
officers were stripped bare. The crowds converged, like
ants, on the sugar repository where Amin hoarded sugar
as a form of payment for his favourites or inducement
for informants. Sugar had long been a scarcity. Anger
turned to greed ... greed following deprivation. The

looters tore down the steel shopfront grilles and smashed the plate glass windows. No single shop escaped plunder. Broken glass, packaging and the paperwork of every business littered the streets. The looters made off with all they could carry—clothing, radios, typewriters, chairs, tables, television sets, refrigerators, mattresses, bedding, liquor ... and what little food they could find. Cars were driven through the smashed frontings of the showrooms. Fire gutted a bicycle shop, and the looters sorted through the smouldering debris, salvaging charred bicycle parts.

A dozen Amin soldiers were caught by mobs and beaten to death. Others captured by the troops were shot on the city golf course, their hands tied behind their backs.

The Uganda National Liberation Front took over the radio station and broadcast its first proclamation. 'The racist fascist is no longer in power. We call on all Ugandans to join hands and eliminate the few remaining murderers. We call on remaining Ugandan soldiers to surrender.'

From Dar es Salaam the UNLF announced a new civilian cabinet naming Yusufu Lule as President of Uganda and Commander-in-Chief of the Armed Forces in place of Idi Amin Dada.

Amin had escaped from Kampala in a convoy of five black limousines. From Jinja he made a broadcast of his own relayed through Uganda radio's external services transmitter at Soroti, 140 miles from Kampala in the country's remote north east. 'Ugandan forces must not surrender their arms. We are giving law and order. No-one in Uganda should be confused or deceived by this so-called rebellion. I am speaking as the President of the Republic and Commander of the Armed Forces. I am still in control.

'I, Idi Amin Dada, would like to denounce the announcement that my government has been over-thrown by the rebellion government in Uganda.'

Amin's last attempt to rally support was as desperate as it was futile. He was on the run.

'Idi Amin has killed hundreds of thousands of our brothers and sisters,' said the UNLF announcer. 'He has done more harm to Uganda than any other person. He deserves the gallows.

'We call on all Ugandans to tell the authorities where he is. He should be handed over to the government for trial and he knows what will happen to him.'

President Lule flew triumphantly to Entebbe. The crowds, waving banana leaves, cheered, sang, danced and beat tribal drums.

'Welcome to liberated Uganda,' they called.

'This Easter we are seeing the resurrection of Uganda. We thought God had forgotten us.'

President Lule's government was formally sworn in at the Parliament Buildings.

The last time Kampala had witnessed similar scenes of public jubilation had been eight years before—when Idi Amin came to power.

Tanzanian forces threw open Amin's prisons. What they found bore harrowing testimony to Amin's reign of terror. At Luzira prison alone 3,800 prisoners were freed: hundreds were young Ugandan soldiers accused of mutiny and teenagers suspected of being guerrillas. Sam Walugembe, a pilot in the Uganda Air Force, was to have been executed on the day the city fell to the invaders. The pilot said he disobeyed orders to bomb Tanzania.

'We couldn't believe it when suddenly our cell doors were opened and the troops said we were free. I had expected to die and instead I find myself celebrating the end of Amin's rule.'

At Makindye prison Ugandan soldiers carried out last acts of brutality as the Tanzanians closed in on the city. Frenzied shootings and bludgeonings ended Makindye's bloody history under Amin. In ultimate defiance, grenades were hurled into cells.

The three-story pink and red-brick villa in the tree-lined district of Nakasero, the headquarters of Amin's secret police, the State Research Bureau—his evil spy network which permeated every sphere of Ugandan life and kept Amin in power through fear and torture: here too, vengeful massacres took place as the Tanzanians approached. Hundreds of corpses, chained or wired together by the neck and horribly mutilated, were removed from the villa in truckloads by State Research agents before they themselves fled. When the provisional government forces came to the abandoned building, five prisoners in the windowless dungeon were still alive—they had survived by eating the flesh of the corpses. 'They could walk, but they couldn't talk. They just wandered off,' said a platoon commander.

More corpses were found in the third-floor torture cells. In drainage gutters lay the bodies of five men and a boy—shot in the gutters so that their blood would flow away.

The walls and floors of the cells were caked thick with dried blood; the floors were scattered with pieces of bone and flesh, and sacking stiff with blood. Pools of dried blood on the stairs, on the stonework outside, in the corridors. Everywhere, the sickly reek of the dead.

In the spacious second-floor office of the head of the State Research Bureau, Major Faruk Minawa, hung the framed epigram, words of his own: 'No Wisdom Is Greater Than Kindness. Those Who Build Their Success On Others' Misfortunes Are Never Successful.'

Ugandans rifled through mounds of secret files searching vainly for signs that missing relatives might be alive.

Amin's Kampala houses were thrown open and ransacked. The Command Post at 12 A, Prince Charles Drive, Kololo, once Amin's pride, was left in a chaos of scattered family photographs, maps, live ammunition, papers marked secret, newly-minted medals and broken wine and whisky bottles. Hundreds of bottles of drugs and medicines filled the bathroom closet. A life-size portrait of Amin bearing the inscription 'Oh God Keep President Idi Amin Dada—Unity, Peace and Justice' had been torn down and defaced.

At Amin's Nakasero Lodge, around the corner from

the State Research Centre, looters discovered toys, board games, dress patterns, the school-books of some of Amin's 35 children and his private film library. Amin apparently enjoyed Tom and Jerry cartoons, tourist films from Eastern Europe, world-title boxing fights, *I Love Lucy, Judy and the Gorilla* . . .

A building which remained intact as Kampala changed hands was the British High Commission, closed three years earlier. The first Foreign Office official to return to Uganda, Richard Posnett, re-opened the High Commission with the help of a soldier's bayonet leverage. Posnett found half an inch of dust on the floor, creepers growing through the windows—and a dust-encrusted cup of tea on the reception desk.

The United States determined to send a diplomatic mission to Uganda.

Outside Kampala's towering, hilltop International Hotel Tanzanian soldiers executed a well-dressed Ugandan, who they said refused to drink to their victory. The man had also been carrying a Libyan passport and had made a number of telephone calls from the hotel, where Amin snipers were still operating.

Soldiers—quite whose nobody knew—blew down the two-foot-thick door of the strongroom at Barclays Bank using plastic explosives and helped themselves to 2½ million Ugandan shillings.

Tanzanian soldiers dug foxholes in the grassy patches between or beside the streets and covered them over with bivouacs. Slowly the civilians returned to pick up the pieces. It had not been the fighting that caused the destruction. Said a Tanzanian officer: 'We were told to do as little damage as possible. Our biggest problem has been how to stop the Ugandans themselves from looting and destroying everything.'

The Tanzanian engineers restored water and electricity supplies to most districts of the capital. Nightclubs re-opened too—the new patrons brought their own supplies of pillaged liquor. They outnumbered the girls—but danced anyway, their rifles and rocket launchers strapped across their backs.

'When we reached Masaka we didn't think we would

be going any further. We wanted to revenge the damage caused by Amin's soldiers in Tanzania...

'The Ugandan Army was highly mechanised. It could only operate along main roads. Our ambushes played havoc with their tanks. Amin's soldiers and then the Libyans ran away.'

Their enemy crumbled. Not more than 1000 Ugandan soldiers died in the entire campaign. The Tanzanians' own casualties were much lower. As many as 400 Libyans died—most of them in the battle for Entebbe. The largest Libyan force was halted in a single ambush where the Entebbe-Kampala road passed between two distinctive hills. A jeep and an APC passed through the position and waved on the rest before the ambushers opened fire.

Libyans who escaped had nowhere to run.

Three were shot dead by a Tanzanian soldier further along the road. An unspecified number were taken alive and flown to Tanzania. Stragglers who escaped into the bush, with no command of English or local dialects, were beaten or panga-slashed to death by villagers as they begged for food or beckoned to surrender.

Two whites drove towards Entebbe to reach colleagues there. Briton Gordon Parrott, head of the Atlas Tower Construction Company, and a Dane, Sven Sorensen, died when their Ugandan escorts opened fire at a Tanzanian roadblock. Retaliating Tanzanian soldiers hit their car with a rocket propelled grenade. (Parrott had been one of the four British businessmen who carried Amin shoulder high in a sedan chair to demonstrate 'the white man's burden.')

The body of a middle-aged white man was found at Kampala Golf course, and a second European lay in the grounds of Nile Mansions hotel, where Amin's advisor Bob Astles had an office. Both bodies were decomposed beyond recognition. At first, Astles was thought to have committed suicide...

While the victorious forces relived their glory in Kampala, men of Idi Amin's army engaged in yet another wave of killings. Desperate for food and shelter, bands of soldiers raided villages off the eastward road to Jinja and the Kenyan border. Six hundred Amin soldiers set up a half-hearted line of defence at Jinja but most of Amin's troops dispersed into the bush. In Busoga district 20 soldiers dragged branches across the road to stop a bus heading for the border. Sixty passengers were ordered out of the bus. They were robbed and shot down. Nearer the border 200 civilians were rounded up in a village market and cut down by machine gun fire.

Amin's desperadoes chanted anti-Amin slogans. They said they were members of the liberation forces. When the villagers joined the chanting the soldiers opened fire.

In the northern town of Lira, according to a Roman Catholic missionary, Nubian State Research Bureau agents also conducted last assassinations. Fifteen men travelling in a Mercedes mini-bus, a Peugeot car and accompanied by a motorcycle outrider roamed the district with impunity and had killed more than 50 townspeople. 'Bodies lie rotting in the fields and beside the roads. Members of the public who tried to bury them were also killed,' the missionary said.

The new Government's radio pleaded: 'If your area is not yet liberated don't give up. Continue praying and hoping. The liberators are on their way any moment now. Keep up your spirits and save life where you can.

'If you are being harrassed by Amin's rebel soldiers try and immediately report their presence in your area. The authorities will help free you from such terror.'

The Government captured Jinja, 50 miles from Kampala, ten days after toppling Amin. Handfuls of Amin soldiers guarded the Owen Falls Dam. Battle was short. Jinja townspeople bedecked the three Tanzanian tanks with bougainvillea blossoms. Gaddafi Barracks, home of Amin's Eagle Battalion, was almost deserted.

But throughout eastern Uganda more than 1000 people had not survived the dreadful reprisals of Amin fugitives.

Where was Idi Amin? Some of his senior officers

escaped to Kenya. Colonel Nasur Abdallah crossed the border with a fleet of Mercedes cars, minibuses and trucks, four wives and 28 children. The former governor of Kampala told the Kenyans: 'All the cars are my personal property. I want to settle in Kenya and use my cars as taxis to educate my children.' Nasur was held in a makeshift camp near the border—along with the former head of Amin's CID, three other former governors, and a number of Army officers, businessmen and civil servants.

Amin's Vice-President Mustafa Aarisi was arrested, still in his hospital bed at Mulago. Kenyan police arrested Astles, who escaped across Lake Victoria to Kisumu in his motor launch. After two weeks of interrogation, Astles, the second most wanted man in Uganda, was returned to the custody of the new Kampala government to answer for his crimes.

Where was Idi Amin?

An early suggestion: he had been picked up by his private jet at Soroti and flown to Libya bound for Iraq by a Libyan crew. But refugees crossing into Kenya said he had been seen with a hardcore of bodyguards near the border town of Busia. Asian contractors, however, reported seeing him at the village of Nebbi in the far West, near Uganda's border with Zaire. A Sudanese newspaper, *Al Ayam*, said Amin had returned to his home region in north western Uganda, and intended to pass through southern Sudan en route to an Arab country. Then the new authorities in Kampala maintained Amin had been smuggled out of Uganda aboard a Libyan airliner via Nairobi.

In Tel Aviv the family of Dora Bloch offered a reward for information leading to Amin's arrest and an Israeli member of parliament, millionaire Samuel Flatto-Sharon, hired 12 detectives in Europe, Africa and the United States to track down Amin. 'We have promised the new Ugandan government that we will deliver Mr Amin Dada to them,' he said.

The American Central Intelligence Agency said Amin's family had arrived in Iraq—but he had not joined them . . . yet.

For eight long and terrible years Amin held sway as one of Africa's most tyrannical and brutal leaders. Yet this most contradictory, elusive and unpredictable of men is to remain an enigma to the last. Even as this book goes to press his whereabouts are uncertain. In the vast, untamed continent of Africa, it is still possible for a man as highly visible, as hated, as wanted as Idi Amin to melt into obscurity, to disappear without trace . . .

But Amin will not be forgotten. His crimes are an indelible scar on the already pitted map of mankind. Amin brought a Satanic dark age to Uganda. How will he atone for it?

For Africa: atone for it he must.

Joseph Kamau & Andrew Cameron
Nairobi, Kenya. 1st May, 1979.

POSTSCRIPT

In the last year of Amin's misrule Uganda's annual inflation had reached a staggering 700 percent. Amin ordered his treasury to print more money. That was his answer. Public administration, health services and education had ground to a standstill as Amin's ruling clique ravaged the country. The aspirations of Ugandans had been mercilessly crushed.

Ahead, the task of social, economic and political reconstruction is immense. The post-Amin government has pledged to hold democratic elections within two years. It needs massive foreign aid. 'The magnitude of aid we need is very, very large,' said Finance Minister Sam Sebagereka. 'But we are going to perform a miracle here.'

President Lule's government quickly received international recognition. President Nyerere, accused of setting a dangerous precedent for Africa, offered to defend the action of Tanzanian forces at the United Nations.

But with Amin gone, imponderables remained. The settling of old scores would be inevitable—but to what degree? And what of old ambitions and old animosities? And what of the man Amin deposed, Nyerere's close friend Milton Obote?

'Dr Obote, like any other citizen of Uganda, can be considered for any position in the government,' said President Lule.

Free elections under the Lule government will be the first since independence in 1962.

How will new, fragile Uganda fare?

In the words of President Lule, the new government's aim is to give Ugandans confidence that they have the right to live and be treated as human beings.

After the fear and suffering, that itself is an immense task.

APPENDIX I

THE SAYINGS OF IDI AMIN—A SELECTION

On himself: 'I am not a politician but a professional soldier. I am therefore a man of few words and I have been very brief throughout my professional career.'

After a visit by Tanzanian President Julius Nyerere to Sudan: 'Nyerere has got a chronic disease of bringing misunderstandings between countries. He might infect the people of Sudan with this disease. He is like a prostitute who has gonorrhoea and every man who sleeps with her is infected with gonorrhoea.'

On the Middle East: 'Arab victory in the war with Israel is inevitable and Prime Minister of Israel Mrs Golda Meir's only recourse is to tuck up her knickers and run away in the direction of New York and Washington.'

'I have sent a telegram to Golda Meir telling her I am not a person who fears anyone. I am six foot three inches tall and a former heavyweight boxing champion. The world is now convinced that I was right when I said sometime ago that Hitler was right to burn six million Jews during the Second World War.'

In a telegram to Moshe Dayan on behalf of Ugandans of the 'Suicide Liberation Organisation who have signed up to die for the Arab cause': 'I cannot communicate with a murderous woman. I have come to the conclusion that it is time for you as a military leader of your country to advise your Prime Minister Mrs Golda Meir, your Government and all the murderers in Israel to withdraw completely from the land forcibly occupied in the 1967 and 1948 Middle East War in order to save the lives of many innocent Israelis.'

On US Secretary of State Henry Kissinger's Middle East peace shuttle: 'His aircraft flying to Arab capitals possesses special instruments recording strategic targets. Dr Kissinger was also accompanied by Israel intelligence and operational officers who were making targets for their next attack.'

Offering to swim the Suez Canal at Ismailia, Egypt: 'The water here is very good. I have been swimming in more rough water.'

To Colonel Baruch Bar-Lev after the Entebbe raid: 'As a professional soldier I must tell you the operation was very good. But you did not get the good MiGs—the planes your soldiers destroyed were waiting for repairs.'

On the Entebbe rescue raid movies: 'It is stupid and ridiculous to feed public opinion on bogus events and deceive anyone with falsehoods for the sake of money. We are not weak or cowards because we failed to hit back. Some people will kneel before me for the action we will take which will never be forgotten. Those who are now rejoicing will one day suffer, and some of them will come and kneel before me for mercy, and they will write a different story.' (telegramme to Israeli Prime Minister Yitzhak Rabin)

'I am portrayed very well.'

On the death of actor Godfrey Cambridge during filming of the ABC production Victory at Entebbe: 'It is a punishment by God and should be a lesson to those who intend to take part in the film and those who want to imitate Field Marshal Amin.'

On the White Man's Burden: 'I am not a racist. Uganda is one of the African countries that loves Europeans.'

'The Europeans carried me on their backs into my reception. Why did they do that? Because they considered me a brilliant, tough African leader who has helped create better understanding between Europeans and Africans.'

On the Uganda Army: 'You should not say bad things about the Ugandan Army. I have served with the British, Italian and Indian armies; even with the US army in Burma and I can tell you Uganda forces are up to international standard. Of course, everyone can make a mistake from time to time, except God.'

On the economy: 'Uganda is a paradise. The most poor man in Uganda today is General Amin. I don't have anything—and I don't want anything. Because otherwise I would not be doing my job as president.'

'If you go into the countryside you will see we have enough food. We have a lot of medicine in the hospitals. We have increased the salary of the people of Uganda. We are growing crops for export and we are getting foreign exchange. You do not hear anywhere Uganda has debts. The world bank is very happy with Uganda.'

On Tanzania: "I have no time to think bad thoughts about Tanzania.'

329

On British Prime Minister Edward Heath: 'He is one of the best Prime Ministers. He is like Hitler—really tough—I admire him.'

To Mr Heath, out of office: 'I understand you have been relegated from prime minister to the obscure rank of bandmaster. Despite that I understand you have established yourself well in your new profession and are one of the best bandmasters in the United Kingdom. Because of this I am taking the liberty of inviting you to come to Uganda with your band to play before me and British nationals at the Command Post. I will assist you with foreign exchange for your excellent performance here. You will get a warm welcome from Ugandans who will give you not only money but also chickens and goats.'

To Mrs Margaret Thatcher, Heath's successor as British Conservative Party leader: 'It was on Tuesday when I happened to look at your photograph which was published in one of the East African papers. You were depicted laughing at Mr Edward Heath whom you have defeated at the party leadership elections. From the photograph you appeared very charming, happy, fresh, intelligent and confident.'

On Britain's Labour Government Prime Minister James Callaghan: 'I love him as my friend, he has been to my house, he has been having coffee with me and he has even been carrying my little baby son Mwanga and I am very happy with him.'

On Britain: 'The British are my best friends. I love them very much but they are annoyed because I kicked out British Asians. They can say what they like. I have no time for imperialists.'

'I am the Conqueror of the British Empire after British have been in power and conquered Uganda for over 100 years. British just removed the union jacks from Uganda and ran away. I am very proud to be called the conqueror. I think I am the only one in the world who conquered British in black Africa and even now they are calling me great black power in the continent of Africa.'

On the expropriation of British assets: 'I will not talk to any British junior officer because I am the top man in Uganda. If Britain wants compensation for their businesses which were taken over because of the Economic War the Prime Minister or the Queen must come personally because the Economic War was declared in Uganda and not in Britain.'

On the Scots: A message copied to Queen Elizabeth, the British Government, UN Secretary General Dr Waldheim, Soviet Party leader Leonid Brezhnev and Chairman Mao Tsetsung of China: 'Unless the Scots achieve their independence peacefully they will take up arms and fight the English until they regain their freedom.'

'Many of the Scottish people already consider me King of the Scots. I am the first man to ask the British Government to end their oppression of Scotland. If the Scots want me to be their King, I will.'

On US President Richard Nixon's efforts to end the Vietnam War: 'You are one of the most brilliant leaders in the Western world and my best friend. I offer the advice that you should not again get involved militarily in Vietnam to assist the solution of the problems between North and South.'

On Nixon's nomination for the Nobel Peace Prize: 'I should like to congratulate you for the nomination. However, I have reason to believe that the organisation that has nominated you merely wishes you to hear of the nomination so that you can recover from the Watergate affair. My reason for holding this view is that it is very discouraging for the real peacemakers in the world to hear of your nomination . . . I am led to the conclusion that your nominators were not serious in their choice.'

To Nixon on US-Uganda aid cuts after Amin's expulsion of Uganda Asians: 'My dear brother, it is quite true that you have enough problems on your plate, and it is surprising that you have the zeal to add on fresh ones. . . . At this moment you are uncomfortably sandwiched in that unfortunate affair (Watergate). . . . I ask Almighty God to help solve your problems.'

To Nixon on Watergate: 'I wish you a speedy recovery from the Watergate affair. We Ugandans hope that the great United States of America does not continue to use its enormous resources especially its military Might to destroy human life on earth, particularly in the developing world.'

'I am sure that any weak leader would have resigned or even committed suicide after being subject to so much harrassment because of the Watergate affair. I take this opportunity to once again wish you a quick recovery from the Watergate affair and join your wellwishers in praying for your success in recovering from it.'

'It is strange Nixon has attacked Uganda in a speech. If he had requested me to help him solve his problem at home I would be willing to help.'

During a visit to Algiers: 'Even prostitutes on the street are more respected than President Nixon today. Nixon is a human being. He has made a mistake. The press shouldn't waste time on Watergate.'

Later: 'President Ford has got a lot of problems. It is too early for me to tell you now because I am still studying his problems, but I have been briefed by the American people. (Nixon) was very sick, he had to be taken to hospital and the people were very worried he was going to die, and he might not give the answers on the case of Watergate for the whole world to know. Because nobody knows, the only person who can answer is Nixon . . . and if he dies I am sure the whole blame will be pushed on him. That is why I wished him a quick recovery, so that he may be in a position to answer all those questions even now. I have actually extended an invitation through President Ford for Nixon to come and rest in Uganda.'

On Jimmy Carter: 'I love Jimmy Carter. He is a very great revolutionary leader and a very great leader. I admire him very much. I loved him even before (his) election. I know he is a great man because black Americans love him. I want Jimmy Carter to visit me in Uganda. He will be very warmly received.'

On the U.N.: 'Everyone knows my speech to the United Nations General assembly covered the whole United Nations agenda for the year.'

On being president of Uganda: 'It is very hard, but I like it very much and enjoy it very much. One must have a very good brain, work very hard and not be a coward. Very many Africans have written to me that I am a hero of Africa. This makes me very proud.'

After sending cabinet ministers on compulsory leave: 'A human being is a human being, and like a car he needs refuelling and fresh air after working for a long time.'

On the killing in Uganda of between 100,000 and 300,000 people: 'Evidence from the report of the Commission of Inquiry into the disappearance of people in Uganda found that 305 people dead and not more.'

'Some criminals pretending to act on my orders are killing drivers and then stealing their cars.'

'We are a government of action. If we have evidence that an army officer is guilty of kidnapping and murder then he will face justice. There is no evidence to back up such a serious allegation.'

On Deposed Ugandan President Milton Obote: 'I was never against him. Had it not been for the help I gave him he would not have managed to rule the country for so long. At one time Obote asked me to take over the government but I refused. He is free to return to Uganda to apply for any job or business.'

On Americans: 'I love the American people very much. I have very many Americans living in Uganda. Some Americans are personal pilots in Uganda. I love Americans very much.'

On his telegrames: 'I send them to different leaders. They are based on the truth and I meant to advise the leaders when I realised they were wrong.'

After the expulsion of Uganda Asians: 'Some Asians in Uganda have been painting themselves black with shoe polish. Asians are our brothers and sisters. If anyone is found painting himself with black polish disciplinary action will be taken against him.'

To Malawi president Dr Hastings Banda: 'I would advise that you should kick out of Malawi the whole lot of economic suckers so as to cure your country of economic cancer as we did in Uganda. I will be happy to receive a Malawi delegation to show them the operational tactics of mass expulsion in imperialist agents and suckers. I wish to assure you from our own experience in Uganda that you should not worry about any external propaganda being mounted against your country, such as direct and implied threats to withhold financial aid to Malawi. You have every sovereign right to boot out from Malawi any criminal residents who are milking the economy of Malawi for their own selfish interests for their own foreign masters.'

On the United Nations: 'UN headquarters should be moved away from the USA and I would like to suggest that it is transferred to Uganda which is geographically located not only in the heart of Africa but in the heart of the world. When it is situated in a non-aligned environment it will be able to discharge its functions without bias, fear or favour.'

On Obote: 'Even Obote knows that I am his best friend. He knows he has lost a great friend.'

On himself: 'I have been made Life President for what I have done for Uganda. I love Uganda and have the insight to lead the country. I do not fear anybody except God.'

Of the Nysamba assassination attempt: 'Three grenades hit me and killed 39 people. My driver was killed and so was my escort—it was only I that escaped. I was saved by God's wish. I will not die until the date God has ordained. I know but I don't tell you to stop your suspense.'

On Religion: 'If you see a people of any country committing a lot of crimes and engaging themselves in bad habits you understand that religious organisations in that country are not with the people and not teaching people the ways of God.'

'Whites from America and the United States enter Uganda under the guise of being religious heads when they are mercenaries who know nothing about the Bible. Some of these so-called missionaries do not even know the Bible.'

'My decision to expel the British Asians was made when God told me to act quickly in a dream if I wanted to save the Ugandan economy for the Ugandan people themselves.'

'I like all the three main religions in Uganda and that is why I donated 10,000 shillings each to everyone of them from my salary.'

On politics: 'We are not Communist. I want my people to be free. In communist countries you do not feel free to talk, there is one spy for every three people. Not here. No-one is afraid here. It's like Uganda girls. I tell them to be proud, not shy. It's no good taking a girl to bed if she is shy....Do you get my point? We have problems but we are proud because no-one is telling us what to do.'

'You should not be like some stupid politicians who cause a lot of damage to property and loss of lives but when it comes to discussing the problem to find out the truth they pretend to be sick and cover themselves under ten blankets.'

'I am a revolutionary. Less talk and more action is better.'

'I do not want to be controlled by any super power. I myself consider myself the most powerful figure in the world and that is why I do not let any superpower control me.'

'Uganda believes in combining the virtues of free enterprise with those of just social policy directed by the Government. The ultimate goal is to establish a democratic progressive society in Uganda which must be accompanied by discipline. Our slogan therefore should be democracy with discipline and we are gradually but firmly moving in this direction. No-one who makes criticisms of government policies will come to grief for doing so.'

Banning the use by Uganda women of beautifying and skin toning creams: 'Women use creams only to change the colour of their faces, legs and arms to look white while other parts of the body remain black. When they undress the parts on which they use cream look different from the other parts. Some even look as if they are suffering from leprosy because of the cream. This is why men chase them away from their homes when they undress because they look unnatural, and look like half-castes.'

On love secrets: 'If women get responsible jobs or have any other job they should avoid associating with spies from foreign countries whose aim is to cause confusion and retard development in our country. It is natural for women to be in love with men or get married. When their love ceases when they separate from their husbands they should not reveal the secrets about their lovers or husbands to Imperialists or Zionists.'

On 'raffia-style' African hairdo's: 'Anyone found with such hair will have her head shaved with a razor.'

On women: 'Women should not sleep while men are working. Even prostitutes can do some work, reporting subversives.'

'Ugandan women should not carry on with white men. Black men are stronger than whites. This is why white girls run after black men.'

To Makerere students: 'You are responsible for teaching people hygiene. You must make yourself very smart, very clean and very healthy. I find that VD is very high. If you are a sick man, sick woman you had better go to hospital, make yourselves clean or you will find that you will infect the whole population. I like you very much and I don't want you spoiled by gonorrhea.'

337

On discipline: 'Our soldiers must behave themselves and not think they are above the law. I have discovered that when some army officers are promoted they run for big cars and stop buying suits. Some of them dress like cowboys in bellbottom trousers. Also, some Makerere students do not even comb their hair, pretending that they are reading books, and have no time to shave. On the other hand you find that these students have time to go to bars and drink.'

To Lord Snowdon, after his separation from Princess Margaret: 'Your experience will be a lesson to all of us men to be careful not to marry ladies in high positions.'

On why he changed the name of Kampala's Grand Hotel back to its pre-independence name, Imperial Hotel: 'It was built by the sweat and labour of Ugandans. The natives of Uganda were forbidden to use it . . . the only nationals allowed in were servants, cooks, waiters and cleaners. We cannot rewrite history.'

On his rejected request to Britain for Harrier jets: 'I was sincere. I asked the Defence Secretary in my meeting with him. I had to go and attack South Africa. I asked them even for a destroyer and an aircraft carrier so I could move to South Africa. The common enemy of all Africa is South Africa and Rhodesia.'

During his 1971 visit to Israel: Amin: 'I would like 24 Phantom jets.' Dayan: 'Why?' Amin: 'I need them to bomb Tanzania.'

On the Uganda Air Force: 'The British told us when I started forming the Uganda Air Force that it will take Uganda 15 years to produce better fighter pilots, but I am producing a better fighter pilot in less than one year. Everything is done in Uganda super-sonic.'

On the opinion that he is mad: 'Well, what do you think?'

On opponents: 'No-one can run faster than a bullet.'

For posterity: 'I am going to write it all down in my book. I am going to write what I did bad and what I did good. Africans will read the book and be very happy.'

APPENDIX II

A SELECTION FROM THE FILES OF UGANDA'S STATE RESEARCH CENTRE
(recovered after the fall of Kampala, April 1979)

1. A letter from Ali Amin, Amin's son, to his father. (It is doubtful that it ever reached him.) A report on Ali from Uganda Government Prison Kigo.

2. An address by Amin to his Cabinet.

3. A confidential S.R.C. report. Note the recommended action.

4. A top secret communication from the Deputy Head of the Public Safety Unit.

5. An address by Amin to the officers and staff of the S.R.C.

H.E. The President
of Uganda

Dear Father

I am healing working very hard.
how to g farm work is good. I am lear ning
how to grow vegetables like cabbages
tomatoes onions and other vegetables.
I am now starting schooling. I like
very much to learn to read and to speak for
I like english and to write it.
I like games very much. We do very
very hard work every day.

your son

Ali Amin

Ref: KGO/GEN/18

UGANDA GOVERNMENT PRISON KIGO,
P.O. BOX 4153,
KAMPALA.

13th July, 1976.

The Commissioner of Prisons,
Prisons Headquarters,
P.O. Box 7182,
Kampala.

SUB: ALLI   AMIN

In accordance with your directive No.S.41 of 23rd April, 1976
I append below a report in connection with the above mentioned lad for
your information please:

(a) GENERAL BEHAVIOUR

Alli is witty and naughty clever boy . Though quiet and
reserved but looks stubborn and argumentative with those
placed in charge of him. He tends to overrate himself.

(b) PERFORMANCE AT WORK

He resents being given orders and tends to argue back when
allocated a task which he has little interest. But generally
he is keen on Vegetable growing. His performance is fairly
satisfactory as he appears too changeable in character.

(c) VISITS BY RELATIVES

He has not received any visit since and he has not registered
any complaint.

(d) OFFENCE AGAINST DISCIPLINE

Though he has not been punished for any offence but he has
signs of misbehavour and takes stock of himself.

(e) GENERAL COMPLAINT

Since given a warning for unnecessary complaints, he has not
ventured to complain of anything. He appears to have gathered
momentum, to behave.

(f) HEALTH

He has been in good health and for the whole month, he has
not reported sick at all. He looks quite healthy and plays
net ball daily.

(g) GENERAL REMARKS

Alli's behaviour is generally satisfactory but requires
close supervision at all times otherwise he is a story teller
and cracks jokes unnecessarily.

As I suggested in my last report, this lad should be
taken to A Reformatory School to avoid him cultivating some
bad behaviours from matured inmates here. Your prompt action
on this point would be greatly appreciated.

(D. G. A. OPELOT) SP
OFFICER in Charge. U.G. Prison Farm, Kigo.

TOP SECRET

**MINUTES OF THE FIRST SPECIAL MEETING OF THE CABINET
OF THE SECOND REPUBLIC OF UGANDA, HELD ON TUESDAY,
14TH MARCH, 1972, AT 10.00 A.M. IN STATE HOUSE, ENTEBBE**

PRESENT: H.E. General Idi Amin Dada, President
of Uganda and Head of the Military
Government

Hon. Prof. W.B. Banage, Minister of
Animal Resources

Hon. J.M. Byagagaire, Minister of Public
Service and Local Administrations

Hon. Y.A. Engur, Minister of Culture and
Community Development

Hon. Dr. J.H. Gesa, Minister of Health

Hon. A.K. Kironde, Minister of Planning and
Economic Development

Hon. W.O. Lutara, Minister of Commerce,
Industry and Tourism

Hon. A.K. Mayanja, Minister of Labour

Hon. W.L. Naburri, Minister of Information
and Broadcasting

Hon. P.J. Nkambo Mugerwa, Attorney General

Hon. Lt. Col. E.A.T. Obitre Gama, Minister
of Internal Affairs

Hon. A.C.K. Oboth-Ofumbi, Minister of Defence

Hon. F.L. Okwaare, Minister of Agriculture,
Forestry and Co-operatives

Hon. E.W. Oryema, Minister of Mineral and
Water Resources

Hon. E.B. Rugumayo, Minister of Education

Hon. E.B. Walhweya, Minister of Finance

Hon. Wanume Kibedi, Minister of Foreign Affairs

Hon. Eng. J.M.N. Zikusoka, Minister of Works,
Communications and Housing.

MINUTE 1 (TSC 1972)   **MINISTERS' SECURITY**

                                         (Cabinet Minute 131 (CT 1972))

     Further to Cabinet Minute 131 (CT 1972) in which
Cabinet discussed the security of Ministers, His Excellency
the President observed that on a number of occasions,
especially when on duty outside Kampala, a Minister's
life could be endangered if he was confronted by unruly
crowd or dissatisfied elements. He, therefore, instructed
the Cabinet that, should any Minister feel that his life
was in danger from unruly crowd or dissatisfied persons,
he was at liberty to shoot to kill.

2.   Cabinet noted the information given by His Excellency
the President that, if a Minister found that his life was
in danger due to confrontation with a person or persons,
he was free to shoot to kill in self-defence.

Signed: **CHAIRMAN**

          , 1972.

DATE: 12/5/75

SURNAME: DRAME

OTHER NAMES: MALAHIYA

DATE OF BIRTH: 1947

PLACE OF BIRTH: KIBAN C/ BANAMBA R.M.

OCCUPATION: BUSINESSMAN

ADDRESS: BRAZAVILLE

NATIONALITY: MALIAN

RELIGION: MOSLEM

STATE:

I arrived in Uganda from Zaire via Goli on the 14/4/75 in transit by lorry (number forgotten) and I stayed in Kisenyi at lodge (name not known) but I know where it is. I stayed there for 5 days and I did not pay anything. After being questioned why I did not pay I said that I had paid 10/= a day. We stayed with DIABY DIARRA.

Afterwards I went to Kenya. I had forgotten to say that I had spent two nights on the way from the border to Kampala. This means that I arrived in Kampala on the 16/4/75. I was arrested with only 33/= without any foreign exchange.

This is all I can state.

Comments: 1) Drame's signature does not appear on the passport

2) When answering questions Drame almost breaks into tears. He does not answer questions properly. He does not explain what type of business he is doing.

3) It seems he is being sponsored by DIABY who has been accomodating him.

Recommendation: Interrogation with intimidation can bring more facts out of him into light.

Ref: CONF/PSU/26/143:   PUBLIC SAFETY UNIT,
                                                 P.O.BOX 7163,
                                                  KAMPALA.

                                          13th April, 1973:

The Head of Public Safety Unit,
Police Headquarters,
P.O.Box 7055,
KAMPALA.

                    TOO SECRET INFORMATION:

1.   A secret information has just been received this afternoon
that; There are two groups of British Troops have just arrived
in Kenya recently early this month APRIL 1973.

2.   These Troops have been devided into two groups e.g.

                         1. GIL-GIL &
                         2. NANYUKI.

3.   The intention of them being brought to East Africa is not
known, but very suspicious.

4.   I therefore bringing this to you knowledge, so that you may
wish to inform our Head of the NATION who may also wish for a check
to be made to find out the trueth and the intention. PREVENTION IS
BETTER THAN CURE.

                              A.Sebi
                         (A.SEBBI) ASP.
                     DEPUTY HEAD OF PUBLIC SAFETY UNIT.

AS/TJO.

ADDRESS BY HIS EXCELLENCY THE LIFE PRESIDENT AL HABI FIELD MARSHAL DR IDDI AMIN DADA V.C., D.S.D., M.C., C.B.E., & COMMANDER IN CHIEF OF THE UGANDA ARMED FORCES TO THE OFFICERS AND STAFF OF S.R.C.

PRESENT:

—MAJOR GENERAL GOWON	—CHIEF OF STAFF
—MAJOR GENERAL MONDO	—SECRETARY FOR DEFENCE
—BRIGADIER MALYAMUNGU	—G.S.O.1—TRAINING & OPERATIONS
—BRIGADIER TABAN	—COMMANDER OF MARINES
—MAJOR MOSES OKELLO	—
—CAPTAIN YOSSA MZEE	—HEAD OF OPERA-TIONS S.R.C.
—CAPTAIN RAPHAEL OSACHA	—O.C. ENTEBBE AIRPORT S.R.C.
—LT. ADAM HAROUN	—HEAD OF TECHNICAL OPERATION S.R.C.
—LT. ABDULATIF JUMA	—THE M.T.O. & ACTING ADJUTANT

Welcoming speech given by Cptain Mzee Yossa who expressed happiness and gratitude for H.Es sacrifice to come and address the staff despite his heavy duty schedule. He also expressed the grief of the staff of this Unit on the accident which befell the Director Lt Col Farouk and prayed that he could get better soon. He then welcomed the President to give his fatherly advice.

His Excellency explained that he had wanted to come to the Unit some time back to congratulate the staff on their recent improvement of their work, and discipline. He noted that he did not hear complaints from people as he used to.

346

Explaining more about the work of an Intelligence person he said that all the staff should try not to show off and give out their covers. He said that due to the nature of Intelligence work, one is bound to have many enemies. He said, he had always advised Officers that whenever they are going for an assignment they should make sure that they go with about two or three cars, to assist in case there is anything. He went on that in case the Director would have gone with escorts of that nature such an accident would easily be solved as the culprits would be found immediately the accident occured. He advised that even if you are to identify yourself just say that you a security officer without giving any details of where you are from. He explained further that an Intelligence man is supposed to be very loyal to the people and the government. Be ready to assist at all times. He advised that in case one happens to come across an accident one should be ready to render any necessary assistance without necessarily identifying oneself. He discouraged the habit of some intelligence officers who go and create rows in bars and other public places and end up in producing pistols at the public. An Intelligence man's actions should speak louder than his words.

Going back to the question of the accident, he praised Professor Kim who performed a very successful operation in the legs of the Director. He added that in was spoken by the surgeon in Tripoli who looked at the operation in this leggs of the Director. He added that in fact they were suggesting that they should get him for their own hospitals in Libya. He explained further that this Professor managed to remove 30 pieces from the right leg and 2 pieces from the left leg of the Director and 1 piece from the leg of Omar.

On co-operation he advised that people should forget their differences, tribal or religious.

Representation in Conferences:

On the point of representation he noted that the Unit was not well represented in Provincial meetings. He advised that arrangements should be made so that

347

whenever there are such meetings some members of the staff should go to attend and give independent reports on the meetings. He added that he wanted this office to be represented in all kinds of gatherings. He then advised that this could be attained if the staff could start mixing with the people in sports clubs and the like so that in case there is a team going out our people can also go when they have an idea of what they are doing. On the side of ladies, he suggested that they should immediately form a netball team and join the National Council of Sports so that whenever there is a team going out they select some from the ones in the team. He added that they should also study the Constitution of Women's Association so that they should join in the association and this could easen matters when they want to send a delegation out they can include some ladies from here. He added that he did not want any delegation to go out without some members from this Unit. He noted that since some members of staff of S.R.C. started working in Embassies embezzlement of funds in Embassies had stopped as one of the signatories of each cheque is a member of this Office.

Adding on this point, he noted that there are some clubs and places which are frequented only by Whites, he advised that such places should be the ones where some of our Case Officers should join membership on different covers. He mentioned Clubs like the Sailing Club of Entebbe, and the one in the Island near Cape Town Villas.

Working Principles:

He urged members working with Technical Operation to study and know how to communicate properly at all times. He noted that there are some who do not know how to express themselves properly in the radio. He advised that they should learn how to talk slowly and clearly and make sure that the message is well received. He suggested that whenever they have to communicate and they find that they are amongst other people who are not members of staff try and separate yourself from them and then communicate without them knowing what you are doing.

He discouraged that habit of letting friends and relatives knowing the secrets of our work. He added that if there is a necessity of combining work and pleasure one should make sure that he finds a way of preventing the others from knowing what your work is. He said that an Intelligence Officer should be ready to do any type of work. One should be ready to work as anything as long as you are able to get some information from that end. He pointed that that was how CIA worked. It uses all people from all walks of life to get any necessary information. Talking on that same line he gave an example of a shop which he had entrusted to a Major in Masaka and directed the Minister of Commerce to fill the shop with goods and sell these goods at government price. This shop has made a profit of one million shillings in no time. This kind of business could be given to any of our Officers on cover and do a job on the cover of a business.

Car Thefts:

He noted that car thefts had increased very much of late. He informed that arrangements would be made so that they organise a combat mission. They will find out what cars are on the market of these robbers then security personnel would be given such cars and try and trap these robbers. He added that in such assignments members of Striking Force would be ready to reinforce in the Office.

He then summarised all his points and stressed more on co-operation and avoiding segregation.

Talking about the people who were arrested from Tanzania, he said that they had promised them One million shillings on any security man they kidnap from Uganda. But, he said revenge of Intelligence is very slow. You leave the enemy to forget about it and then attack effectively then you keep quiet but very alert.

On foreign visitors coming to Uganda he noted that many Whites coming here come on different covers but many have been known to be Israelis and Americans. He suggested that whenever you suspect anybody, you can approach him politely and identify yourself as a security man and find out his true identity. This can also be done to suspected vehicles. With the maximum politeness nobody will have any cause for complaint.

He noted that there are times when he goes on functions, he sees some Case Officers covering the place, but there was a practice of leaving as soon as they see H.E. leaving the place which is very bad because that is when they know who are the security officers. He advised that when they see him leaving they should stay behind because that is when they start talking anything they want knowing that security people are gone. That is the only way information can be obtained from the public.

Adding on attendance on functions, he noted that intelligence from different Units come and that is duplication of work. He advised that when there are functions intelligence officers going to cover the area should first report to the Commanding Officer of that place so that he can organise to combine them with other intelligence officers of that area. This will stop the duplication of work.

He suggested that intelligence officers should befriend people from all walks of life. He gave an example of Muscians who have access to many people of the public. He urged the staff to learn languages from neighbouring tribes and even neighbouring countries like Ruanda and Zaire. This will in future assist in our work. Here he suggested that officers should buy Lingala books to learn what they can from it. He asked Case Officers to try and cover all areas where the High ranking officers go to address people or for any function, as you can never know anything might turn up and you might be of assistance. He added that he wanted some Case Officers to go to Shaba to go and see the progress.

Talking about publicity, he advised that whenever a Case Officer is at a function he should avoid cameramen and TV men because these pictures might somehow go out of the country. On rumour mongering, he discouraged that habit saying that it had been going around saying that Major General Lumaga was going to be dismissed. He stressed that any Officer can be posted anywhere where the government thinks that they can be of assistance.

He then closed the meeting urging them to work harder and have more discipline, avoid rumour mongering and too much talking.